THE ARAB-ISRAELI CONFLICT

The War/Peace Bibliography Series
Richard Dean Burns, Editor

This series has been developed in cooperation with the Center for the Study of Armament and Disarmament, California State University, Los Angeles.

Songs of Protest, War & Peace
A Bibliography & Discography
    R. Serge Denisoff

Warfare in Primitive Societies
A Bibliography
    William Tulio Divale

The Vietnam Conflict
Its Geographical Dimensions, Political Traumas, & Military Developments
    Milton Leitenberg & Richard Dean Burns

Modern Revolutions and Revolutionists
A Bibliography
    Robert Blackey

The Arab-Israeli Conflict
A Historical, Political, Social, & Military Bibliography
    Ronald M. DeVore

THE ARAB-ISRAELI CONFLICT

A Historical, Political,

Social, & Military Bibliography

Ronald M. DeVore

Clio Books

Santa Barbara, California / Oxford, England

© 1976 by Ronald M. DeVore
All rights reserved.

No part of this book may be reproduced in any form without the written permission of the publishers.

DeVore, Ronald M
   The Arab-Israeli conflict.

   (The War/peace bibliography series)
   Includes index.
   1. Jewish-Arab relations—Bibliography.   I. Title.
Z3479.R4D48   [DS119.7]   016.95694   76-17575
ISBN 0-87436-229-6

American Bibliographical Center—Clio Press, Inc.
2040 Alameda Padre Serra
Santa Barbara, California 93103

European Bibliographical Center—Clio Press
Woodside House, Hinksey Hill
Oxford OX1 5BE, England

Manufactured in the United States of America

ACKNOWLEDGMENTS

Numerous people have assisted in the preparation of this work and it is impossible to acknowledge all of them. Ms. Christine Soto spent innumerable hours completing the thankless task of sorting and alphabetizing nearly 5,000 cards. I am deeply appreciative for the encouragement and continuing understanding of Dr. Richard D. Burns, Director of the Center for the Study of Armament and Disarmament, California State University, Los Angeles. Continuing moral support which made this work possible was provided by my wife Audrey D. DeVore. She also contributed her valuable time at every stage of development from original cards to the submission of the final manuscript to the publisher. The author is, however, fully responsible for the selection of material and its organization.

Ronald M. DeVore

CONTENTS

Foreword xv
Brief Chronology of the Arab-Israeli Conflict xvii
Introduction xxii
Note on Use as a Research Tool xxxiii

I / REFERENCES & GENERAL WORKS   3

    A / Bibliographies   3
            Middle East   4
            Arab Topics   7
            Israel Topics   8
            Review Articles   9

    B / Indexes   11
            Newspaper Indexes   12
            Middle East   12

    C / Documentary Collections   13
            Middle East   13

    D / Atlases & Geography   15

    E / Yearbooks   16

    F / Journals   16

    G / Biography   22
            Arab Biographies   22
            Zionist-Israeli Biographies   23

CONTENTS

      H / General References   25
           Arab-Islamic History   26
           Military in Politics   27
           Modernization: Social & Anthropological   28
           Palestine: Arabs & Israelis   30
           Economics   30

II / ARAB COUNTRY SURVEY   32

      A / Arab Middle East   33

      B / Egypt   35
           Egypt & Britain to 1952   36
           Egyptian Revolution   37
           Politics & Government   38
           Foreign Policy   39
           Social & Economic History   40
           Egypt Since 1967   43

      C / Jordan   44

      D / Syria   47

      E / Lebanon   49
           Lebanese Crisis, 1958   50

      F / Iraq   51

      G / Saudi Arabia   52

      H / Libya   53

      I / North Africa   54

      J / Arab League   54

      K / Arab Unity Efforts   56

III / PALESTINE: ISRAEL & THE PALESTINIANS, 1948–1974   58

      A / Israel: Creation & First Decade, 1948–1958   59
           Israeli Society   61

CONTENTS

      The Kibbutz   61
      Immigration   62
      Economy   62
      Politics & Government   63
      Israel & the World   63

B / Israel: Evolving Nation, 1958–1974   64
      Israeli Society   66
      Arabs in Israel   69
      The Kibbutz   72
      Immigration   73
      Oriental Jews in Israel   74
      Economy   75
      Politics & Government   77
      Israel & the Arabs   79
      Israel's Reprisal Raid Policy   79
      Israel & the World   80
          Israel & the Third World   81
      Foreign Policy   83
      Israel & the Diaspora   83

C / Palestinian Arabs   84

D / Palestinian Refugees   86
      Origins   86
      Existence & Continuing Problem   87
      Settlement & Compensation   89
      United Nations Relief & Works Agency (UNRWA)   90
      1967 Refugees   91
      Palestinians & the United Nations   92
      Problem without End? Post–1967   93

E / Palestine Entity   94

F / Palestinian Arab Solutions   95

G / Territories Occupied by Israel, 1967   96
      Israeli Administration   96
      The West Bank   100
      Hussein's Plan   101
      Gaza   101

CONTENTS

IV / CLASH OF NATIONALISMS   102

    A / Zionism   102
        Jewish History in Ancient Times   102
        The Jewish Diaspora   102
        The Rise of Zionism: Theory & Environment   104
        Zionist Political Efforts, 1890–1922   105
        Zionism under the Mandate, 1922–1948   105
        Jewish Anti-Zionism   106
        Zionism in the United States   107
        Zionism after Israel   108

    B / Arab Nationalism   111
        Origins   111
        Islam & Nationalism   111
        Nationalism under the Mandates   112
        Post–World War II Arab Nationalism   112

V / WORLD WARS & MANDATE   115

    A / Palestine: Pre–World War I Period   115

    B / Middle East: World War I Period   115
        Sykes-Picot Agreement   116
        Hussein-McMahon Correspondence   117
        Balfour Declaration   117
        The Arab Revolt   118
        The Kingdom of Greater Syria   119
        Paris Peace Conference   120
        Partition of the Ottoman Empire   120

    C / Mandate Period, 1922–1948   121
        Immediate Postwar Rule in Palestine   121
        Establishment of the Mandates in the
            Middle East   122
        Britain & the Arabs   122

    D / Mandate for Palestine   123
        Britain Mandatory Power   125
        Mandate in the 1920s   126
        Arab Society in Mandatory Palestine   127
        Jewish Immigration   128

Mandate in the 1930s   129
Arab Revolt in Palestine, 1936–1939   130
1939 White Paper   132
United States & Palestine   132

E / World War II in Palestine & the Middle East   133
    Jewish Terrorism in Palestine during World War II   134

F / The Destruction of Jews in Europe   135

G / End of the Mandate, 1940–1948   136
    Palestine Question, 1940–1948   136
    British Palestine Policy   137
    Zionism in Palestine   138
    Arab Society, 1940–1948   138
    United States & Zionism after World War II   139
    Solutions Never Tested   140

H / Partition of Palestine   140

I / The Palestine War, 1948   142
    Israeli Views of the 1948 War   143
    Arab Views of the 1948 War   143
    Count Folke Bernadotte & Conciliation   144
    Armistice   145

J / British Policies: An Overview   145
    Britain in the Middle East   145
    Britain & Palestine   147
    Britain & the Arabs   147

VI / ARAB-ISRAELI WARS   149

A / Military Developments, 1948–1955   149

B / Suez-Sinai War, 1956   150
    History of Suez Canal   150
    Aswan Dam   151
    Suez Canal Nationalization   152
    1956 Suez Crisis   154
    Prelude to November 1956   155

        Israel's Sinai Campaign   155
        British & French Intervention   156
        United States, U.S.S.R., & Evacuation   158
        Aftermath   158

C / Military Evolution to 1967   160

D / Six-Day War, 1967   161
        The Buildup, May 1967   163
        United Nations Emergency Force (UNEF)   164
        Straits of Tiran & Gulf of Aqaba   165
        The War   166
        Aftermath   168
        Six-Day War: World Effects   170
        The Great Powers & the Six-Day War   171

E / Palestinian Resistance   172
        Palestine Liberation Organization (PLO) to 1968   174
        Origins & Rise of Resistance, 1964–1970   174
        Jordanian Civil War, 1970–1971   175
        Lebanon, the Resistance, & Israel   176
        Guerrillas to World Terrorism   177
        Israeli Counteractions   179
        Black September   180

F / Military Evolution Since the Six-Day War   180
        The Arms Balance   180
        Israel Defense Forces (IDF)   182
            Doctrine & Tactics   182
            Air Force   184
            Weapons   185
        War of Attrition (Suez Canal), 1969–1970   186
        Arab Armed Forces   187
        Nuclear Weapons   188
        Soviets Out of Egypt, 1972   188
        October 1973 War   189
        Strategic Considerations, Post–1973: Suez, Red Sea, Sinai   191
        Spies   192

VII / THE UNITED NATIONS & PEACE EFFORTS   194

    A / The United Nations & the Arab-Israeli Problem   194
        International Military Force   195

United Nations Truce Supervision Organization
    (UNTSO)   196

B / Prospects for Peace   196

C / Peace Efforts   199
    United Nations Resolution 242   199
    Jarring Mission   199
    Rogers Plan   200
    Kissinger's Efforts   202

VIII / THE WEST, THE SUPERPOWERS, & THE MIDDLE EAST   204

A / Superpowers in the Middle East   205

B / United States & the Middle East   207
    Historical Ties   207
    Policy in the Contemporary Middle East   207
    United States Interests & Policy Goals   210
    Relations with the Arab World   214
    Eisenhower Doctrine & Lebanon, 1958   215
    United States Policy toward Israel   216
    Zionism: Israel & American Jewry   216
    United States Economic & Military Aid   217
    United States Mediterranean Fleet   218

C / Soviet Union & the Middle East   219
    Historical Ties   219
    Relations with Contemporary Middle East   220
    Soviet Interests & Policy   223
    Attitudes toward the Arab World   224
    Soviet Union & Israel   225
    Soviet Jewry Question   226
    Soviet Military Aid   226
    Economic Policy & Aid   226
    Soviet Mediterranean Fleet   227

D / Communism in the Middle East: Arab World   229

E / China, Sino-Soviet Relations, & the Middle East   230

F / Europe & the Arabs & Israel   231

CONTENTS

IX / CONTINUING PROBLEMS   233

    A / Jordan Waters Conflict   233
          The Johnston Plan   234
          Water Diversion   235

    B / Jerusalem   236
          Jerusalem Holy City   237
          Jerusalem, 1948–1967   238
          Jerusalem, 1967–1973   238
          Jerusalem Solution   240

    C / Middle East Oil   241
          Concessions & Early Efforts to 1950   241
          Oil Developments, 1950–1970   242
          Organization of Petroleum Exporting Countries
            (OPEC)   245
          Oil in the 1970s   245
          Oil as a Political Weapon   247
          Soviet Interests in Middle East Oil   248

    D / Conflict Continued, 1967–1973   249
          Israeli Positions & Views   252
          Arab Positions & Views   254

Index   256

FOREWORD

With this bibliographical series, the Center for the Study of Armament and Disarmament, California State University, Los Angeles, seeks to promote a wider understanding of martial violence and the alternatives to its employment. The Center, which was formed by concerned faculty and students in 1962–1963, has as its primary objective the stimulation of intelligent discussion of war/peace issues. More precisely, the Center has undertaken two essential functions: (1) to collect and catalogue materials bearing on war/peace issues; and (2) to aid faculty, students, and the public in their individual and collective probing of the historical, political, economic, philosophical, technical, and psychological facets of these fundamental problems.

This bibliographical series is, obviously, one tool with which we may more effectively approach our task. Each issue in this series is intended to provide a comprehensive "working," rather than definitive, bibliography on a relatively narrow theme within the spectrum of war/peace studies. While we hope this series will prove to be a useful tool, we also solicit your comments regarding its format, contents, and topics.

Richard Dean Burns
Series Editor

BRIEF CHRONOLOGY OF THE ARAB-ISRAELI CONFLICT

70 A.D.	Romans destroy the Second Temple in Jerusalem Beginning of the Jewish Diaspora
636 A.D.	Muslim-Arab conquest of Palestine
1882	Pinsker's *Autoemancipation* published
1896	Theodor Herzl's *Der Judenstaat* published
1897	First Zionist Congress, Basel, Switzerland; World Zionist Organization founded
1903	Sixth Zionist Congress Great Britain offers territory in East Africa
1904	(July) Theodor Herzl dies
1905	N. Azouri, an Arab publisher in Paris, advocates Arab independence from Ottoman rule
1915	Ottoman Empire joins Central Powers in war against Entente Powers Hussein-McMahon correspondence
1916	Arab Revolt led by the Sherif of Mecca Sykes-Picot Agreement between Britain and France on division of Ottoman territory after the war
1917	(November 2) Balfour Declaration (private letter from Lord Balfour, British Foreign Secretary, to Lord Rothschild)
1919	King-Crane Commission investigates wishes of peoples in the Middle East
1920	San Remo Conference (victorious powers divide Ottoman territory)
1922	(July) Britain granted League of Nations mandate over Palestine The Churchill White Paper (Churchill Colonial Secretary)
1929	Arab riots in Palestine against Zionist aims
1930	British White Paper on Palestine

1933	(January 30) Adolf Hitler becomes Chancellor of Germany
1936	Arab general strike in Palestine
1937	Peel Commission (Palestine Royal Commission) proposes partition of Palestine
	Members of Arab High Committee arrested and exiled
1939	British White Paper, proposed restriction of Jewish immigration
1940	New land transfer regulations aimed at controlling Zionist land acquisition in Palestine
1944	Jewish Brigade Group organized by Allies
1946	Anglo-American Committee of Inquiry
	(July 22) Irgun blows up wing of King David Hotel, Jerusalem
1947	(April 28) Special session of U.N. General Assembly on Palestine at request of Britain
	(November 29) U.N. General Assembly adopts plan for partition of Palestine with internationalized Jerusalem
1948	(May 14) British High Commissioner leaves Palestine; state of Israel proclaimed; U.S. recognizes state of Israel
	(May 17) U.S.S.R. recognizes Israel
	(May–February 1949) Palestine War, interspersed with truces
1949	(February) Armistice agreements between Israel and various Arab states
	(May) Israel admitted to the U.N.
	(September 17) U.N. mediator, Count Folke Bernadotte, killed by Zionist terrorists
1950	Israel's "Law of Return" enacted (every Jew has the right to immigrate to Israel)
	(April 25) Jordan annexes West Bank area and Jerusalem
	(May 25) Tripartite agreement (France, Britain, and U.S.) to limit arms to Israel and Arab states
1951	(July 20) King Abdullah of Jordan assassinated by Arab extremists
1952	Coup d'etat in Egypt removes King Farouk from the throne
1955	(February 28) Israeli raid into Egyptian-administered Gaza Strip
	(September) Egyptian-Czech arms deal announced
	(December) Egypt assured of financing for initial stages of Aswan Dam project by U.S. and Britain
1956	(June 13) Suez Canal Zone turned over to Egypt
	(July) U.S. and Britain withdraw promise to assist initial financing of Aswan Dam
	Egypt nationalizes the Suez Canal Company
	(October 29) Israel launches attack into Sinai

(November) British-French attack on Egyptian forces in Suez Canal Zone
(December 22) Last British and French troops leave Egypt

1957 (March) U.N. Emergency Force stationed in Gaza and Sinai
(March) Israel evacuation of Sinai and Gaza completed (assurances to Israel of free passage in Straits of Tiran)

1958 (February 1) United Arab Republic (U.A.R.) formed by Egypt and Syria
(July 14) Military coup in Iraq, monarchy destroyed
(July 15) U.S. Marines land in Lebanon
(July 17) British paratroopers enter Jordan at request of government
(October-November) U.S. and British troops withdrawn from Lebanon and Jordan

1961 (April) Adolf Eichmann tried in Jerusalem
(September) Syria withdraws from U.A.R. following coup d'etat in Damascus

1962 U.S. agrees to supply Israel Hawk antiaircraft missiles
(September) Army revolt in Yemen against rule of the Imam; beginning of the Yemeni civil war
(October) Egyptian troops sent to Yemen to aid Republican forces

1963 (November) Crown Prince Faisal assumes complete control of Saudi Arabia

1964 (January) Unified Arab Command created by meeting of Arab leaders to strengthen Arab forces in relation to Israel
(May) Palestine Liberation Organization created after meeting of Arab states in Jerusalem
(September) Arab plan to divert headwaters of the Jordan River adopted at Arab summit conference (Cairo) to counter Israeli diversion plan

1965 (February) West Germany announces halt of arms shipments to Israel
(March 7) West Germany announces diplomatic recognition of Israel
(September) U.S. Agricultural Assistance Act (PL 480) amended by Congress to exclude U.A.R. unless "... the President determines that such sale is in the national interests of the United States"

1966 (February 23) Left wing of Baath party takes power in Syria
(April 2) U.S. to sell F-104 Starfighter aircraft to Jordan

(April 30) Israelis retaliate against Jordanian villages for six incidents during April
(May 19) U.S. to sell A-4 Skyhawk aircraft to Israel
(September-November) Continuing incidents on Syrian-Israeli border
(November 4) U.A.R. and Syria sign mutual defense pact
(November 13) Israelis invade Jordan and destroy town of Samu; villagers evacuated before homes blown up; U.N. toll of raid—18 killed, 134 wounded, 127 buildings destroyed
(December) Israel announces abolition of military government in border areas (only partially carried out)

1967 (January-April) Continued incidents on Syrian-Israeli border
(April 17) Six Syrian MIGs shot down by Israeli aircraft
(May 15) Egypt moves forces into Sinai
(May 19) U.N. Emergency Force withdrawn by U.N. Secretary General at Egyptian request
(May 23) Egyptian President Nasser declares Straits of Tiran closed to Israel
(June 5) Israeli aircraft attack Arab airfields, destroying Arab air forces on the ground; beginning of Six-Day War
(June 7) East Jerusalem and West Bank captured by Israel
(June 8) Israelis reach Suez Canal
(June 10) Israelis storm Golan Heights;
cease-fire ends Six-Day War
(October) Egyptians sink Israeli destroyer *Eilat;* Israelis shell Egyptian oil refineries at Suez
(November 22) U.N. Resolution 242 calling for Middle East settlement passed

1968 (March 22) Karameh, Jordan, attacked in Israeli raid against Palestinian bases across Jordan River

1969 (April 1) "War of Attrition" announced by President Nasser

1970 (January-April) Israeli deep penetration raids into Nile Valley begin
(April) U.S.S.R. assumes responsibility for Nile Valley air defense
(April 13) Israel suspends deep penetration raids
(May-August) Intensified "War of Attrition" along Suez Canal; Israeli air power vs. Egyptian artillery
(June-August) Intense U.S. efforts to gain a cease-fire
(June-August) Egyptian and Soviet forces extend missile defenses into Canal zone
(August 7) Suez Canal cease-fire

	(August) Multiple aircraft hijackings by Popular Front for the Liberation of Palestine
	Jordanian civil war
	(September) President Nasser dies
1971	(May 27) U.S.S.R.-Egypt pact of friendship and cooperation
	(December) Long-term U.S.-Israeli arms procurement accord
1972	(March 15) King Hussein of Jordan proposes a United Arab Kingdom to embrace the Palestinian Arabs
	(July) Egyptian President Anwar Sadat announces the expulsion of Soviet military units and advisors
1973	(October 6) Egyptian troops cross Suez Canal; Syrian forces attack on Golan Heights (fourth Arab-Israeli war)
	(October 22) U.N. call for cease-fire
	(October 24) Cease-fire goes into effect on Suez front
	(November 11) Egypt and Israel sign cease-fire accord
	(December 21) Arab-Israeli Peace Conference convenes in Geneva (many parties not represented)
1974	(April) Government crisis in Israel over conduct of October War
	(May 29) Syrian-Israeli disengagement agreement announced
	(May) Palestinian units focus actions on suicide attacks against settlements inside pre–June 1967 Israel

INTRODUCTION

The Arab-Israeli conflict is a modern Gordian knot that continues to complicate recent history and current international politics. Regrettably, no modern Alexander (not even Henry Kissinger) has appeared capable of solving the problem with a single decisive stroke. The vast complexities of the Arab-Israeli conflict are rooted in the history of Palestine, for centuries a critical area of cultural transition. Some commentators extend the issue almost back to Creation although they rarely agree as to when even that event took place. The Arab-Israeli problem evokes heated discussion of its exact nature, whether it is a clash of religions or races, or a territorial dispute involving demographic goals. Recent analysis tends to focus on the clash of nationalisms which arose during the late nineteenth and twentieth centuries. The imbroglio which developed has become more critical, its repercussions ever-widening. The problem was brought into sharper focus during the Mandate period and following the creation of the state of Israel. But definition of the problem has not brought a solution. According to an often-used description, the continuing conflict has three separate levels. First, the dispute between the Arab states and Israel; second, the involvement of the United States and the Soviet Union with the risk of a nuclear confrontation between the superpowers; third, the conflict among Arab states over the solution to the Palestine problem, which has caused continuing turmoil in the Arab world. This useful taxonomy, however, neglects the Palestinian Arabs as a factor.

The continuing dispute has resulted in four wars of increasing ferocity and expanded consequences. For example, in October 1973 the Soviet Union and the United States went on military alert and the Arab oil-exporting nations, far from the place of conflict, imposed an oil embargo on most industrial nations. In this unique conflict men have received the Nobel Peace Prize for merely effecting brief cessations of the fighting. The problems will take years to resolve—indeed, there may not be a peaceful solution.

Origins & Rise of Nationalism

In its most rudimentary form, the Arab-Israeli conflict is the result of two peoples attempting to occupy the same parcel of land at the same time. The Zionists claim that Palestine or Zion was the Promised Land. The area was inhabited when the Hebrew tribes moved in initially and elements of this population remained. Because of its geographical position, Palestine has been a mixing bowl of people.

The Kingdom of Israel, established under the Maccabees in 141 B.C., was short-lived. It fell under the hegemony of the Roman Empire, and when the Jews revolted, the Romans crushed the rebellion, destroying the Second Temple and expelling most of the Jews in 70 A.D. A small Jewish population remained in Palestine after the dispersion but the vast bulk of the population was not Jewish. Many of the people spoke Semitic languages, including some dialects of Arabic. Palestine, and especially Jerusalem, became a center of Christian pilgrimage under Emperor Constantine I in the fourth century A.D. and it has continued in that role.

The next signal event was the conquest of Palestine, then under Byzantine domination, by the Muslim-Arab armies in 636 A.D.—four years after the death of the prophet Muhammad. In the centuries that followed, the population, having ethnic, linguistic, and even religious affinities with the Muslims, easily accepted the language and religion of the new rulers. The people of Palestine adopted the Arabic language and a large majority became Muslim, although a substantial Arab Christian minority remained. Palestine has since been ruled by various conquerors: by Muslims, briefly by Christians during the Crusades, and again by a series of Muslim dynasties. The last Muslim rulers were the Ottoman Turks, who captured Palestine in 1517 and ruled until 1918.

The current Arab-Israeli conflict germinated during the last quarter of the nineteenth century. During that period the rise of ethnic nationalism in central and eastern Europe created a dual problem. The Jews were persecuted because they lacked the required ethnic, religious, and linguistic credentials. At the same time the Jews were caught up by the same emotions of ethnic nationalism but they lacked land upon which to establish a state—although they felt that it should be located in Zion—the Promised Land. Zionism emerged from these persecutions as an expression of the desire among many

Jews to have their own state. Most Zionists, however, were unaware of what had happened in Zion since 70 A.D. and this would result in grave problems. But nationalist fervor did not require, it even negated, the asking of some pragmatic questions.

Similar feelings of nationalism were stirring among Arab intellectuals in the Middle East. The Arabs had been relatively content under the Ottomans because they were part of a great Muslim empire. The decline of the Ottoman regime and the Young Turk Revolution during the first decade of the 1900s, however, brought the Arab position into question. The Young Turks came increasingly to emphasize their Turkish origins and adopt Pan-Turkic ideas. The Arabs consequently began thinking in terms of their own national identity and a small but influential Arab nationalist movement was formed. The aims of both the Arabs and the Zionists included the territory of Palestine.

World War I & the Mandate Period

During World War I, one of the most intense and confusing periods in the evolution of the Arab-Israeli problem began. The Turks allied themselves with the Central Powers against the Triple Entente. Turkish control over Palestine threatened Britain's lifeline to India, the Suez Canal. The British were also concerned because the sultan, acting as caliph (the successor of Muhammad), declared a holy war (jihad) against Turkey's enemies. Britain feared the effects this might have on the large Muslim population they controlled in India. The British negotiations with Hussein ibn 'Ali, the Sherif of Mecca, a direct descendant of Muhammad and the protector of the Muslim holy places in Arabia, were generally aimed at the Sherif's leading an Arab revolt against the Turks in return for Arab independence after the war. Although the correspondence between the Sherif Hussein and the British High Commissioner in Egypt, Sir Henry McMahon, was vague, the Arabs clearly expressed their intention that Palestine was to be part of the new Arab state. The British did not make a firm commitment.

The Arab Revolt was declared and the Turkish garrison at Medina was attacked in 1916. But in May 1916, in order to avoid postwar disputes, the British and French negotiated the Sykes-Picot Agreement, one of a series of secret treaties dividing Ottoman territory among the Allies. The treaty created "spheres of influence" clearly in conflict with the British correspondence with the Sherif Hussein.

Among the many remarkable and contradictory documents produced during World War I which confused the Palestine issue was the Balfour Declaration of November 2, 1917. As the position of the Entente Powers became critical, the British Foreign Secretary, Lord Arthur J. Balfour, responded to Zionist pressure by addressing a letter to banker Lord Rothschild which stated that the British government viewed with favor "the establishment in Palestine of a national home for the Jewish people and will use their best endeavors to facilitate the achievement of that object . . ."[1] The words "national home" were not defined and the Balfour Declaration further blurred Palestine's future if the Entente won the war.

After the defeat of Turkey and the Central Powers, the determination of the future of Ottoman land was delayed. Finally, at the San Remo Conference in 1920, and agreement was reached which generally paralleled the terms of the Sykes-Picot Agreement. The League of Nations (created by the Paris Peace Conference), technically responsible for the disposition of the territories of the defeated nations, created the mandate system to deal with the problem. Britain was granted the mandate for Palestine in 1922 and the Balfour Declaration was included in the charter. The British were thus placed in the delicate situation of preparing Palestine for independence while at the same time viewing with favor the establishment of a Jewish "national home" in Palestine.

The contradiction soon became manifest. The Zionists openly sought to establish a Jewish majority in the area as the basis for the creation of a Jewish state. The Arab nationalist leaders immediately perceived that the British policies, if carried out, implied a dire future for them. Thus, the major issues during the mandate period were the immigration of Jews into Palestine; the acquisition of land by Jews and especially Zionist agencies; and the form of government that would follow the British departure. From 1918 through 1947 there were sporadic outbursts of violence in Palestine that usually evoked either a commission of inquiry or an official British white paper or both. During this thirty-year period several contradictory recommendations were formulated: to encourage or to restrict Jewish immigration; to permit or to forbid Jewish land acquisition; to partition Palestine or create a unitary state, i.e., a state dominated by the Arab majority. None of these recommendations was ever fully implemented because of countervailing pressures. The situation reached a critical stage in 1936, when the Arabs declared a general strike which they maintained for several months.

---

1. J. C. Hurewitz, *Diplomacy in the Near and Middle East: A Documentary Record*, vol. 2 (New York: Octagon Books, 1972), p. 26.

Active resistance to British rule continued until 1939. The new Arab determination was prompted by a vast increase in Jewish immigration that accompanied the rise of Nazism in Germany. In October 1937, the British attempted to break organized Arab resistance by arresting the members of the Arab High Committee of Palestine and deporting them to islands in the Indian Ocean. This critical move stripped the Arab community in Palestine of its traditional leadership and that loss was to be felt following the end of World War II. The Arabs won a point, on paper at least, when the British White Paper of 1939 proposed the restriction of Jewish immigration and the establishment of controls over Zionist land acquisition. But World War II intervened to prevent the implementation of the proposed policies.

World War II & the Partition of Palestine

During World War II British attention was diverted from Palestine but the mandated area remained in political turmoil. The Palestinian Arabs held the British responsible for the incursion of Zionism and considered them their enemy. Consequently, there was some Arab flirtation with Germany. The Jewish community was split; most Jews viewed Germany as their primary foe because of the Nazi persecutions. Many Palestinian Jewish youths enlisted in the Jewish brigade of the British army to fight Nazism and to acquire military skills which would be needed in the contest for Palestine. A small but violent group dissented, contending that Britain was the real enemy because the British controlled Palestine. These Jewish paramilitary groups, the Irgun and the Stern Gang, waged a campaign of terror against British authorities throughout the war.

Britain emerged from the war exhausted economically and militarily. Palestine constituted a continuing drain on Britain's limited resources while other areas of traditional British interests called for attention and resources. The British position in Palestine was further weakened because Britain had no friends in the area. Zionist efforts were given an increased sense of urgency when the full scope of Nazi efforts to exterminate Europe's Jews became known with the end of the war. There was the immediate problem of over 100,000 Jewish displaced persons in Europe whom the Jewish Agency wanted to transport to Palestine.

During the war Zionist political and diplomatic efforts shifted from Britain to the United States. The 1939 White Paper led the Zionists to believe that British policy was "pro-Arab" and this feeling was reinforced as oil from the Arab countries appeared to be increasingly important to Britain's economic well-being. Although the Arabs lacked effective spokesmen for their position, they clearly did not want to be dominated by either Britain or the Zionists.

A joint Anglo-American committee of inquiry was appointed in 1946 but its recommendations pleased neither local group. Zionist terrorism directed at the British forces increased. Britain then referred the Palestine problem to the United Nations in April 1947 and the General Assembly voted in November 1947 to partition the country into Jewish and Arab states and to place the city of Jerusalem under international control. The Zionists accepted the proposal; the Arabs did not. The Zionists anticipated the Arab rejection and were confident that the plan would not be implemented, so they felt there was no danger in accepting it even though the plan did not meet their objectives.

The Mandate ended on May 14, 1948, and the state of Israel proclaimed its existence. But sporadic fighting had broken out months before and there was no doubt that might of arms, not a United Nations resolution, would determine the future of Palestine. The Arab states pledged to aid their Palestinian brethren and the Zionists had long been working to establish a strong fighting force.

The Palestine War (1948-1949) was a small-scale conflict by any standard, but it had all the elements of violence, hatred, and tragedy of war. The fighting, interspersed with truces, eventually resulted in a state of Israel containing more territory than allotted by the United Nations partition plan and part of the city of Jerusalem. The war was halted by various armistice agreements and in May 1949 Israel was admitted to the United Nations.

The war created hundreds of thousands of Palestinian Arab refugees. Initially numbering about 750,000, most were lodged in camps located in the neighboring Arab states; in the West Bank region annexed by the Kingdom of Trans-Jordan (renamed the Hashimite Kingdom of Jordan); and in the Gaza Strip under Egyptian administration. Within two decades the Palestinian refugees and their descendants numbered about one and a half million (not including the refugees from the 1967 war).

The Continuing Conflict

The continuing Arab-Israeli conflict is based on the problems unresolved in 1948-1949. Will the Jewish state of Israel exist? What will happen to the Palestinian refugees? Who is responsible for them? What will be the status of Jerusalem, the holy city of three monotheistic religions?

Since 1949 almost nothing has been accomplished to ameliorate the situation or resolve these questions. Actually, subsequent developments have exacerbated the situation. Israel's Knesset (Parliament) passed the "Law of Return" in 1950, which proclaimed the right of any Jew to immigrate to Israel and be granted automatic citizenship. The Arabs interpreted the law as an indication of future expansion. Arab nationalism was on the rise, as signaled by the coup d'etat led by Colonel Nasser which overthrew the Egyptian monarchy in 1952. Arab nationalists have always paid lip service to the cause of the Palestinian Arabs but there have been no tangible results.

The efforts of the major Western powers (i.e., the United States, Britain, and France) to control the situation by regulating the flow of weapons into the area were never entirely successful. They failed completely following Nasser's conclusion of an arms agreement with Czechoslovakia in 1955. After Nasser's assumption of power in Egypt, it was evident that Egyptian nationalism and foreign control of the Suez Canal were incompatible. The years 1955 and 1956 were punctuated by a critical sequence of events: Israel's large-scale reprisal raid into the Gaza Strip (February 1955); Egyptian-Czechoslovakian arms agreement (September 1955); United States withdrawal of its offer to Egypt to finance preliminary stages of the Aswan High Dam (July 1956); Egypt nationalizes Suez Canal Company to provide revenue to pay for the Aswan High Dam (July 1956); armed forces of Israel, Britain, and France invade Egypt (October–November 1956). This sequence of events is simplified but considerable controversy swirls around each stage.

Britain and France were clearly the losers of the Suez-Sinai war because they failed to gain their objective and suffered adverse world opinion. Egypt, defeated militarily, won a huge diplomatic victory. Strong pressure from the United States accompanied by ostentatious Soviet "rocket rattling" forced the invaders to withdraw from the territory they had occupied. Israel gained access to the Red Sea when the Straits of Tiran came under the control of the newly created United Nations Emergency Force (UNEF). The stationing of UNEF troops on the Egyptian side of the border neutralized the Egyptian Israeli border as an area of conflict. Israel refused to permit UNEF on its soil. Nothing was resolved in 1956. All the basic issues of the Arab-Israeli dispute remained. In an international context, the events of 1956 weakened the mutual confidence of the members of NATO.

During the next decade the Arab-Israeli conflict continued to simmer but it often seemed to be submerged by regional inter-Arab conflicts. During 1958 regional instability was emphasized by the overthrow of the monarchy in Iraq; the landing of United States Marines in Lebanon; and the airlift of British troops into Jordan. The Imam of Yemen was overthrown in a military coup and both Egypt and Saudi Arabia became involved in the civil war which followed. Syria was wracked by a series of coups. During this period the Arab-Israeli dispute appeared to center on such controversies as the use of the Jordan River and its tributaries. The Palestinian refugees continued to subsist in camps administered by the United Nations, supported by contributions. The Palestinian Arabs began forming paramilitary organizations during the mid-1960s with the intent of retaking their homeland by violence. Arab politics during this period consigned the Arab-Israeli problem to the future.

Israeli reprisal raids against Jordan and Syria increased the tempo of events in 1966. These raids were partly in response to attacks launched by Palestinian-organized fedayeen beginning in 1965. A coup d'etat brought the left wing of the Baath party to power in Damascus and Syria's stance toward Israel became more bellicose. The U.A.R. (Egypt) concluded a mutual defense pact with Syria in November 1966. Violence continued to flare along the Syrian-Israeli border; the most dramatic event was the shooting down by Israeli fighters of six Syrian MIGs in April 1967. Damascus now challenged Cairo to prove its claim to leadership of the Arab cause. The events of spring 1967 seemed to move inexorably toward war. Nasser requested the removal of the UNEF and the United Nations Secretary General complied immediately. Once the UNEF left Sinai, Nasser as an Arab leader had no choice but to close the Straits of Tiran to Israel, a move which Israel stated would be an act of war. To much of the world Israel appeared a small state threatened with extinction by a numerically overwhelming enemy. During six days in June, Israel shocked the world with its lightning victory over the armed forces of its three Arab neighbors. Israel was able to satisfy almost all of its strategic and territorial goals: control of the Straits of Tiran, unification of the city of Jerusalem, and occupation of the Golan Heights. Controversy has since engulfed the origins of the Six-Day War. Israeli generals have stated that Israel's existence was not endangered by the might of the Arab states arrayed against it. There is little reason to believe the Arabs planned full-scale war.

The magnitude of the victory in the Six-Day War surprised the world, the Arab countries, the Palestinians, and probably the Israelis. Israel was clearly the dominant military power in its continuing dispute with the Arabs. The Israelis controlled the Straits of Tiran along with the remainder of the Sinai peninsula. Israeli forces on the banks of the blocked Suez Canal resulted in that waterway being closed to commerce, thereby depriving Egypt of a significant source of revenue. The occupation of the Golan Heights meant that Israelis in the valley below no longer needed to fear Syrian artillery. Jerusalem was no longer a city divided by barbed wire and fortifications. Israel took the West Bank area from Jordan and the Gaza Strip from Egyptian forces; but occupation of these last two areas was viewed with mixed feelings in Israel. On one hand, in a military-geographical perspective Israelis felt more secure; on the other, approximately one million Arab inhabitants were now under Israeli control. What was the Jewish state to do with them?

The swift victory did not bring peace to the area with equal speed. The fighting stopped after six days because of mounting international pressure on Israel and because Israel had already accomplished almost all its military objectives. But the United Nations required over five months to approve a resolution as to how the events of June should be resolved. On November 22, 1967, the Security Council passed Resolution 242. The resolution called for an Israeli withdrawal from the territories occupied in the war, implied there was to be a reciprocal recognition of the state of Israel, and requested that the problems of guaranteed frontiers and settlement of the refugees be resolved through negotiations.[2] The opposing sides interpreted Resolution 242 differently: the Arab states demanded withdrawal prior to negotiations; Israel, negotiations prior to withdrawal. The United Nations sent Swedish diplomat Gunnar V. Jarring into this maelstrom; he met almost total frustration in three years of effort.

During this period the Arab-Israeli arena became the focal point of the most intense arms race in the world. The United States became the chief supplier of arms to Israel and the Soviet Union continued to supply Egypt and Syria. Each side was provided sophisticated modern weapons. Israel retained a dominant military position by increasing its air power and armored corps despite significant Arab gains in equipment and training. The occasional outbreaks of fighting along the Suez Canal became almost continuous in 1969, when President Nasser declared a "War of Attrition" against Israel. Israel responded with raids deep into the Nile Valley and Delta and the Soviet Union countered by dispatching a force of 15,000 air defense troops to Egypt in April 1970. The involvement of the superpowers was continuing to grow. After intensive efforts by the United States

---

2. "Security Council Adopts Resolution: With Text," *U.N. Monthly Chronicle* 4 (Dec. 1967): 20.

in mid-1970, a cease-fire went into effect along the Suez Canal in August 1970. The peace initiatives of Secretary of State William Rogers were, however, blocked by the activities of the Palestinian Arabs, the death of President Nasser, and the civil war in Jordan. Both sides continued to expand their arms inventories.

Perhaps the most significant result of the Six-Day War was the emergence of the Palestinian resistance movement. Prior to 1967 most Palestinian refugees placed their faith in the armies of the Arab states to eventually return them to their homes. The Six-Day War completely discredited conventional Arab military forces, and the Palestinian Arab refugees turned to the fedayeen commando groups formed to fight Israel. These groups, regarded as terrorists by the Israelis, have captured the imagination of Palestinian Arabs and much of the Arab world—in spite of the fact that the fedayeen movement has never been strongly centralized and their activities are characterized by a vast diversity of goals and methods. Yet, the fedayeen have galvanized the collective consciousness of Palestinians whether they are in the refugee camps, successful bureaucrats and technicians in the Persian Gulf states, or scholars in Western universities. The fedayeen pose no military threat to Israel but they have infused in the Palestinian Arab refugees a lasting sense of identity and determination.

The Six-Day War introduced another significant change which the Israelis have been slow to recognize. Israel, for the first time, occupied territory which traditionally was part of an Arab state, i.e., the Sinai peninsula belonging to Egypt, and the Golan Heights belonging to Syria. The occupation created a new issue in dealing with the Palestine question for these Arab states because they were now strongly motivated to recover their lost lands.

The inflexibility of Israel's policy between 1967 and 1973 was perhaps the most disappointing result of the Six-Day War. The surprisingly easy victory required an almost complete reversal in the thinking of Israeli leaders. Israel was no longer a small and helpless David; it had become a regional Goliath. But since Israeli policy-makers were steeped in the Zionist movement, their policy concepts were forged during the Mandate and tempered in the 1948 war and the Sinai campaign, it is understandable that they could not grasp the new situation and the need for a more flexible policy vis-à-vis their neighbors. It is possible that if they had acted magnanimously they might have contrived a peaceful resolution and gained the recognition they desired. No such gesture was forthcoming. Arab statesmen were humiliated by the crushing defeat and could not bring themselves to plead with their victorious enemy.

The six-year period of no progress frustrated Egypt and Syria. The October 1973 war was a direct result, as Arab leaders resorted to the ultimate diplomatic tool—military force. It is doubtful that the leaders of Egypt and Syria believed they could crush Israel; they probably felt that their only alternative was to fight, win or lose. The October 1973 war was initiated by Egypt and Syria and their armed forces exploited tactical surprise to retake territory on the Golan Heights and on the east bank of the Suez Canal. Israel's military forces overcame their opponents' initial advantage and eventually dominated the fighting. But some diplomatic movement resulted from the hostilities. Once again, as in 1967, the Arab-Israeli conflict almost drew the United States and the Soviet Union into confrontation, and those superpowers were apparently powerless to restrain their respective "clients."

Despite some of the steps taken to alleviate the problems resulting from the Six-Day War, the major problems remain. Israel has not been accepted by its neighbors. There has been no resolution of the plight of the Palestinian Arab refugees—they have not been compensated for the loss of their homes, and it is not likely they will be repatriated. The three million Jews in Israel have nowhere else to go, and one and a half million Palestinian Arabs claim the right to live there. The Arab-Israeli conflict is a tinderbox that threatens continued unrest and war.

The issues must be studied if they are to be resolved—or if they are to be discussed intelligently. It is hoped that this bibliography will contribute to a measure of understanding. With understanding there is hope.

NOTE ON USE AS A RESEARCH TOOL

"On no area of the Middle East has so much been written by so many with so little concern for objective appraisal and analysis as on Palestine. Any attempt to analyze exhaustively the books, pamphlets, official documents, and articles of even the last dozen years would demand a volume in itself and the collective effort of many scholars, for no one can pretend to have read—let alone digested—all of this material."[1] This statement (made in 1949) was only a warning; the stream of literature on Palestine and the Arab-Israeli conflict has become an ever-increasing torrent. Scholars in the field are tempted to consider building an ark to keep their heads above the deluge of paper.

This bibliography is intended as a preliminary "working" guide to the literature for scholars and especially for graduate and undergraduate students. It will be useful to the reader interested in various aspects of the Arab-Israeli conflict. In order to keep the published volume to a manageable length, utility and availability of sources became criteria for inclusion. In each category, an attempt has been made to cite critical sources about which the user should be aware. The selections are confined almost completely to English-language materials, since most undergraduate students are unfamiliar with Arabic, Hebrew, and the East European languages, and since materials in those languages are not generally available. Some items which appear in a major European language in a well-known scholarly publication are included when they concern some unique aspect of the subject matter. Unfortunately, many articles of possible interest appear in journals of very restricted circulation and they are

---

1. J. C. Hurewitz, "Recent Books on the Problem of Palestine," *Middle East Journal* 3 (Jan. 1949): 86.

not cited. The user will find references to this kind of serial literature in *Historical Abstracts,* Part B, *Twentieth Century Abstracts* (published by the American Bibliographical Center).

In general, items are cited which the user might reasonably expect to find in a university library of about 500,000 volumes. Even that criterion, however, required selectivity to ensure that the bibliography would be broad in scope and variety. Therefore, an attempt was made to include works which present a diversity of views on a given subject in order to give the user a broad perspective on the evolution of the conflict. For example, some articles of average quality written during the mid-1950s have been retained, while a few of many first-rate articles which have appeared since 1967 have been deliberately omitted.

This bibliography is not definitive but it attempts to be comprehensive in that virtually all of the factors involved in the Arab-Israeli conflict are covered. It is intended as a reference tool that will permit the student and interested reader to quickly find items which are of concern and to establish a basis for further research.

As a first step in using the bibliography, the user should consult the extensive Table of Contents, classified to facilitate reference to particular subjects. The headings are necessarily arbitrary, and the user will then find it profitable to seek references under less directly related headings. Every effort has been made to maintain consistency in the citations of periodicals, but it should be noted that many periodicals publishing on the topic do not follow a consistent pattern of reference.

The Arab-Israeli conflict has generated a vast collection of historical literature—but it also continues to "make history" on an almost daily basis. Bibliographies as well as the primary literature become dated even as they are in the process of publication. Most of this bibliography is "historical" in that it cites sources published prior to 1974. The user will find it necessary to consult the surveys of books and periodical literature available to keep abreast of new works and current events. The user's attention is therefore directed especially to the periodicals in review sections of *Middle East Journal* and *Journal of Palestine Studies* (published quarterly). Excellent articles on the subject appear frequently in indexed newspapers: *The New York Times, Christian Science Monitor,* and *The Times* (London) are also valuable sources.

The comments and advice of users on this "working" bibliography, concerning contents, organization, and topics covered, are encouraged and most welcome. These comments will play an important role in revisions incorporated in future editions.

THE ARAB-ISRAELI CONFLICT

I / REFERENCES & GENERAL WORKS

A / Bibliographies

1 Besterman, Theodore. *World Bibliography of Bibliographies.* 3d ed. Geneva: Societas Bibliographica, 1965–1966.

2 *Bibliographic Index.* New York: H. W. Wilson, 1937–. [Annual]

3 *Foreign Affairs Bibliography: A Selected and Annotated List of Books on International Relations.* 4 vols. New York: Council on Foreign Relations, 1933–1964.

4 Geddes, C. L. *An Analytical Guide to the Bibliographies on Islam, Muhammad, and the Qur'an.* Bibliographic Series, no. 3. Denver: American Institute of Islamic Studies, 1973.

5 ———. *An Analytical Guide to the Bibliographies on Modern Egypt and the Sudan.* Bibliographic Series, no. 2. Denver: American Institute of Islamic Studies, 1972.

6 Gray, Richard A. *Serial Bibliographies in the Humanities and Social Sciences.* Ann Arbor, Michigan: Pierian, 1969.

7 *International Bibliography of Political Science.* Chicago: Aldine, 1953. [Annual]

8 Kennedy, James R., Jr. *Guide to Reference Sources on Africa, Asia, Latin America and the Caribbean, Middle East and North Africa, Russia and East Europe: Selected and Annotated.* Williamsport, Pennsylvania: Bro-Dart, 1972.

4 / REFERENCES & GENERAL WORKS

9   Plischke, Elmer. *American Foreign Relations: A Bibliography of Official Sources.* College Park: Bureau of Governmental Research, University of Maryland, 1955.

10   United Nations. Dag Hammarskjöld Library. *Current Issues: A Selected Bibliography on Subjects of Concern to the United Nations.* New York: United Nations, 1965–.

11   U.S. Department of State. *International Politics: A Selective Monthly Bibliography.* 6 vols. Washington, D.C.: U.S. Department of State, 1956–1961.

12   U.S. Department of State. Division of Publications. *Publications of the Department of State, October 1, 1929 to January 1, 1950.* Washington, D.C.: U.S.G.P.O., 1951.

13   U.S. Department of State. Historical Office. *Major Publications of the Department of State: An Annotated Bibliography.* Washington, D.C.: U.S.G.P.O., 1966.

Middle East

14   Al-Abid, Ibrahim. *A Handbook to the Palestine Question.* Palestine Books, no. 17. Beirut: Palestine Liberation Organization Research Center, Oct. 1969.

15   Anthony, John D. *North Africa in Regional and International Affairs: A Selected Bibliography.* Washington, D.C.: Middle East Institute, 1974.

16   ———. *The States of the Arabian Peninsula and the Gulf Littoral: A Selected Bibliography.* Washington, D.C.: Middle East Institute, 1973.

17   Bartsch, William H., and Julian Bharier. *The Economy of Iran, 1940–1970: A Bibliography.* Durham: University of Durham, 1971.

18   Bethman, Erich W. *Catalogue: Specialized Lending Library on the Middle East and Supplement.* Washington, D.C.: American Friends of the Middle East, 1966.

19   "Bibliographie." In *Archiv für Orientforschung: Internationale Zeitschrift für die Wissenschaft von Vorderen Orient*. Berlin, 1924–. [Annual]

20   "Bibliography." *Palestine Affairs* 3 (Feb. 1948): 13–19.

21   *Bibliography of Asian Studies*. Ann Arbor, Michigan: Association for Asian Studies, 1957–. [Annual]

22   "Bibliography of Periodical Literature." In *Middle East Journal*. Washington, D.C.: Middle East Institute, 1947–. [Quarterly]

23   Boardman, Francis. "Recent AUB Publications on Economic Research." *Middle East Journal* 15 (Summer 1961): 329–33.

24   Dotan, Uri, and Avigdor Levy. *A Bibliography of Articles on the Middle East, 1959–1967*. Tel Aviv: Tel Aviv University, 1970.

25   Ettinghausen, Richard. *A Selected Bibliography of Books and Periodicals in Western Languages Dealing with the Near and Middle East with Special Emphasis on Medieval and Modern Times*. Washington, D.C.: Middle East Institute, 1954.

26   "Handbook on the Middle East." *Intercom* 9:6 (1967): 32–68.

27   Hopwood, Derek, and D. Grimwood-Jones. *Middle East and Islam: A Bibliographical Introduction*. Zug, Switzerland: Inter-Documentation, 1972.

28   Howard, Harry N. *The Middle East: A Selected Bibliography of Recent Works: 1960–1969*. 3 supplements. Washington, D.C.: Middle East Institute, 1969–1974.

29   ———, et al., eds. *Middle East and North Africa: A Bibliography for Undergraduate Libraries*. Williamsport, Pennsylvania: Bro-Dart, 1971.

30   Legault, Albert. *Peace-keeping Operations: Bibliography.* Paris: International Information Center on Peace-keeping Operations, 1967.

31   Leiden, Carl. "What to Read on the Middle East." *U.S. Naval Institute Proceedings* 84 (Jan. 1958): 99–102.

32   *Middle East: A Bibliography of Selected RAND Publications.* Santa Monica, California: RAND, SB–1034, Aug. 1972. [Revised periodically]

33   *Middle East Social Science Bibliography: Books and Articles on the Social Sciences Published in Arab Countries of the Middle East in 1955–1960.* Cairo: Middle East Science Cooperation Office, UNESCO, 1961.

34   "Periodicals in Review: The Arab-Israeli Conflict in Periodical Literature." *Journal of Palestine Studies.* Beirut. [Quarterly]

35   *A Select Bibliography: Asia, Africa, Eastern Europe, Latin America.* New York: American Universities Field Staff, 1963.

36   *A Selected Bibliography of Articles Dealing with the Middle East.* 2 vols. (1939–1950; 1951–1954). Jerusalem: Economic Research Institute, Hebrew University, 1954.

37   Singer, Jeanne G. "Focus on the Middle East." *Intercom* 6:2 (1964): 1–76.

38   Sweet, Louise E., ed. *The Central Middle East: A Handbook of Anthropology and Published Research on the Nile Valley, the Arab Levant, Southern Mesopotamia, the Arabian Peninsula, and Israel.* New Haven, Connecticut: Human Relations Area Files, 1971.

39   Thomsen, Peter. *Die Palastina-Literatur.* Leipzig: [various publishers], 1908–1938; Berlin: Akademie-Verlag, 1953–. [Irregular]

40   U.S. Department of the Army. *Area Handbook for the Peripheral States of the Arabian Peninsula*. Washington, D.C.: U.S.G.P.O., 1971.

41   ———. *Middle East: Tricontinental Hub: A Bibliographic Survey*. 2 vols. Washington, D.C.: U.S.G.P.O., 1965.

42   U.S. Library of Congress. Near East Section. *The Arabian Peninsula: A Selected Annotated List of Periodicals, Books, and Articles in English*. New York: Greenwood Reprint, 1969.

43   University of the State of New York. State Education Department. Foreign Area Materials Center. *Bibliographies of the Middle East and North Africa*. Williamsport, Pennsylvania: Bro-Dart. [Irregular]

Arab Topics

44   al-Eran, Tahany. *References Dealing with the Arab World: A Selected and Annotated List*. New York: Organization of Arab Students, 1966.

45   *An Annotated Bibliography of Books and Periodicals in English Dealing with Human Relations in the Arab States of the Middle East (1945–54)*. Beirut: American University of Beirut, 1956.

46   *A Bibliographical List of Works about Syria*. Cairo: National Library, 1965.

47   Grassmuck, George. "Selected Materials on Iraq and Jordan." *American Political Science Review* 51 (Dec. 1957): 1067–90.

48   Kabeel, Soraya M., comp. *Selected Bibliography on Kuwait and the Arabian Gulf*. Kuwait: Libraries Dept., Kuwait University, 1969.

49   *A Selected and Annotated Bibliography of Economic Literature on the Arab Speaking Countries of the Middle East*

(1938-1952). Beirut: Economic Research Service, American University of Beirut, 1954.

50 *A Selected and Annotated Bibliography of Economic Literature on the Arab Speaking Countries of the Middle East: Supplement.* Beirut: Economic Research Service, American University of Beirut, 1955-.

51 Selim, George Dimitri, comp. *American Doctoral Dissertations on the Arab World, 1883-1968.* Washington, D.C.: Library of Congress, 1970.

Israel Topics

52 University of London. School of Oriental and African Studies. *A Cumulation of a Selected and Annotated Bibliography of Economic Literature on the Arabic Speaking Countries of the Middle East, 1938-1960.* Boston: G. K. Hall, 1967.

53 Alexander, Yonah. *Israel: Selected, Annotated, and Illustrated Bibliography.* Gilbertsville, New York: V. Buday, 1968.

54 Cohen, Iva, comp. *Israel: A Bibliography: Selected, Annotated Listing of Works on Israel's Past History and Present Structure and Culture.* New York: Anti-Defamation League of B'nai B'rith, 1970.

55 Emanuel, Muriel. *Israel: A Survey and Bibliography.* London: St. James, 1971.

56 Gioell, Yohal. *Bibliography of Modern Hebrew Literature in English Translation.* Jerusalem: Israel Universities Press, 1968.

57 Jutkowski, A. "A Bibliography in English on Public Administration in Israel, 1948-1967." *Public Administration in Israel and Abroad* 8 (1967): 205-19.

58 Kutten, A. *Bibliography on Physical Planning of Cooperative and Collective Agricultural Settlements in Israel: A Selection of Publications in Foreign Languages.* 3d ed. Haifa:

Faculty of Architecture and Town Planning, Technion-Israel Institute of Technology, 1970.

59 Landau, Jacob M. "Israeli Studies on the Middle East." *Middle East Journal* 19 (Summer 1965): 354–62.

60 Pickering, Peter E., comp. *A Brief Bibliography of Reference Works Containing Data on the Land of Israel, Past and Present.* Melbourne: Alphega, 1969.

61 Rabin, Albert I. *Kibbutz Studies: A Digest of Books and Articles on the Kibbutz by Social Scientists, and Others.* East Lansing: Michigan State University Press, 1971.

62 Reich, Bernard. *Israel in Paperback.* New York: Middle East Studies Association of North America, 1971.

63 *Selected Bibliography of Israel Educational Materials.* Jerusalem: Israel Program for Scientific Translation for the U.S. Office of Education, 1966–.

64 Wenner, Manfred W. *Israeli Foreign Policy: A Selected Bibliography of Recent Works.* Washington, D.C.: Legislative Reference Service, U.S. Library of Congress, 1966.

65 World Zionist Organization. Research Section. *Bitfutzot Hagolah: Surveys and Monographs on the Zionist Movement and the Jewish World Issued on the Occasion of the Twenty-Fifth Zionist Congress.* Jerusalem: World Zionist Organization, 1960.

Review Articles

66 Bochenski, Feliks. "Post-War Economic Writings on the Middle East." *Middle East Journal* 7 (Winter 1953): 100–106.

67 "Books about Israel and by Israeli Writers Published in the U.S. and England." *Israel Book World* 8 (June 1972): 12–13.

68 Busch, Briton C. "A Bibliographical Review of the Modern History of the Powers in the Middle East." *Middle East Information Series* 21 (Dec. 1972): 41–44.

69   Cottrell, A. "The Soviet Union as a Major Power in the Middle East: A Review of Recent Literature." *World Affairs* 133:4 (Mar. 1971): 315–20.

70   Howard, Harry N. "The Middle East in Paperback." *Middle East Journal* 18 (Summer 1964): 355.

71   ———. "Recent Books on International Relations." *Middle East Journal* 3 (July 1949): 337–41.

72   ———. "Some Recent Works on the Near East." *Journal of Modern History* 21 (Mar. 1949): 35–43.

73   Hurewitz, J. C. "Recent Books on the Problem of Palestine." *Middle East Journal* 3 (Jan. 1949): 86–91.

74   Lehrman, Hal. "Recent Books on Israel." *Middle East Journal* 5 (Spring 1951): 239–43.

75   Lenczowski, George. "Literature on the Clandestine Activities of the Great Powers in the Middle East." *Middle East Journal* 8 (Spring 1954): 205–11.

76   McClanahan, Grant Y. "Recent Books on Contemporary Egypt." *Middle East Journal* 5 (Winter 1951): 101–7.

77   Nolte, Richard H. "Recent Books in International Relations: Middle East." *Foreign Affairs* 43 (Jan. 1965): 373–74.

78   "Recent Soviet Books on Africa, the Middle East and South-East Asia." *Mizan* 9:6 (Nov.–Dec. 1967): 258–65.

79   Simpson, Dwight J. "New Books on the Middle East." *Current History* 30 (June 1956): 360–62.

80   Ziadeh, Nicola A. "Recent Arabic Literature on Arabism." *Middle East Journal* 6 (Autumn 1952): 468–73.

81   ———. "Recent Books on the Interpretation of Islam." *Middle East Journal* 5 (Autumn 1951): 505–10.

B / Indexes

82 *ABS Guide to Recent Publications in the Social and Behavioral Sciences.* New York: American Behavioral Scientist, 1965.

83 *ABS Guide to Recent Publications in the Social and Behavioral Sciences, Supplement.* Beverly Hills, California: Sage, 1966–. [Annual]

84 *Air University Library Index to Military Periodicals.* Maxwell Air Force Base, Alabama: Air University Library, 1949–. [Quarterly]

85 *Current Digest of the Soviet Press.* New York: Joint Committee on Slavic Studies, 1949–.

86 *Index to Foreign Legal Periodicals and Collections of Essays.* Chicago: William D. Murphy, 1960–.

87 *Index to Periodical Articles Related to Law.* Hackensack, New Jersey: Fred B. Rothman, 1958–.

88 *International Information Service: A Quarterly Annotated Index of Selected Materials on Current International Affairs.* Chicago: Library of International Affairs, 1963–.

89 *International Political Science Abstracts.* Oxford: Blackwell, 1951–. [Quarterly]

90 *International Relations Digest of Periodical Literature.* Berkeley: Bureau of International Relations, University of California, 1950–.

91 Kujoth, Jean Spealman. *Subject Guide to Periodical Indexes and Review Indexes.* Metuchen, New Jersey: Scarecrow, 1969.

92 *Public Affairs Information Service Bulletin.* New York: Public Affairs Information Service, 1915–. [Weekly]

93   *Reader's Guide to Periodical Literature.* New York: H. W. Wilson, 1905–.

94   *Social Science and Humanities Index.* New York: H. W. Wilson, 1913–. [Quarterly]

95   United Nations. Dag Hammarskjöld Library. *United Nations Documents Index.* New York: United Nations, 1950–.

Newspaper Indexes

96   *The Christian Science Monitor Index.* Corvallis, Oregon: Helen M. Cropsey, 1960–.

97   *Index to the Times.* London: The Times, 1906–.

98   *The New York Times Index.* New York: The New York Times, 1851–.

99   *The Wall Street Journal Index.* New York: Dow Jones, 1958–.

Middle East

100   "Abstracta Islamica." In *Revue des Etudes Islamiques.* Paris: Geuthner, 1927–. [Biennial]

101   *African Abstracts.* London: International African Institute, 1950–. [Quarterly]

102   *Index Islamicus: A Catalogue of Articles on Islamic Subjects in Periodicals and Other Collective Publications.* 3 supplements. Cambridge: Heffer, 1958–.

103   *Index to Jewish Periodicals.* Cleveland Heights, Ohio: College of Jewish Studies Press, 1963–. [Quarterly]

104   *Palestine and Zionism: A Cumulative Author, Title and Subject Index to Books, Pamphlets and Periodicals.* 2 vols. New York: Palestine Foundation Fund, 1946. [Supplements, 1946–1948]

C / Documentary Collections

105   Council on Foreign Relations. *Documents on American Foreign Relations*. New York: Harper's, 1952–. [Annual]

106   Great Britain. Foreign Office. *Documents on British Foreign Policy, 1919–1939*. London: H.M.S.O., 1963.

107   *Public Papers of the Presidents of the United States*. Washington, D.C.: U.S.G.P.O., 1945–; 1957–. [Truman, Eisenhower, Kennedy, Johnson, Nixon]

108   Royal Institute of International Affairs. *Documents on International Affairs, 1928–*. London: Oxford University Press, 1929–. [Annual]

109   U.S. Department of State. *American Foreign Policy: Current Documents*. Washington, D.C.: U.S.G.P.O., 1957–. [Annual]

110   ———. *American Foreign Policy, 1950–55: Basic Documents*. 2 vols. Washington, D.C.: U.S.G.P.O., 1957.

111   ———. Historical Office. *The Foreign Relations of the United States: Diplomatic Papers*. Washington, D.C.: U.S.G.P.O., 1866–. [Annual]

Middle East

112   "Arab Documents on Palestine, November 15, 1971–February 15, 1972." *Journal of Palestine Studies* 1:3 (1972): 158–74.

113   Christman, Henry M. *This is Our Strength: The Selected Papers of Golda Meir*. New York: Macmillan, 1962.

114   ———, ed. *The State Papers of Levi Eshkol*. New York: Funk & Wagnalls, 1969.

115   Davis, Helen. *Constitutions, Electoral Laws, Treaties of States in the Near and Middle East*. Durham, North Carolina: Duke University Press, 1947.

14 / REFERENCES & GENERAL WORKS

116   Diab, Zuhair, ed. *International Documents on Palestine, 1968.* Beirut: Institute for Palestine Studies, 1971.

117   *Dustur: A Survey of the Constitutions of the Arab and Muslim States.* Leiden: E. J. Brill, 1966.

118   Hurewitz, J. C. *Diplomacy in the Near and Middle East: A Documentary History.* 2 vols. (1535–1914; 1914–1956). New York: Octagon Books, 1972.

119   Khalidi, Walid, and Yusuf Ibish. *Arab Political Documents, 1963.* Beirut: Khayats, 1964.

120   Laqueur, Walter, ed. *The Israel-Arab Reader: A Documentary History of the Middle East Conflict.* New York: Bantam, 1969.

121   Litvinoff, Barnet, ed. *The Letters and Papers of Chaim Weizmann.* Vol. 3. *September 1903–December 1904.* New York: Oxford University Press, 1972.

122   Mansoor, Menahem. *Political and Diplomatic History of the Arab World, 1900–1967: A Chronological Study.* 7 vols. Washington, D.C.: NCR/Microcard Editions, 1972.

123   *Middle East Record.* 4 vols. Jerusalem: Israel Universities Press, 1960–1973.

124   *Palestine International Documents on Human Rights, 1948–1972.* Basic Documents Series, no. 9. Beirut: Institute for Palestine Studies, 1972.

125   United Nations. *Studies on Selected Development Problems in Various Countries in the Middle East.* New York: United Nations, 1970.

126   U.S. Congress. Senate. Committee on Foreign Relations. *A Select Chronology and Background Documents Relating to the Middle East.* 91st Cong., 1st sess., May 1969.

127   *Zeev Jabotinsky's Letters.* Vol. 1. Tel Aviv: Chaim Weizmann Institute for Zionist Research and Jabotinsky Institute, 1972.

D / Atlases & Geography

128 *Atlas of the Arab World and the Middle East.* New York: St. Martin's Press, 1960.

129 *Atlas of Israel: Cartography, Physical Geography, Human and Economic Geography, History.* Amsterdam: Elsevier, 1970.

130 Bartholomew, John, ed. *The Times Atlas of the World.* Vol. 2. *South-West Asia and Russia.* Boston: Houghton Mifflin, 1959.

131 Fisher, W. B. *The Middle East: A Physical, Social, and Regional Geography.* London: Methuen, 1961.

132 Karmon, Yehuda. *Israel: A Regional Geography.* London: Wiley-Interscience, 1971.

133 Kingsbury, Robert C., and Norman J. G. Pounds. *An Atlas of Middle Eastern Affairs.* New York: Praeger, 1963.

134 Longrigg, Stephen H. *The Middle East: A Social Geography.* Chicago: Aldine, 1963.

135 Orni, Ephraim. *Geography of Israel.* Jerusalem: Israel Universities Press, 1971.

136 *Oxford Regional Economic Atlas of the Middle East and North Africa.* London: Oxford University Press, 1960.

137 Roolvink, R. *Historical Atlas of the Muslim Peoples.* Cambridge, Massachusetts: Harvard University Press, 1957.

E / Yearbooks

138   International Institute for Strategic Studies. *Military Balance*. London: International Institute for Strategic Studies, 1959–.

139   Jacoby, F. J., and I. A. Abbady, eds. *The Anglo-Palestine Year Book, 1946*. London: Anglo-Palestine, 1946.

140   *The Jewish Year Book*. London: Greenberg, 1896–.

141   London Institute of World Affairs. *Year Book of World Affairs*. London: Stevens & Sons, 1947–.

142   *The Middle East and North Africa*. London: Europa, 1948–. [Formerly *The Middle East*]

143   *The New International Year Book: A Compendium of the World's Progress for the Year*. New York: Funk & Wagnalls, 1932–.

144   Royal Institute of International Affairs. *Survey of International Affairs*. London: Oxford University Press, 1925–.

145   Stockholm International Peace Research Institute [SIPRI]. *World Armaments and Disarmament, SIPRI Yearbook*. New York: Humanities Press, 1968/69–.

146   United Nations. Statistical Office. *Statistical Year Book*. New York: United Nations, 1949–.

147   ———. *Yearbook of International Trade Statistics*. New York: United Nations, 1949–.

F / Journals

148   *American Political Science Review*. Washington, D.C.: American Political Science Association, 1906–.

149 *American Universities Field Staff Reports.* Southwest Asian Series, North African Series, Northeast African Series, South Asian Series. Hanover, New Hampshire: American Universities Field Staff Service. [Irregular]

150 *American Zionist.* New York: Zionist Organization of America. 1921–. [Monthly]

151 *An-Nahar Arab Report.* Beirut: An-Nahar Press Services SARL, 1970–.

152 *Annals of the American Academy of Political and Social Science.* Philadelphia: American Academy of Political and Social Science, 1889–.

153 *Arab Journal.* New York: Organization of Arab Students in the U.S.A., 1964–1973.

154 *The Arab World.* New York: Arab Information Center, League of Arab States, ceased 1973.

155 *Asian Affairs.* London: Royal Central Asian Society, 1903–. [Triennial; formerly *Royal Central Asian Society Journal*]

156 *Commentary.* New York: American Jewish Committee, 1945–. [Monthly]

157 *Current History.* Philadelphia: Current History, Inc., 1914–. [Monthly]

158 *Economist.* London: Economist Newspaper Ltd., 1843–. [Weekly]

159 *Facts on File: A Weekly News Guide, with Cumulative Index.* New York: Facts on File, Inc., 1940–.

160 *Foreign Affairs.* New York: Council on Foreign Relations, Inc., 1922–. [Quarterly]

161 *Foreign Policy.* New York: National Affairs, Inc., 1971–. [Quarterly]

162   *Foreign Policy Association.* Headline Series. New York: Foreign Policy Association, 1935–.

163   *International Affairs.* London: Royal Institute of International Affairs, 1922–. [Quarterly]

164   *International Affairs: A Monthly Journal of Political Analysis.* Moscow: All-Union Society Znaniye, 1955–.

165   *International Conciliation.* New York: Carnegie Endowment for International Peace, 1907–1972.

166   *International Journal of Middle East Studies.* New York: The Middle East Studies Association of North America, 1970–. [Quarterly]

167   *International Relations.* London: David Davies Memorial Institute of International Studies, 1954–.

168   *Israel Digest.* Jerusalem and New York: World Zionist Organization, 1948–. [Fortnightly]

169   *Israel Economist.* Jerusalem, 1945–. [Monthly]

170   *Israel Export and Trade Journal.* Tel Aviv, 1949–. [Monthly]

171   *Issues.* New York: American Council for Judaism, ceased 1968.

172   *Jeune Afrique.* Paris: Presse Africaine Associée, 1960–. [Biweekly]

173   *Jewish Journal of Sociology.* London: World Jewish Congress, 1959–. [Semiannual]

174   *Jewish Observer and Middle East Review.* London: 36–38 White Friars St., 1952–.

175   *Jewish Social Studies.* New York: Conference on Jewish Social Studies, 1939–.

176   *Journal of Conflict Resolution.* Beverly Hills, California: Sage Publications, 1957–. [Formerly *Conflict Resolution*]

177   *Journal of Contemporary History.* London: Sage Publications Ltd., 1966–.

178   *Journal of International Affairs.* New York: School of International Affairs, Columbia University, 1947–.

179   *Journal of Modern History.* Chicago: University of Chicago Press, 1929–.

180   *Journal of Palestine Studies.* Beirut: Institute for Palestine Studies and the University of Kuwait, 1971–.

181   *Journal of Peace Research.* Oslo: International Peace Research Institute, Universitetsforlaget, University of Oslo, 1964–. [Formerly *Journal of Peace*]

182   *Keesing's Contemporary Archives: Weekly [Indexed] Diary to World Events.* London: Keesing's Publications, 1931–.

183   *Link.* New York: Americans for Middle East Understanding, 1968–. [Bimonthly]

184   *Middle East Economic Survey.* Beirut: Middle East Research and Publishing Center, 1957–.

185   *Middle East Forum.* Beirut: Alumni Association of the American University of Beirut, 1954–.

186   *Middle East Information Media Brief.* Tel Aviv, 1972–. [Fortnightly]

187   *Middle East Information Series.* New York: American Academic Association for Peace in the Middle East, 1972–. [Supersedes: *American Academic Association for Peace in the Middle East Bulletin*]

188   *Middle East International.* London: Middle East International Publishers, 1971–. [Monthly]

189   *Middle East Journal.* Washington, D.C.: Middle East Institute, 1947–. [Quarterly]

190 *Middle East Monitor*. Washington, D.C.: Middle East Institute, 1971–. [Bimonthly]

191 *Middle East Newsletter*. Beirut: Americans for Justice in the Middle East, 1967–. [Bimonthly]

192 *Middle East Perspective*. New York, 1970–. [Monthly]

193 *Middle Eastern Affairs*. Elmont, New York: Council for Middle Eastern Affairs, 1950–1963. [Monthly]

194 *Middle Eastern Studies*. London: Frank Cass & Co. Ltd., 1964–.

195 *Mid East: A Middle East-North African Review*. Washington, D.C.: American Friends of the Middle East, 1961–1970. [Semimonthly; formerly *Viewpoints*]

196 *Mid East Report*. New York: MidEast Report, Inc., 1967–.

197 *Midstream: A Monthly Jewish Review*. New York: Theodor Herzl Foundation, Inc., 1955–.

198 *Military Review*. Ft. Leavenworth, Kansas: U.S. Army Command and General Staff School, 1922–. [Monthly]

199 *Mizan*. London: Central Asian Research Center, 1959–1971. [Triennial]

200 *Muslim World*. Hartford, Connecticut: Hartford Seminary Foundation, 1911–.

201 *National Geographic*. Washington, D.C.: National Geographic Society, 1888–. [Monthly]

202 *Naval War College Review*. Newport, Rhode Island: U.S. Naval War College, 1948–. [Bimonthly]

203 *Near East Report: A Washington Newsletter on American Policy in the Near East*. Washington, D.C.: American Israel Public Affairs Committee, 1957–. [Weekly]

204 *New Middle East.* London: New Middle East Publishing Co. Ltd., 1968–1973.

205 *New Outlook: Middle East Monthly.* Tel Aviv: Hevart Tazpiot Ltd., 1957–. [Monthly]

206 *New Times.* Moscow: New Times, 1943–.

207 *Orbis.* Philadelphia: Foreign Policy Research Institute, 1957–. [Quarterly]

208 *Orient.* Paris: 11 rue Saint Sulpice, 1957–.

209 *Palestine Digest.* Washington, D.C.: Arab Information Center, League of Arab States, 1971–. [Bimonthly]

210 *Political Science Quarterly.* New York: Academy of Political Science, 1886–.

211 *Round Table: The Commonwealth Journal of International Affairs.* London: Round Table Ltd., 1910–.

212 *Survival.* London: International Institute for Strategic Studies, 1959–. [Bimonthly]

213 *Swiss Review of World Affairs.* Zurich: Neue Zuercher Zeitung, 1951–.

214 *U.S. Department of State Bulletin.* Washington, D.C.: U.S. Department of State, 1939–.

215 *Vital Speeches of the Day.* Pelham, New York: City News Publishing Co., 1948–. [Weekly]

216 *World Affairs.* Washington, D.C.: American Peace Society, 1834–. [Quarterly]

217 *World Today.* London: Oxford University Press, 1945–.

G / Biography

218   Slocum, Robert B. *Biographical Dictionaries and Related Works.* Detroit: Gale, 1967. [Organized by nation; indexed]

Arab Biographies

219   Abdullah, King (of Jordan). *My Memoirs Completed.* Translated by Harold Glidden. Washington, D.C.: American Council of Learned Societies, 1954.

220   Birdwood, Lord (Christopher Bromhead). *Nuri as-Said: A Study in Arab Leadership.* London: Cassell, 1959.

221   Graves, Philip P., ed. *Memoirs of King Abdullah of Transjordan.* New York: Philosophical Library, 1950.

222   Hussein, King (of Jordan). *My War with Israel.* Translated by June P. Wilson and Walter B. Michaels. New York: Morrow, 1969.

223   ———. *Uneasy Lies the Head.* London: Heinemann, 1962.

224   Khadduri, Majid. *Arab Contemporaries: The Role of Personalities in Politics.* Baltimore: Johns Hopkins Press, 1973.

225   Nutting, Anthony. *Nasser.* New York: Dutton, 1972.

226   St. John, Robert. *The Boss.* New York: McGraw-Hill, 1960. [Nasser]

227   Semaan, K. "A New Source for the Biography of Jamal Abd al-Nasir." *Muslim World* 58 (July 1968): 242–52.

228   Snow, Peter. *Husain: A Biography.* London: Barrie & Jenkins, 1972.

229   Stephens, Robert. *Nasser: A Political Biography.* Manchester: Penguin, 1971.

230 Weiss, Samuel. *Men and Ideas in the Middle East Today: A Biographical Dictionary of 183 Arab Statesmen.* Jerusalem: Israel Universities Press, 1966.

231 *Who's Who in the Arab World.* Beirut: Publitec Editions, 1965-1966.

232 *Who's Who in U.A.R. and the Near East.* Cairo: Le Mondain égyptien, 1947-. [Irregular; title varies]

Zionist-Israeli Biographies

233 Bar-David, Molly Lyons. *My Promised Land.* New York: Putnam, 1953.

234 Bar-Zohar, Michael. *The Armed Prophet: A Biography of Ben-Gurion.* London: Barker, 1967.

235 Bein, Alex. *Theodor Herzl: A Biography.* Philadelphia: Jewish Publication Society of America, 1942.

236 Ben-Gurion, David. *Ben-Gurion Looks Back.* New York: Simon & Schuster, 1965.

237 Ben-Horin, Meir. *Max Nordau: Philosopher of Solidarity.* New York: Conference on Jewish Social Studies, 1956.

238 Bentwich, Norman. *For Zion's Sake: A Biography of Judah L. Magnes.* Philadelphia: Jewish Publication Society of America, 1954.

239 Bodenheimer, Henriette Hanna. *Prelude to Israel: The Memoirs of M. I. Bodenheimer.* Translated from the German by Israel Cohen. New York: Yoseloff, 1963.

240 Bransten, Thomas R., ed. *Recollections of David Ben-Gurion.* London: Macdonald, 1970.

241 Dayan, Yael. "Father and Hero: General Moshe Dayan." *Look* (Aug. 22, 1967): 15-19.

242 Edelman, Maurice. *Ben Gurion.* London: Hodder & Stoughton, 1964.

243 Goldmann, Nahum. *The Autobiography of Nahum Goldmann: Sixty Years of Jewish Life.* New York: Holt, Rinehart & Winston, 1969.

244 Lau-Lavie, Naphtali. *Moshe Dayan: A Biography.* London: Vallentine, Mitchell, 1968.

245 Litvinoff, Barnet. *Ben-Gurion: The Biography of a Statesman.* New York: Praeger, 1954.

246 ———. *The Story of David Ben-Gurion.* New York: Oceana, 1960.

247 Mann, Peggy. *Golda: The Life of Israel's Prime Minister.* New York: Pocket Books, 1973.

248 Meir, Golda. *This Is Our Strength.* New York: Macmillan, 1963.

249 Noble, Iris. *Israel's Golda Meir: Pioneer to Prime Minister.* New York: Messner, 1972.

250 Patai, Josef. *Star over Jordan: The Life and Calling of Theodor Herzl.* New York: Philosophical Library, 1946.

251 Patai, Raphael, ed. *The Complete Diaries of Theodor Herzl.* 5 vols. New York: Herzl-Yoseloff, 1961.

252 Pearlman, Moshe, ed. *Ben Gurion Looks Back in Talks with Moshe Pearlman.* New York: Simon & Schuster, 1965.

253 Prittie, Terence. *Eshkol: The Man and the Nation.* New York: Pitman, 1969.

254 Rosensaft, Menachem Z. *Moshe Sharett: Statesman of Israel.* New York: Shengold, 1966.

255 St. John, Robert. *Ben-Gurion.* New York: Doubleday, 1959.

256 Samuel, Edwin. *A Lifetime in Jerusalem: The Memoirs of the Second Viscount Samuel.* London: Vallentine, Mitchell, 1970.

257 Schechtman, Joseph B. *Fighter and Prophet: The Vladimir Jabotinsky Story: The Last Years.* New York: Yoseloff, 1961.

258 ———. *Rebel and Statesman: The Jabotinsky Story.* New York: Yoseloff, 1956.

259 Shihor, Schmuel. *Hollow Glory: The Last Days of Chaim Weizmann, First President of Israel.* New York: Yoseloff, 1960.

260 Syrkin, Marie. *Golda Meir: Israel's Leader.* New York: Putnam, 1969.

261 Taslitt, Israel I. *Soldier of Israel: The Story of General Moshe Dayan.* New York: Funk & Wagnalls, 1969.

262 Teveth, Shabtai. *Moshe Dayan: The Soldier, the Man, the Legend.* Translated by Leah and David Zinder. Boston: Houghton Mifflin, 1973.

263 Weisgal, Meyer W., and Joel Carmichael, eds. *Chaim Weizmann: A Biography by Several Hands.* New York: Atheneum, 1963.

264 Weizmann, Chaim. *Trial and Error: The Autobiography of Chaim Weizmann.* New York: Harper, 1949.

265 Weizmann, Vera. *The Impossible Takes Longer: The Memoirs of the Wife of Israel's First President.* London: Hamish Hamilton, 1967.

266 *Who's Who, Israel.* Jerusalem, 1945/46– . [Title varies]

H / General References

267 Fisher, S. N. *The Middle East: A History.* New York: Knopf, 1959.

268 Halpern, Manfred. *The Politics of Social Change in the Middle East and North Africa.* Princeton, New Jersey: Princeton University Press, 1963.

269 Karpat, Kemal H., ed. *Political and Social Thought in the Contemporary Middle East.* New York: Praeger, 1969.

270 Khouri, Fred J. *Arab-Israeli Dilemma.* Syracuse, New York: Syracuse University Press, 1969.

271 Kirk, George E. *A Short History of the Middle East: From the Rise of Islam to Modern Times.* 7th rev. ed. New York: Praeger, 1964.

272 Lenczowski, George. *Middle East in World Affairs.* Ithaca, New York: Cornell University Press, 1962.

273 Mansfield, Peter. *The Middle East: A Political and Economic Survey.* New York: Oxford University Press, 1973.

274 Morrison, S. A. *Middle East Tensions: Political, Social and Religious.* New York: Harper, 1954.

275 Peretz, Don. *The Middle East Today.* London: Holt, Rinehart, & Winston, 1963.

276 Roosevelt, Kermit. *Arabs, Oil and History: The Story of the Middle East.* Port Washington, New York: Kennikat, 1949.

277 Rustow, Dankwart A. *Middle Eastern Political Systems.* Englewood Cliffs, New Jersey: Prentice-Hall, 1970.

278 Sharabi, Hisham B. *Government and Politics in the Middle East in the Twentieth Century.* Princeton, New Jersey: Van Nostrand, 1962.

Arab-Islamic History

279 Cragg, Kenneth. "The Intellectual Impact of Communism upon Contemporary Islam." *Middle East Journal* 8 (Spring 1954): 127–38.

280 Gabrieli, Francesco. *The Arabs: A Compact History.* New York: Hawthorn, 1963.

281 Gibb, H. A. R. *Modern Trends in Islam.* Chicago: University of Chicago Press, 1947.

282 Hitti, Philip K. *History of the Arabs.* London: St. Martin's Press, 1970.

283 Hourani, Albert H. *Arabic Thought in the Liberal Age, 1798-1939.* New York: Oxford University Press, 1962.

284 Izzeddin, Nejla. *The Arab World: Past, Present and Future.* Chicago: Regnery, 1953.

285 Lewis, Bernard. *The Arabs in History.* London: Hutchinson, 1956.

286 Von Grunebaum, Gustave E. *Modern Islam: The Search for Cultural Identity.* Los Angeles: University of California Press, 1962.

Military in Politics

287 Be'eri, Eliezer. *Army Officers in Arab Politics and Society.* New York: Praeger, 1970.

288 Binder, Leonard. *The Ideological Revolution in the Middle East.* New York: Wiley, 1964.

289 Brill, J. "The Military and Modernization in the Middle East." *Comparative Politics* 2:1 (Oct. 1969): 41-62.

290 Haddad, George M. *Revolutions and Military Rule in the Middle East: Egypt, the Sudan, Yemen, and Libya.* New York: Speller, 1973.

291 ———. *Revolutions and Military Rule in the Middle East.* Vol. 2 *The Arab States, Part 1: Iraq, Syria, Lebanon and Jordan.* New York: Speller, 1971.

292 Hurewitz, J. C. *Middle East Politics: The Military Dimension.* New York: Praeger, 1969.

293 Johnson, John J., ed. *The Role of the Military in Underdeveloped Countries*. Princeton, New Jersey: Princeton University Press, 1962.

294 Khadduri, Majid. "The Role of the Military in Middle East Politics." *American Political Science Review* 47 (June 1953): 511–24.

295 Koury, Enver M. *The Patterns of Mass Movements in Arab Revolutionary-Progressive States*. The Hague: Mouton, 1970.

296 Luttwak, Edward. *Coup d'Etat: A Practical Handbook*. New York: Knopf, 1968.

Modernization: Social & Anthropological

297 Baer, Gabriel. *Population and Society in the Arab East*. New York: Praeger, 1964.

298 Berger, Monroe. *The Arab World Today*. New York: Doubleday, 1962.

299 Bonne, Alfred. "Land and Population in the Middle East: Trends and Prospects." *Middle East Journal* 5 (Winter 1951): 39–55.

300 Carmichael, J. "The Shaping of the Arabs." *Midstream* 13:3 (Mar. 1967): 24–37.

301 Childers, Erskine B. *Common Sense about the Arab World*. New York: Macmillan, 1960.

302 Churchill, Charles W., and Abdulla M. Lutfiyya. *Readings in Arab Middle Eastern Societies*. New York: Humanities Press, 1970.

303 Coon, Carleton S. *Caravan: The Story of the Middle East*. New York: Holt, 1951.

304 Cressey, George. *Crossroads: Land and Life in Southwest Asia*. New York: Lippincott, 1962.

GENERAL REFERENCES / 29

305 *Demographic Measures and Population Growth in Arab Countries.* Research Monograph Series, no. 1. Cairo: Demographic Center, 1970.

306 Granqvist, Hilma. *Child Problems among the Arabs.* Copenhagen: Munksgaard, 1951.

307 Hourani, Albert H. *Minorities in the Arab World.* London: Oxford University Press, 1947.

308 Malik, Charles. "The Meaning of the Near East." *Journal of International Affairs* 6:2 (1952): 32–36.

309 Patai, Raphael. *Golden River to Golden Road.* Philadelphia: University of Pennsylvania Press, 1969.

310 ———. "The Middle East as a Culture Area." *Middle East Journal* 6 (Winter 1952): 1–21.

311 Polk, William R. "The Nature of Modernization: The Middle East and North Africa." *Foreign Affairs* 44 (Oct. 1965): 100–110.

312 Sharabi, Hisham. "The Transformation of Ideology in the Arab World." *Middle East Journal* 19 (Autumn 1965): 471–85.

313 Shouby, E. "The Influence of the Arabic Language on the Psychology of the Arabs." *Middle East Journal* 5 (Summer 1951): 284–302.

314 Speiser, E. A. "Cultural Factors in Social Dynamics in the Near East." *Middle East Journal* 7 (Spring 1953): 133–52.

315 Thompson, Jack H., and Robert D. Reischauer, eds. *Modernization of the Arab World.* Princeton, New Jersey: Van Nostrand, 1966.

316 Yaukey, David. *Fertility Differences in a Modernizing Country.* Princeton, New Jersey: Princeton University Press, 1961.

Palestine: Arabs & Israelis

317   Abu-Lughod, Ibrahim, ed. *The Transformation of Palestine: Essays on the Origin and Development of the Arab-Israeli Conflict.* Evanston, Illinois: Northwestern University Press, 1971.

318   Arnoni, M. S. *Rights and Wrongs in the Arab-Israeli Conflict: To the Anatomy of the Forces of Progress and Reaction in the Middle East.* Passaic, New Jersey: Minority of One, 1968.

319   Burdett, Winston. *Encounter with the Middle East: An Intimate Report on What Lies Behind the Arab-Israeli Conflict.* New York: Atheneum, 1969.

320   Cohen, Aharon. *Israel and the Arab World.* New York: Funk & Wagnalls, 1970.

321   Dodd, C. H., and M. E. Sales. *Israel and the Arab World.* New York: Barnes & Noble, 1970.

322   Goitein, S. D. *Jews and Arabs: Their Contacts through the Ages.* New York: Noonday Press, 1955.

323   Great Britain. Admiralty. Naval Intelligence Division. *A Handbook of Syria, Including Palestine.* London: H.M.S.O., 1920.

324   Suleiman, M. "Attitudes of the Arab Elite toward Palestine and Israel." *American Political Science Review* 67 (July 1973): 482–89.

325   Taylor, Alan R., and Richard N. Tetlie, eds. *Palestine: A Search for Truth.* Washington, D.C.: Public Affairs, 1970.

Economics

326   Baster, Albert S. J. *The Introduction of Western Economic Institutions into the Middle East.* Oxford: Oxford University Press, 1960.

327 Bonne, Alfred. *State and Economics in the Middle East: A Society in Transition.* London: Routledge & Kegan Paul, 1948.

328 Clawson, Marion; Hans H. Landsberg; and Lyle T. Alexander. *The Agricultural Potential of the Middle East.* New York: American Elsevier, 1971.

329 El-Ghonemy, Mohamad Riad. *Land Policy in the Near East.* Rome: Food and Agriculture Organization of the United Nations, 1967.

330 Fried, Jerome J., and Milton C. Edlund. *Desalting Technology for Middle Eastern Agriculture: An Economic Case Study.* New York: Praeger, 1971.

331 Meyer, A. J. *Middle East Capitalism.* Cambridge, Massachusetts: Harvard University Press, 1959.

332 Preston, Lee E. *Trade Patterns in the Middle East.* Washington, D.C.: American Enterprise Institute, 1970.

333 United Nations. *Economic Developments in the Middle East, 1945 to 1954.* New York: United Nations, 1955.

334 Warriner, Doreen. *Land and Poverty in the Middle East.* New York: Royal Institute of International Affairs, 1948.

335 Zartman, I.; J. Paul; and J. Entelis. "An Economic Indicator of Socio-Political Unrest." *International Journal of Middle East Studies* 2 (Oct. 1971): 293–310.

II / ARAB COUNTRY SURVEY

336 Badeau, J. S. "The Sovereign Arab World Faces the Future." *Arab World* 12:4 (Apr. 1966): 2.

337 Harrison, Joseph G. "Middle East Instability." *Middle Eastern Affairs* 5 (Mar. 1954): 73–80.

338 Hoskins, Halford L. *The Middle East: Problem Area in World Politics.* New York: Macmillan, 1954.

339 Hurewitz, J. C. *Unity and Disunity in the Middle East.* International Conciliation, no. 481. New York: Carnegie, May 1952.

340 Kerr, Malcolm H. *The Arab Cold War, 1958–1967.* 3d ed. New York: Oxford University Press, 1967.

341 Khadduri, Majid. *Political Trends in the Arab World: The Role of Ideas and Ideals in Politics.* Baltimore: Johns Hopkins Press, 1970.

342 Nawfal, S. "The Arab Summits and Inter-Arab Cooperation." *Middle East Forum* 41:2 (1965): 57–60.

343 Rabbath, Edmond. "The Problem of Arab Unity." *Middle East Forum* 3 (Apr. 1956): 9–11.

344 Rouleau, E. "The Arabs: Between Unity and Division." *New Outlook* 9:8 (Oct.–Nov. 1966): 5–9.

345 Trevelyan, Humphrey. *The Middle East in Revolution.* London: Macmillan, 1970.

A / Arab Middle East

346 Antoun, R. "On the Modesty of Women in Arab Muslim Villages: A Study of the Accommodation of Traditions." *American Anthropologist* 70 (Aug. 1968): 671–97.

347 Arab Information Center. *Education in the Arab States.* New York: Arab Information Center, 1966.

348 Be'eri, E. "A Note on *coups d'état* in the Middle East." *Journal of Contemporary History* 5:2 (Apr. 1970): 123–30.

349 Ben-Zur, A. "What Is Arab Socialism?" *New Outlook* 8:5 (July–Aug. 1965): 37–45.

350 Capil, M. "Political Survey 1962: Arab Middle East." *Middle Eastern Affairs* 14 (Feb. 1963): 34–46.

351 Diqs, Isaak. *A Bedouin Boyhood.* London: Allen & Unwin, 1967.

352 Fisher, Sydney Nettleton, ed. *The Military in the Middle East: Problems in Society and Government.* Columbus: Ohio State University Press, 1963.

353 ———, ed. *Social Forces in the Middle East.* Ithaca, New York: Cornell University Press, 1955.

354 Glubb, Lt. Gen. Sir John. "The Role of the Army in the Traditional Arab State." *Journal of International Affairs* 19:1 (1965): 8–15.

355 Haddad, George M. "Revolutions and *coups d'état* in the Middle East: A Comparative Study." *Welt des Islams* 10:1–2 (1965): 17–32.

356 Hurewitz, J. C. "The Politics of Rapid Population Growth in the Middle East." *Journal of International Affairs* 19:1 (1965): 26–38.

357 Kerr, Malcolm H. "Who Speaks for the Arabs?" *Middle East Forum* 31 (May 1956): 15–17.

358 Lenczowski, George. "Radical Regimes in Egypt, Syria, and Iraq: Some Comparative Observations on Ideologies and Practices." *Journal of Politics* 28:1 (Feb. 1966): 29–56.

359 Patai, Raphael. "Relationship Patterns Among the Arabs." *Middle Eastern Affairs* 2 (May 1951): 180–85.

360 Peretz, Don. "Nonalignment in the Arab World." *Annals of the American Academy of Political and Social Science* 362 (Nov. 1965): 36–43.

361 Perlmann, M. "Higher Education in the Arab Countries." *Palestine Affairs* 2 (Jan. 1947): 4–6.

362 Polk, William R. *The Opening of South Lebanon, 1788–1840.* Cambridge, Massachusetts: Harvard University Press, 1963.

363 Rosenthal, E. I. J. *Islam in the Modern National State.* New York: Cambridge University Press, 1966.

364 St. John, Robert. *Roll Jordan Roll: The Life Story of a River and Its People.* Garden City, New York: Doubleday, 1965.

365 Salem, Elie. "Emerging Government in the Arab World." *Orbis* 6:1 (1962): 102–18.

366 Sharabi, Hisham B. *Nationalism and Revolution in the Arab World.* Princeton, New Jersey: Van Nostrand, 1966.

367 Tannous, Afif I. "Land Reform: Key to the Development and Stability of the Arab World." *Middle East Journal* 5 (Winter 1951): 1–20.

368 Williams, Keith. "Commercial Aviation in Arab States." *Middle East Journal* 11 (Spring 1957): 123–38.

B / Egypt

369 American University. Foreign Area Studies Division. *Area Handbook for the United Arab Republic (Egypt)*. Washington, D.C.: U.S.G.P.O., 1970.

370 Ammar, Hamed. *Growing Up in an Egyptian Village*. New York: Grove, 1954.

371 Ayrout, Father Henry Habib. *The Egyptian Peasant*. Boston: Beacon, 1968.

372 Baer, Gabriel. *A History of Landownership in Modern Egypt, 1800-1950*. New York: Oxford University Press, 1962.

373 Berger, Monroe. *Military Elite and Social Change: Egypt Since Napoleon*. Princeton, New Jersey: Princeton University Press, 1960.

374 Berque, Jacques. *Egypt: Imperialism and Revolution*. New York: Praeger, 1972.

375 Dekmejian, Hrair R. *Egypt under Nasir: A Study in Political Dynamics*. Albany: State University of New York Press, 1971.

376 Harris, George L., ed. *Egypt*. New Haven, Connecticut: Human Relations Area Files, 1957.

377 Holt, Peter. *Egypt and the Fertile Crescent, 1516-1922*. Ithaca, New York: Cornell University Press, 1966.

378 Lane, Edward W. *The Manners and Customs of the Modern Egyptians*. 1836. London: Everyman's Library, 1954.

379 Little, Tom. *Egypt*. New York: Praeger, 1958.

380 Mansfield, Peter. *Nasser's Egypt*. Baltimore: Penguin, 1966.

381 Peck, M. "American Policy and Interest in Egypt, 1918-1939." *Arab Journal* 4:2-4 (1967): 30-37.

382   Vatikiotis, P. J. *The Modern History of Egypt.* New York: Praeger, 1969.

383   Waterfield, Gordon. *Egypt.* New York: Walker, 1967.

384   Young, George. *Egypt.* New York: Scribners, 1927.

Egypt & Britain to 1952

385   Adams, C. C. *Islam and Modernism in Egypt.* London: Oxford University Press, 1933.

386   al-Sayyid, Afaf Lutfi. *Egypt and Cromer: A Study in Anglo-Egyptian Relations.* London: Murray, 1968.

387   Blunt, Wilfrid S. *A Secret History of the English Occupation of Egypt.* London: Unwin, 1907.

388   Cumberbatch, A. N. *Egypt: Economic and Commercial Conditions in Egypt, October, 1951.* London: H.M.S.O., 1952.

389   "Egypt's Shortage of Leaders." *Great Britain and East* 63 (May 1947): 47-48.

390   Faulkner, Brian. "Is Egypt Planning a Second Round?" *Commentary* 9 (Aug. 1950): 308-14.

391   Galatoli, Anthony M. *Egypt in Midpassage.* Cairo: Urwand, 1950.

392   Issawi, Charles. *Egypt: An Economic and Social Analysis.* London: Oxford University Press, 1947.

393   Kitchen, Helen A. "Al-Ahram: The *Times* of the Arab World." *Middle East Journal* 4 (Apr. 1950): 155-69.

394   Landau, Jacob M. *Parliaments and Parties in Egypt.* Tel Aviv: Israel Oriental Society, 1953.

395   Lloyd, George Ambrose L. *Egypt Since Cromer.* 2 vols. London: Macmillan, 1933-1934.

396   Marlowe, John. *Anglo-Egyptian Relations, 1800-1953.* London: Cresset, 1954.

397 ———. *A History of Modern Egypt and Anglo-Egyptian Relations, 1800–1956*. Hamden, Connecticut: Archon, 1965.

398 Milner, Alfred M. *England in Egypt*. New York: Fertig, 1970.

399 Quraishi, Zaheer M. *Liberal Nationalism in Egypt: Rise and Fall of the Wafd Party*. Delhi: Alwaz, 1967.

400 Rifaat, Mohammed. *The Awakening of Modern Egypt*. London: Longmans, Green, 1947.

401 Roosevelt, Kermit. "Egypt's Inferiority Complex." *Harper's* (Oct. 1947): 357–64.

402 Royal Institute of International Affairs. *Great Britain and Egypt, 1914–1951*. London: Oxford University Press, 1952.

403 Wilson, John A. *The Burden of Egypt*. Chicago: University of Chicago Press, 1951.

404 Zayid, Mahmoud Y. *Egypt's Struggle for Independence*. Beirut: Khayats, 1965.

Egyptian Revolution

405 al-Barawy, Rashed. *The Military Coup in Egypt: An Analytic Study*. Cairo: Renaissance Book Shop, 1952.

406 Atyeo, Henry C. "Egyptian Nationalism." *Current History* 23 (Nov. 1952): 312–15.

407 Badeau, John S. "A Role in Search of a Hero: A Brief Study of the Egyptian Revolution." *Middle East Journal* 9 (Autumn 1955): 373–84.

408 Batal, James. "Notes on the New Egypt." *Muslim World* 44 (July–Oct. 1954): 227–35.

409 Colombe, Marcel. "Egypt from the Fall of King Farouk to the February 1954 Crisis." *Middle Eastern Affairs* 5 (June–July 1954): 185–92.

410 Copeland, Miles. *The Game of Nations*. New York: Simon & Schuster, 1969.

411 Heikal, Mohamed H. *The Cairo Documents.* Garden City, New York: Doubleday, 1973.

412 Moore, Austin L. *Farewell Farouk.* Chicago: Scholars, 1954.

413 Naguib, Mohammed. *Egypt's Destiny: A Personal Statement.* New York: Doubleday, 1955.

414 Nasser, Gamal Abdel. *Egypt's Liberation: The Philosophy of the Revolution.* Washington, D.C.: Public Affairs, 1959.

415 ———. "The Egyptian Revolution." *Foreign Affairs* 33 (Jan. 1955): 199–211.

416 ———. "What Should the U.S. Do in the Middle East?" *U.S. News & World Report* (Sept. 3, 1954): 26–32.

417 Sadat, Anwar. *Revolt on the Nile.* New York: Day, 1957.

418 Vatikiotis, P. J. *The Egyptian Army in Politics: Pattern for New Nations.* Bloomington: Indiana University Press, 1961.

Politics & Government

419 Ayres, Henry F. "Egypt Today." *Royal Central Asian Journal* 41 (July–Oct. 1954): 200–211.

420 Berger, Monroe. *Bureaucracy and Society in Modern Egypt: A Study of the Higher Civil Service.* Princeton, New Jersey: Princeton University Press, 1957.

421 "Egypt's Defense Policy." *Economist* (Jan. 5, 1952): 4.

422 Harris, Christina Phelps. *Nationalism and Revolution in Egypt.* The Hague: Mouton, 1964.

423 Kerr, Malcolm H. *Egypt under Nasser.* New York: Foreign Policy Association, 1963.

424 Lacoutre, Jean, and Simone Lacoutre. *Egypt in Transition.* New York: Criterion, 1958.

425 Leiden, Carl. "Egypt: The Drift to the Left." *Middle Eastern Affairs* 13 (Dec. 1962): 290-98; 14 (Jan. 1963): 2-9.

426 Lenczowski, George. "The Objects and Methods of Nasserism." *Journal of International Affairs* 19:1 (1965): 63-76.

427 Loya, A. "Radio Propaganda of the United Arab Republic: An Analysis." *Middle Eastern Affairs* 13 (Apr. 1962): 98-110.

428 Mayfield, James B. *Rural Politics in Nasser's Egypt.* Austin: University of Texas Press, 1971.

429 Peretz, Don. "Democracy and the Revolution in Egypt." *Middle East Journal* 13 (Winter 1959): 26-40.

430 Safran, Nadav. *Egypt in Search of Political Community.* Cambridge, Massachusetts: Harvard University Press, 1961.

431 Sharabi, H. B. "The Egyptian Revolution." *Current History* 42 (Apr. 1962): 233-37.

432 Torrey, Gordon H. "Nasser's Egypt." *Current History* 48 (May 1965): 290.

433 Vatikiotis, P. J. "Egypt 1966: The Assessment of a Revolution." *World Today* 22 (June 1966): 242-51.

434 ———. "Egypt's Politics of Conspiracy." *Survey* 18 (Spring 1972): 83-99.

435 Wilber, D. *United Arab Republic—Egypt.* New York: Taplinger, 1968.

436 Wynn, Wilton. *Nasser of Egypt: The Search for Dignity.* Cambridge: Arlington, 1959.

Foreign Policy

437 Bruegel, J. "Israel and South Africa." *Venture* 23:8 (Sept. 1971): 6-8.

438 Churba, J. "U.A.R.-Israeli Rivalry in East Africa." *Military Review* 48 (Sept. 1968): 91–96.

439 Cremeans, Charles D. *The Arabs and the World: Nasser's Arab Nationalist Policy.* New York: Praeger, 1963.

440 Ismael, Tareq. "Religion and U.A.R. African Policy." *Journal of Modern African Studies* 6 (May 1968): 49–57.

441 ———. *The U. A. R. in Africa: Egypt's Policy under Nasser.* Evanston, Illinois: Northwestern University Press, 1971.

442 Kerr, Malcolm H. "'Coming to Terms with Nasser'—Attempts and Failures." *International Affairs* 43 (Jan. 1967): 65–84.

443 ———. *The United Arab Republic: Domestic Political and Economic Background of Foreign Policy.* Santa Monica, California: RAND, RM–5967, 1969.

444 Nasser, Gamal Abdel. "Where I Stand and Why." *Life* (July 20, 1959): 96.

445 Perlmann, M. "Egypt Versus the Bagdad Pact." *Middle Eastern Affairs* 7 (Mar. 1956): 95–101.

446 Rubinstein, Alvin Z. "Egypt's Foreign Policy." *Current History* 66 (Feb. 1974): 53–56.

447 Scholz, P. "Cooperation between the German Democratic Republic and the United Arab Republic." *German Foreign Policy* 6:4 (1967): 304–8.

448 Stevens, Georgiana G. "Arab Neutralism and Bandung." *Middle East Journal* 11 (Spring 1957): 139–52.

449 Wissa-Wassef, C. "Les relations entre l'Egypte et les deux états allemands depuis la seconde guerre mondiale." *Politique Etrangère* 5 (1972): 609–38.

Social & Economic History

450 Baer, Gabriel. *Studies in the Social History of Modern Egypt.* Publications of the Center for Middle Eastern Studies, no. 4. Chicago: University of Chicago Press, 1969.

451 Barbour, Nevill. "Impressions of the United Arab Republic." *International Affairs* 36 (Jan. 1960): 21-34.

452 Berger, Monroe. *Islam in Egypt Today: Social and Political Aspects of Popular Religion.* Cambridge: Cambridge University Press, 1970.

453 Carson, William Morris. "The Social History of an Egyptian Factory." *Middle East Journal* 11 (Autumn 1957): 361-70.

454 Cleland, Wendell. *The Population Problem in Egypt: A Study of Population Trends and Conditions.* Lancaster, Pennsylvania: Science Press, 1936.

455 Crecelius, Daniel. "Al-Azhar in the Revolution." *Middle East Journal* 20 (Winter 1966): 31-49.

456 El Daly, S. "The Problem of Population in the United Arab Republic." *Arab Journal* 3:2 (1966): 42-45.

457 El-Kammash, Magdi. *Economic Development and Planning in Egypt.* New York: Praeger, 1968.

458 Elliott, Ward. "The Peacock Syndrome: Barriers to Economic Development in Egypt." *Public Policy* 15 (1966): 212-62.

459 El Serafy, Salah. "Economic Development by Revolution: The Case of the UAR." *Middle East Journal* 17 (Summer 1963): 215-30.

460 Flapan, Simha. "Development vs. Militarism in Egypt." *New Outlook* 7:6 (July-Aug. 1964): 5-15.

461 Halpern, M. "Egypt and the New Middle Class: Reaffirmation and No Explorations." *Comparative Studies in Sociology and History* 11:1 (Jan. 1968): 97-108.

462 Hussein, Aziza. "The Role of Women in Social Reform in Egypt." *Middle East Journal* 7 (Autumn 1953): 440-50.

463 Issawi, Charles. *Egypt at Mid-Century: An Economic Survey.* New York: Oxford University Press, 1954.

464 ———. *Egypt in Revolution: An Economic Analysis.* New York: Oxford University Press, 1963.

465 Iwan, James L. "From Social Welfare to Local Government: The United Arab Republic (Egypt)." *Middle East Journal* 22 (Summer 1968): 265-77.

466 Kardouche, George K. *The U.A.R. in Development: A Study in Expansionary Finance.* New York: Praeger, 1967.

467 Kerr, Malcolm H. "The Emergence of a Socialist Ideology In Egypt." *Middle East Journal* 16 (Spring 1962): 127-44.

468 Lichstenstadter, Ilse. "An Arab-Egyptian Family." *Middle East Journal* 6 (Autumn 1952): 379-99.

469 Meinardus, Otto F. A. *Christian Egypt—Faith and Life.* Cairo: American University Press, 1970.

470 Mohy Ed-Din, K. "The Course of the Egyptian Revolution and Its Future." *World Marxist Review* 9 (Aug. 1966): 35-43.

471 Neame, Alan. "The Christian Dilemma in Egypt and Lebanon." *New Middle East,* no. 51 (Dec. 1972): 19-22.

472 O'Brien, Patrick. *The Revolution in Egypt's Economic System: From Private Enterprise to Socialism, 1952-1965.* New York: Oxford University Press, 1966.

473 Rejwan, Nissim. "Building the New Egyptian Man." *New Middle East,* no. 41 (Feb. 1972): 16-18.

474 ———. "Egypt's Educational Problems." *Midstream* 18:3 (Mar. 1972): 46-51.

475 Robbins, P. K. "Nasser's Quest for Foreign Aid, 1957-1958." *Middle East Forum* 41:2 (1965): 61-70.

476 Saab, Gabriel S. *The Egyptian Agrarian Reform, 1952-1962.* New York: Oxford University Press, 1967.

477 Samaan, Sadek H. *Value Reconstruction and Egyptian Education.* New York: Columbia University Press, 1955.

478 Wakin, Edward. *A Lonely Minority: The Modern Story of Egypt's Copts.* New York: Morrow, 1963.

479 Warriner, Doreen. "Land Reform in Egypt and Its Repercussions." *International Affairs* 29 (Jan. 1953): 1–10.

Egypt Since 1967

480 Abdel-Malek, Anouar. *Egypt: Military Society.* Translated by Charles L. Markmann. New York: Random House, 1968.

481 "After Abdul Nasser·Everything Has Changed: An Interview with Professor J. L. Talmon." *New Middle East* no. 26 (Nov. 1970): 11–16.

482 Dodd, Peter C. "Youth and Women's Emancipation in the United Arab Republic." *Middle East Journal* 22 (Spring 1968): 159–72.

483 El-Ayouty, Yassin. "Egypt and the Palestinians." *Current History* 64 (Jan. 1973): 9–12.

484 Fernea, Elizabeth Warnock. *A View of the Nile.* Garden City, New York: Doubleday, 1970.

485 Freeman, R. "Soviet Policy toward Sadat's Egypt from the Death of Nasser to the Fall of General Sadek." *Naval War College Review* 26:3 (Nov.–Dec. 1973): 63–79.

486 Hopkins, Harry. *Egypt: The Crucible: The Unfinished Revolution in the Arab World.* Boston: Houghton Mifflin, 1969.

487 Howard, Harry N. "The United Arab Republic." *Current History* 58 (Jan. 1970): 8–12.

488 Mansfield, Peter. "Egypt after Nasser." *World Today* 27 (July 1971): 302–9.

489 ———. "Egypt since June 1967." *World Today* 24 (Oct. 1968): 414-20.

490 ———. "Nasser and Nasserism." *International Journal* 28:4 (1973): 670-88.

491 "Nasser and After: A Symposium." *Royal Central Asian Journal* 58 (Feb. 1971): 12-23.

492 Rouleau, Eric. "Egypt from Nasser to Sadat." *Survival* 14 (Nov.-Dec. 1972): 284-86.

493 Rubinstein, A. "Egypt since Nasser." *Current History* 62 (Jan. 1972): 6-13.

494 Sadat, Anwar el. "Where Egypt Stands." *Foreign Affairs* 51 (Oct. 1972): 114-23.

495 Smith, H. "Where Egypt Stands." *Atlantic Monthly* (Jan. 1971): 39-45.

496 Stevens, Georgiana G. "Egypt." *Atlantic Monthly* (Jan. 1972): 12-16.

497 ———. "What Nasser Did." *Atlantic Monthly* (Jan. 1971): 45-47.

498 Vatikiotis, P. J. "Two Years after Nasser: The Chance of a New Beginning." *New Middle East,* no. 48 (Sept. 1972): 7-9.

499 ———, ed. *Egypt since the Revolution.* New York: Praeger, 1968.

C / Jordan

500 Abidi, Aqil Hyder Hasan. *Jordan: A Political Study 1948-1957.* New York: Asia Publishing House, 1965.

501 Abu Jaber, K. S. "The Legislature of the Hashemite Kingdom of Jordan: A Study in Political Development." *Muslim World* 59 (July-Oct. 1969): 120-50.

502 Aruri, Naseer H. *Jordan: A Study in Political Development, 1921-1965*. The Hague: Nijhoff, 1972.

503 Baratz, Joseph. *A Village by the Jordan: The Study of Degania*. New York: Roy, n.d.

504 Baster, James. "The Economic Problems of Jordan." *International Affairs* 31 (Jan. 1955): 26-35.

505 Beecher, William. "Jordan: On the Razor's Edge." *Army* 22:1 (Jan. 1972): 41-44.

506 Campbell, D. "Jordan: The Economics of Survival." *International Journal* 23:1 (1967-1968): 109-23.

507 Carr, Winifred. *Hussein's Kingdom*. London: Frewin, 1966.

508 Copeland, Paul W. *The Land and the People of Jordan*. Philadelphia: Lippincott, 1965.

509 Dann, U. "The Beginning of the Arab Legion." *Middle Eastern Studies* 5 (Oct. 1969): 181-91.

510 Dearden, Ann. *Jordan*. London: Hale, 1958.

511 "Facts and Figures: Jordan." *Middle Eastern Affairs* 14 (May 1963): 145-47.

512 Furlonge, Geoffrey. "Jordan Today." *Royal Central Asian Journal* 53 (Oct. 1966): 277-85.

513 Glubb, John B. *A Soldier with the Arabs*. New York: Harper, 1958.

514 ———. *The Story of the Arab Legion*. London: Hodder & Stoughton, 1948.

515 Harris, George L. *Jordan: Its People, Its Society, Its Culture*. New Haven, Connecticut: Human Relations Area Files, 1958.

516 Howard, Norman F. "The Uncertain Kingdom of Jordan." *Current History* 66 (Feb. 1974): 62–65.

517 Hussein, King (of Jordan). "Holy Land, My Country." *National Geographic* (Dec. 1964): 784–89.

518 International Bank for Reconstruction and Development. *The Economic Development of Jordan.* Baltimore: Johns Hopkins Press, 1957.

519 Jarvis, Claude Scudamore. *Arab Command: The Biography of Lt. Col. F. G. Peake Pasha.* London: Hutchinson, 1942.

520 Johnston, Sir Charles Hepburn. *The Brink of Jordan.* London: Hamilton, 1972.

521 "King Abdullah's Assassins." *World Today* 7 (Oct. 1951): 411–19.

522 Marden, Luis. "The Other Side of Jordan." *National Geographic* (Dec. 1964): 790–825.

523 Mogannam, E. Theodore. "Developments in the Legal System of Jordan." *Middle East Journal* 6 (Spring 1952): 194–206.

524 Morris, James. *The Hashimite Kings.* New York: Pantheon, 1959.

525 Patai, Raphael. *The Kingdom of Jordan.* Princeton, New Jersey: Princeton University Press, 1958.

526 Peake, Frederick G. *History and Tribes of Jordan.* Coral Gables, Florida: University of Miami Press, 1958.

527 Pepper, C. "Hussein Approaches 'A Point of No Return'." *New York Times Magazine* (Apr. 7, 1968): 24.

528 Phillips, Paul G. *The Hashimite Kingdom of Jordan: Prolegomena to a Technical Assistance Program.* Chicago: University of Chicago Press, 1954.

529   Prjla, A. "The Lessons of the Drama in Jordan." *Review of International Affairs* (Belgrade) (Nov. 5, 1970): 24–27.

530   Rouleau, Eric. "Crisis in Jordan." *World Today* 23 (Feb. 1967): 62–70.

531   Sanger, Richard H. *Where the Jordan Flows*. Washington, D.C.: Middle East Institute, 1964.

532   Shwadran, Benjamin. *Jordan: A State of Tension*. New York: Council for Middle Eastern Affairs, 1959.

533   Sparrow, Gerald. *Modern Jordan*. London: Allen & Unwin, 1961.

534   Streithorst, Tom. "Hashemite Jordan Today." *Middle East Forum* 31 (Jan. 1956): 12–20.

535   Vatikiotis, P. J. *Politics and the Military in Jordan: A Study of the Arab Legion, 1921–1957*. New York: Praeger, 1967.

536   Wright, Esmond. "Abdullah's Jordan: 1947–1951." *Middle East Journal* 5 (Autumn 1951): 439–60.

537   Young, Peter. *Bedouin Command with the Arab Legion, 1953–1956*. London: Kimber, 1956.

D / Syria

538   Abouchdid, Eugenie Elie. *Thirty Years of Lebanon and Syria, 1917–1947*. Beirut: Soder Rihani, 1948.

539· Abu Jaber, Kamel S. *The Arab Ba'th Socialist Party: History, Ideology, and Organizations*. Syracuse, New York: Syracuse University Press, 1966.

540 American University. Foreign Area Studies Division. *Area Handbook for Syria.* Washington, D.C.: U.S.G.P.O., 1965.

541 Armstrong, Harold Courtenay. *Turkey and Syria Reborn.* London: Lane, 1930.

542 Bell, Gertrude M. L. *Syria: The Desert and the Sown.* New York: Dutton, 1907.

543 Field, M. "Syria under Assad." *Middle East International* (July 1972): 26.

544 Gordon, Helen C. *Syria as It Is.* London: Methuen, 1939.

545 Hitti, Philip K. *History of Syria Including Lebanon and Palestine.* New York: Macmillan, 1951.

546 Hourani, Albert H. *Syria and Lebanon.* London: Oxford University Press, 1946.

547 Kerr, M. "Hafiz Asad and the Changing Patterns of Syrian Politics." *International Journal* 28:4 (1973): 689–706.

548 Khouri, Fred J. "Friction and Conflict on the Israeli-Syrian Front." *Middle East Journal* 17 (Winter–Spring 1963): 14–34.

549 Longrigg, Stephen H. *Syria and Lebanon under French Mandate.* London: Oxford University Press, 1958.

550 Ma'oz, Moshe. "Attempts at Creating a Political Community in Modern Syria." *Middle East Journal* 26 (Autumn 1972): 389–404.

551 MacCallum, Elizabeth P. *The Nationalist Crusade in Syria.* New York: Foreign Policy Association, 1928.

552 Makdisi, Samir A. "Syria: Rate of Economic Growth and Fixed Capital Formation, 1936–1968." *Middle East Journal* 25 (Spring 1971): 157–79.

553 Rabinovich, Itamar. *Syria under the Ba'th, 1963–66: The Army-Party Symbiosis.* New York: Halsted, 1973.

554 Sanjian, Avedis K. "The Sanjak of Alexandretta (Hatay): Its Impact on Turkish-Syrian Relations (1939-1956)." *Middle East Journal* 10 (Autumn 1956): 379-94.

555 Seale, Patrick. *The Struggle for Syria: A Study in Post-War Arab Politics, 1945-1958*. London: Oxford University Press, 1965.

556 Tibawi, A. L. *A Modern History of Syria Including Lebanon and Palestine*. New York: St. Martin's Press, 1969.

557 Torrey, G. H. "Instability in Syria." *Current History* 58 (Jan. 1970): 13-15.

558 ———. *Syrian Politics and the Military, 1945-1958*. Columbus: Ohio State University Press, 1964.

559 Van Dusen, Michael H. "Political Integration and Regionalism in Syria." *Middle East Journal* 26 (Spring 1972): 123-36.

560 Yamak, Labib Zuwiyya. *The Syrian Social Nationalist Party: An Ideological Analysis*. Cambridge, Massachusetts: Harvard University Press, 1966.

561 Ziadeh, Nicola A. *Syria and Lebanon*. New York: Praeger, 1957.

E / Lebanon

562 Binder, Leonard, ed. *Politics in Lebanon*. New York: Wiley, 1966.

563 Grassmuck, George, and Kamal Salibi. *Reformed Administration in Lebanon*. Ann Arbor: University of Michigan Press, 1967.

564 Gubser, Peter. "The Zu'ama' of Zahlah: The Current Situation in a Lebanese Town." *Middle East Journal* 27 (Spring 1973): 173-89.

565   Guenther, H. P. "The Beirut Management College: An Experiment in Management Training for a Developing Nation." *Middle East Journal* 17 (Autumn 1963): 368–82.

566   Gulick, John. *Social Structure and Culture Change in a Lebanese Village*. New York: Johnson Reprint, 1971.

567   Hess, Clyde G., Jr., and Herbert L. Bodman, Jr. "Confessionalism and Feudality in Lebanese Politics." *Middle East Journal* 8 (Winter 1954): 10–26.

568   Hudson, Michael C. "The Electoral Process and Political Development in Lebanon." *Middle East Journal* 20 (Spring 1966): 173–86.

569   Meo, Leila M. T. *Lebanon: Improbable Nation: A Study in Political Development*. Bloomington: Indiana University Press, 1965.

570   Salibi, K. S. *The Modern History of Lebanon*. New York: Praeger, 1965.

571   Sayegh, Yusif A. *Entrepreneurs of Lebanon: The Role of Business Leaders in the Middle East*. Cambridge, Massachusetts: Harvard University Press, 1962.

Lebanese Crisis, 1958

572   Agwani, M. S., ed. *The Lebanon Crisis, 1958: A Documentary Study*. New York: Asia Publishing House, 1965.

573   Qubain, Fahim I. *Crisis in Lebanon*. Washington, D.C.: Middle East Institute, 1961.

574   Sights, Col. Albert P., Jr. "Lessons of Lebanon: A Study in Air Strategy." *Air University Review* 16:5 (July–Aug. 1965): 28–43.

F / Iraq

575   Adamson, David. *The Kurdish War.* London: Allen & Unwin, 1964.

576   al-Marayati, Abid A. *A Diplomatic History of Modern Iraq.* New York: Speller, 1961.

577   American University. Foreign Area Studies Division. *Area Handbook for Iraq.* Washington, D.C.: U.S.G.P.O., 1971.

578   Arfa, Hassan. *The Kurds: An Historical and Political Study.* New York: Oxford University Press, 1964.

579   Cohen, H. "University Education among Iraqi-born Jews." *Jewish Journal of Sociology* 11:1 (June 1969): 59–66.

580   Dann, Uriel. *Iraq under Qassem: A Political History, 1958-63.* New York: Praeger, 1969.

581   Edmonds, C. J. "The Kurds of Iraq." *Middle East Journal* 11 (Winter 1957): 52–62.

582   Fernea, Elizabeth W. *Guests of the Sheik: An Ethnography of an Iraqi Village.* Garden City, New York: Doubleday, 1969.

583   Fernea, Robert A. *Shaykh and Effendi: Changing Patterns of Authority among the El Shabana of Southern Iraq.* Cambridge, Massachusetts: Harvard University Press, 1970.

584   Gallman, Waldemar. *Iraq under General Nuri.* Baltimore: Johns Hopkins Press, 1964.

585   Habermann, Stanley John. "The Iraq Development Board: Administration and Program [Economic Review]." *Middle East Journal* 9 (Spring 1955): 179–86.

586   Ireland, Philip. *Iraq: A Study in Political Development.* New York: Russell & Russell, 1970.

587 Kedourie, E. "The Jews of Baghdad in 1910." *Middle Eastern Studies* 7 (Oct. 1971): 355–62.

588 Khadduri, Majid. *Independent Iraq, 1932–1958.* New York: Oxford University Press, 1961.

589 Lloyd, Seton. *Iraq.* New York: Oxford University Press, 1944.

590 Longrigg, Stephen H. *Iraq, 1900 to 1950: A Political, Social and Economic History.* New York: Oxford University Press, 1953.

591 Marr, P. "The Iraqi Revolution: A Case Study of Army Rule." *Orbis* 14:3 (1970): 714–19.

592 Schmidt, Dana Adams. *Journey among Brave Men.* Boston: Little, Brown, 1964. [Kurdish Revolt]

593 Thoman, Roy E. "Iraq and the Persian Gulf Region." *Current History* 64 (Jan. 1973): 21–25.

594 Vinogradov, A. "The 1920 Revolt in Iraq Reconsidered: The Role of Tribes in National Politics." *International Journal of Middle East Studies* 3 (Apr. 1972): 123–39.

595 Wenner, Lettie M. "Arab-Kurdish Rivalries in Iraq." *Middle East Journal* 17 (Winter–Spring 1963): 68–82.

G / Saudi Arabia

596 American University. Foreign Area Studies Division. *Area Handbook for Saudi Arabia.* Washington, D.C.: U.S.G.P.O., 1966.

597 De Gaury, Gerald. *Faisal: King of Saudi Arabia.* New York: Praeger, 1967.

598 Gaspard, J. "Feisal's Arabian Alternative." *New Middle East,* no. 6 (Mar. 1969): 15–19.

599 Howarth, David. *The Desert King: Ibn Saud and His Arabia.* New York: McGraw-Hill, 1964.

600 Philby, H. St. John. *Saudi Arabia.* New York: Praeger, 1955.

601 Sheean, Vincent. "King Faisal's First Year." *Foreign Affairs* 44 (Jan. 1966): 304-13.

602 Twitchell, Karl Saben. *Saudi Arabia: With an Account of the Development of Its Natural Resources.* 3d ed. New York: Greenwood Press, 1958.

603 Winder, R. Bayly. *Saudi Arabia in the Nineteenth Century.* New York: St. Martin's Press, 1966.

H / Libya

604 "Another Arab Country That Worries U.S." *U.S. News & World Report* (Dec. 8, 1969): 81-82.

605 Cecil, Charles O. "The Determinants of Libyan Foreign Policy." *Middle East Journal* 19 (Winter 1965): 20-34.

606 Lenczowski, George. "Popular Revolution in Libya." *Current History* 66 (Feb. 1974): 57-61.

607 Lewis, W. H. "Libya: The End of the Monarchy." *Current History* 58 (Jan. 1970): 34-40.

608 "The Libyan Revolution in the Words of Its Leaders." *Middle East Journal* 24 (Spring 1970): 203-19.

609 Sheehan, E. "Colonel Qadhafi—Libya's Mystical Revolutionary." *New York Times Magazine* (Feb. 6, 1972): 10-11.

610 Stanford Research Institute. *Area Handbook for Libya.* Prepared for the American University. Washington, D.C.: U.S.G.P.O., Sept. 1969.

I / North Africa

611 Cooley, John K. "Playing for High Stakes South of the Med." *Christian Science Monitor* (Sept. 9, 1972): 7.

612 Gallagher, Charles F. *The Maghrib and the Middle East.* Santa Monica, California: RAND, RM–5962, 1969.

613 ———. *The United States and North Africa.* Cambridge, Massachusetts: Harvard University Press, 1963.

614 Lewis, William. "North Africa and the Power Balance." *Current History* 64 (Jan. 1973): 30–32.

615 "Mohammed Yazid on Algeria and the Arab-Israeli Conflict." *Journal of Palestine Studies* 1:2 (1972): 1–18.

J / Arab League

616 "The Arab League: Development and Difficulties." *World Today* 7 (May 1951): 187–96.

617 Atiyah, E. "The Arab League." *World Affairs* (London) 1 (Jan. 1947): 34–47.

618 Boutros-Ghali, B. Y. *The Arab League, 1945–1955.* International Conciliation, no. 498. New York: Carnegie, May 1955.

619 Cleland, Wendell. "The League of Arab States after Fifteen Years." *World Affairs* 123 (Summer 1960): 49–52.

620 "Development of the Arab League." *U.S. Department of State Bulletin* (May 18, 1947): 963–70.

621 Hourani, Cecil A. "The Arab League in Perspective." *Middle East Journal* 1 (Apr. 1947): 125–36.

622 "Joint Defense and Economic Cooperation Treaty between the States of the Arab League [Document]." *Middle East Journal* 6 (Spring 1952): 238–40.

623 Khadduri, Majid. "The Arab League as a Regional Arrangement." *American Journal of International Law* 40 (Oct. 1946): 756–77.

624 Khalil, Muhammad, ed. *The Arab States and the Arab League: A Documentary Record.* Vol. 1. *Constitutional Developments;* Vol. 2. *International Affairs.* Beirut: Khayats, 1962.

625 Little, T. R. "The Arab League: A Reassessment." *Middle East Journal* 10 (Spring 1956): 138–50.

626 MacDonald, Robert W. *The League of Arab States: A Study in the Dynamics of Regional Organization.* Princeton, New Jersey: Princeton University Press, 1967.

627 McKay, Vernon. "The Arab League in World Politics." *Foreign Policy Reports* (Nov. 15, 1946): 206–15.

628 Marlowe, John. "What Next for the Arab League?" *Commentary* 6 (Oct. 1948): 305–12.

629 Perrett, Michael. "The Arab League." *Contemporary Review*, no. 1028 (Aug. 1951): 84–88.

630 ———. "King Abdullah and the Arab League." *Contemporary Review*, no. 1000 (Apr. 1949): 207–10.

631 Radmilovic, T. "The Arab League and Arab Antagonisms." *Review of International Affairs* (Belgrade) (May 5, 1967): 17–19.

632 Raleigh, J. S. "Ten Years of the Arab League." *Middle Eastern Affairs* 6 (Mar. 1955): 65–77.

633 Saab, H. "The League of Arab States: An Innovation in Arab Institutional History." *World Justice* 7 (July 1966): 449–70.

634 Sharif, Amer A. *A Statistical Study on the Arab Boycott of Israel*. Monograph Series, no. 26. Beirut: Institute for Palestine Studies, 1970.

K / Arab Unity Efforts

635 Bechtold, Peter K. "New Attempts at Arab Cooperation: The Federation of Arab Republics, 1971–?" *Middle East Journal* 27 (Spring 1973): 152–72.

636 Binder, Leonard. "Radical Reform Nationalism in Syria and Egypt." *Muslim World* 49 (Apr. 1959): 96–109; 49 (July 1959): 213–31.

637 Chejne, Anwar G. "Egyptian Attitudes Toward Pan-Arabism." *Middle East Journal* 11 (Summer 1957): 253–68.

638 "The Constitution of the Federal of Arab Republics (FAR)." *Middle East Journal* 25 (Autumn 1971): 523–29.

639 "Declaration of Libyan-Egyptian Unity, 2 August 1972." *Survival* 14 (Nov.–Dec. 1972): 287–88.

640 "Egyptian-Syrian Mutual Defense Pact (October 10, 1955); Egyptian-Saudi Arabian Mutual Defense Pact (October 27, 1955) [Document]." *Middle East Journal* 10 (Winter 1956): 77–79.

641 Ionides, Michael. *Divide and Lose: The Arab Revolt, 1955 to 1958*. London: Geoffrey Bles, 1960.

642 Issawi, Charles. "The Bases of Arab Unity." *International Affairs* 31 (Jan. 1955): 36–47.

643 Kanovsky, E. "Arab Economic Unity." *Middle East Journal* 21 (Spring 1967): 213-35.

644 Kerr, Malcolm H. "The Convenient Marriage of Egypt and Libya." *New Middle East,* no. 48 (Sept. 1972): 4-6.

645 Khadduri, Majid. "The Problem of Regional Security in the Middle East: An Appraisal." *Middle East Journal* 11 (Winter 1957): 12-22.

646 "The Manifesto of the United Arab Republic [Document]." *Middle East Forum* 39:7 (July 1963): 11-15.

647 Palmer, Monte. "The United Arab Republic: An Assessment of Its Failure." *Middle East Journal* 20 (Winter 1966): 50-67.

648 Parker, J. S. F. "The United Arab Republic." *International Affairs* 38 (Jan. 1962): 15-28.

649 Radouanouic, L. "Conference in Rabat." *Review of International Affairs* (Belgrade) (Oct. 5, 1969): 13-19.

650 Sayegh, Fayez A. *Arab Unity: Hope and Fulfillment.* New York: Devin-Adair, 1958.

651 Seale, Patrick. "The Break-Up of the United Arab Republic." *World Today* 17 (Nov. 1961): 471-79.

III / PALESTINE: ISRAEL & THE PALESTINIANS, 1948–1974

652 Berger, Earl. *The Covenant and the Sword: Arab-Israeli Relations 1948–1956*. Toronto: University of Toronto Press, 1965.

653 Eban, Abba. "Reality and Vision in the Middle East: An Israeli View." *Foreign Affairs* 43 (July 1965): 626–38.

654 Harkabi, Y. "The Arab-Israeli Confrontation." *Midstream* 12:3 (Mar. 1966): 3–12.

655 ———. "The Withering Prospects for a Palestinian State." *New Outlook* 16:4 (May 1973): 23–26.

656 Howard, Harry N. "The Bourguiba Proposals: Time's Erosion of the Arab-Israeli Conflict." *Issues* 19:2 (1965): 5–11.

657 Hurewitz, J. C. *Middle East Dilemmas*. New York: Harper, 1953.

658 Issawi, Charles. "The Arab World's Heavy Legacy." *Foreign Affairs* 43 (Apr. 1965): 501–12.

659 Jackh, Ernest, ed. *Background of the Middle East*. Ithaca, New York: Cornell University Press, 1962.

660 Kenny, L. "The United Nations and the Palestine Question." *International Journal* 28:4 (1973): 766–83.

661 Laqueur, Walter Z., ed. *The Middle East in Transition.* New York: Praeger, 1958.

662 Marks, J. H. "The Problem of Palestine." *Muslim World* 60 (Jan. 1970): 25–46.

663 Peretz, Don. "Israel and the Arab Nations." *Journal of International Affairs* 19:1 (1965): 100–110.

664 Stone, I. F. "The Arab-Israeli Conflict: Implications." *Canadian Dimension* 4:5 (Summer 1967): 4.

665 Yin'am, S. "The Middle East in 1953: Annual Political Survey." *Middle Eastern Affairs* 5 (Jan. 1954): 1–17.

666 Zvyagin, Y. "'Total Diplomacy' in the Near East." *New Times* 26 (June 1950): 11–15.

A / Israel: Creation & First Decade, 1948–1958

667 Ben-Gurion, David. *History of Israel.* New York: Funk & Wagnalls, 1970.

668 ———. *Israel: Years of Challenge.* New York: Holt, Rinehart & Winston, 1963.

669 Bentwich, Norman. *Israel.* New York: McGraw-Hill, 1952.

670 ———. *Israel Resurgent.* New York: Praeger, 1960.

671 Bermant, Chaim. *Israel.* London: Thames & Hudson, 1967.

672 Bilby, Kenneth W. *New Star in the Near East.* New York: Doubleday, 1950.

673 Davis, Moshe, ed. *Israel: Its Role in Civilization.* New York: Harper, 1956.

674 De Gaury, Gerald. *The New State of Israel.* New York: Praeger, 1952.

675 Elston, D. R. *Israel: The Making of a Nation.* New York: Oxford University Press, 1963.

676 Feis, Herbert. *The Birth of Israel: The Tousled Diplomatic Bed.* New York: Norton, 1969.

677 Gruber, Ruth. *Israel without Tears.* New York: Wyn, 1950.

678 Horowitz, David. *State in the Making.* Translated by Julian Meltzer. New York: Knopf, 1953.

679 Kac, Arthur W. *The Rebirth of the State of Israel: Is It of God or of Men?* Chicago: Moody, 1967.

680 Lehrman, Hal. *Israel: The Beginning and Tomorrow.* New York: Sloane, 1951.

681 McDonald, James G. *My Mission in Israel, 1948-1951.* New York: Simon & Schuster, 1951.

682 McGill, Ralph. *Israel Revisited.* Atlanta, Georgia: Tupper & Love, 1950.

683 Mikes, George. *Milk and Honey, or Israel Explored.* London: Wingate, 1951.

684 Noth, Martin. *The History of Israel.* New York: Harper, 1958.

685 Riciotti, Giuseppe. *The History of Israel.* Milwaukee, Wisconsin: Bruce, 1958.

686 Rosenne, Shabtai. *Israel's Armistice Agreements with the Arab States.* Tel Aviv: Israel Branch, International Law Association, 1951.

687 Sacher, Harry. *Israel: The Establishment of a State.* New York: British Book Centre, 1952.

688 Williams, L. F. Rushbrook. *The State of Israel.* New York: Macmillan, 1958.

Israeli Society

689 Baly, D. "Christians and Israel." *Mid East* 10:6 (Dec. 1970): 33–36.

690 Bentwich, Norman. "The Hebrew University of Jerusalem and Education in Israel." *Quarterly Review*, no. 584 (Apr. 1950): 206–16.

691 Blanc, Haim. "Hebrew in Israel: Trends and Problems." *Middle East Journal* 11 (Autumn 1957): 397–409.

692 Byford-Jones, W. *Forbidden Frontiers*. London: Hale, 1958.

693 Florsheim, Joel. *Development of the Jewish People in Israel, 1948–1964*. Tel Aviv: Central Bureau of Statistics, n.d.

694 Frank, M. Z. "From Deborah to Kurt: The Story of Hebrew in Israel." *Middle East Journal* 6 (Summer 1952): 315–28.

695 ———. "God of Abraham in the State of Israel." *Middle East Journal* 5 (Autumn 1951): 407–23.

696 Spender, Stephen. *Learning Laughter*. New York: Harcourt, Brace, 1953.

697 Teller, Judd L. "Modern Hebrew Literature of Israel." *Middle East Journal* 7 (Spring 1953): 182–95.

698 Weinryb, Bernard D. "The Lost Generation in Israel." *Middle East Journal* 7 (Autumn 1953): 415–29.

The Kibbutz

699 Fishman, Aryei, ed. *The Religious Kibbutz Movement*. New York: Jewish Agency for Palestine, 1957.

700 *A New Way of Life: The Collective Settlements of Israel*. London: Shindler & Golomb, 1949.

701 Weingarten, Murray. *Life in a Kibbutz*. New York: Reconstructionist Press, 1955.

Immigration

702   Eisenstadt, S. N. *The Absorption of Immigrants: A Comparative Study Based Mainly on the Jewish Community in Palestine and the State of Israel.* London: Routledge & Kegan Paul, 1954.

703   Farrell, James Thomas. *It Has Come to Pass.* New York: Herzl Press, 1958.

704   Frankenstein, Carl, ed. *Between Past and Future: Essays and Studies on Aspects of Immigrant Absorption in Israel.* Jerusalem: Henrietta Szold Foundation, 1953.

705   "How the Iraqi Jews Came to Israel." *Middle East International* (Jan. 1973): 18–20.

706   Klausner, Samuel Z. "Immigrant Absorption and Social Tension in Israel: A Case Study of Iraqi Jewish Immigrants." *Middle East Journal* 9 (Summer 1955): 281–94.

707   Schechtman, Joseph B. "The Jews of Aden." *Jewish Social Studies* 13:2 (Apr. 1951): 133–48.

708   Sicron, Moshe. *Immigration to Israel, 1948–53.* Jerusalem: Falk Project for Economic Research in Israel, 1957.

709   Weingrod. Alex. "Change and Continuity in a Moroccan Immigrant Village in Israel." *Middle East Journal* 14 (Summer 1960): 277–91.

710   Wigoder, G. "Jews from the Land of Frankincense." *Israel Magazine* 5: 3–4 (1973): 25–31.

Economy

711   Bonne, A. "Entrepreneurial Problems in Israel." *Middle East Journal* 12 (Winter 1958): 89–95.

712   Darin-Drabkin, H. *Housing in Israel.* Tel Aviv: Gadish, 1957.

713   Granott, A. *Agrarian Reform and the Record of Israel.* London: Ayre & Spottiswoode, 1956.

714 Janowsky, Oscar I. *Foundations of Israel: Emergence of a Welfare State.* Princeton, New Jersey: Van Nostrand, 1959.

715 Ottensooser, Robert David. *The Palestine Pound and the Israel Pound.* Geneva: E. Droz, 1955.

716 Rosenberg, Leonard G. "Industrial Exports: Israel's Requirement for Self-Support." *Middle East Journal* 12 (Spring 1958): 153-65.

717 Rubner, Alex. *The Economy of Israel: A Critical Account of the First Ten Years.* New York: Praeger, 1960.

Politics & Government

718 Bernstein, Marver H. *The Politics of Israel: The First Decade of Statehood.* Princeton, New Jersey: Princeton University Press, 1957.

719 Caiden, Gerald E. *Israel's Administrative Culture.* Berkeley: Institute of Governmental Studies, University of California, 1970.

720 Peretz, Don. "Reflections on Israel's Fourth Parliamentary Elections." *Middle East Journal* 14 (Winter 1960): 15-27.

721 Perlmutter, Amos. "The Institutionalization of Civil-Military Relations in Israel: The Ben Gurion Legacy and Its Challengers, 1953-1967." *Middle East Journal* 22 (Autumn 1968): 415-32.

722 Rackman, Emanuel. *Israel's Emerging Constitution, 1948-1951.* New York: Columbia University Press, 1955.

723 Samuel, Edwin. "The Government of Israel and Its Problems." *Middle East Journal* 3 (Jan. 1949): 1-16.

Israel & the World

724 Brecher, M. "Ben Gurion and Sharett's Contrasting Images of the Arabs." *New Middle East,* no. 18 (Mar. 1970): 28-34.

725   Cooke, Hedley V. *Israel: A Blessing and a Curse.* London: Stevens, 1960.

726   Eban, Abba. "The Middle East in World Affairs." *Journal of International Affairs* 6:2 (1952): 25-27.

727   ———. *The Tide of Nationalism.* New York: Horizon, 1959.

728   Ellis, Harry B. *Israel and the Middle East.* New York: Ronald, 1957.

729   Eytan, Walter. *The First Ten Years: A Diplomatic History of Israel.* New York: Simon & Schuster, 1958.

730   Rosenblatt, Bernard A. *The American Bridge to the Israeli Commonwealth.* New York: Farrar, Straus & Cudahy, 1959.

731   Samuel, Edwin. "Israel and the Arab States." *Political Quarterly* 28 (Apr.–June 1957): 179-87.

732   Shimoni, Yaacov. "Israel in the Pattern of Middle East Politics." *Middle East Journal* 4 (July 1950): 277-95.

733   Weigert, Gideon. "Arab Writers Look at Israel." *World Today* 15 (Dec. 1959): 501-8.

B / Israel: Evolving Nation, 1958-1974

734   Alder, Bill, ed. *Israel: A Reader.* Philadelphia: Chilton, 1969.

735   Appel, Benjamin. *Ben-Gurion's Israel.* New York: Grosset, 1965.

736   Arian, Alan. *Ideological Change in Israel.* Cleveland, Ohio: Press of Case Western Reserve University, 1968.

737   Badi, Joseph, ed. *Fundamental Laws of the State of Israel.* New York: Twayne, 1961.

738 "Chronicle [of Israeli population statistics]." *Jewish Journal of Sociology* 14:2 (Dec. 1972): 262.

739 Dadiani, L., and G. Musaelyan. "Israel as a Militarist Aggressive State." *International Affairs* (Moscow) (Oct. 1972): 89-93.

740 Evenari, Michael, et al. *The Negev: The Challenge of a Desert.* Cambridge, Massachusetts: Harvard University Press, 1971.

741 Finbert, Elian-J. *Israel.* New York: Oxford University Press, 1968.

742 Fletcher-Cooke, J. "The United Nations and the Birth of Israel." *International Journal* 28:4 (1973): 612-29.

743 Lewis, F. "Israel." *Atlantic Monthly* (July 1971): 14-25.

744 Moskin, J., and A. Newman. "Israel: Twenty years of Siege and Struggle—The Next Twenty Years." *Look* (Apr. 30, 1968): 28-42.

745 Naamani, Israel T.; David Rudavsky; and Abraham I. Katsh, eds. *Israel through the Eyes of Its Leaders: A Socio-Political Reader.* Tel Aviv: Meorot, 1971.

746 Prittie, Terence. *Israel: Miracle in the Desert.* Baltimore: Penguin, 1968.

747 Rodinson, Maxime. *Israel, a Colonial-Settler State?* New York: Monad, 1973.

748 Rubinstein, Amnon. "Who's a Jew, and Other Woes." *Encounter* 36:3 (Mar. 1971): 84-92.

749 Safran, Nadav. *Israel Today: A Profile.* New York: Foreign Policy Association, 1965.

750 Schweid, E. "Israel as a Zionist State." *Dispersion & Unity* 11 (1970): 51-60.

751 Scofield, John. "Israel: Land of Promise." *National Geographic* (Mar. 1965): 395-434.

752 Simpson, Dwight J. "Israel: A Garrison State." *Current History* 58 (Jan. 1970): 1-7.

753 ———. "Israel: The State of Siege." *Current History* 48 (May 1965): 263-68.

754 ———. "Israel: The Unrelenting Battle." *Current History* 52 (Feb. 1967): 78-83.

755 ———. "Israel after Twenty-Five Years." *Current History* 64 (Jan. 1973): 1-4.

756 Smith, Harvey H., et al. *Area Handbook for Israel*. Prepared by Foreign Area Studies Division, American University. Washington, D.C.: U.S.G.P.O., Sept. 1970.

757 Tamarin, Georges R. *Three Studies on Prejudice in Israel*. Tel Aviv: Shikpul Press, 1969.

758 Van Cleef, Eugene. "The Status of Israel—and a Look Ahead." *Middle East Journal* 18 (Summer 1964): 306-12.

759 Willner, Dorothy. *Nation-Building and Community in Israel*. Princeton, New Jersey: Princeton University Press, 1969.

760 Zmora, Ohad, ed. *Days of Ben Gurion*. New York: Grossman, 1967.

Israeli Society

761 Akzin, Benjamin, and Yehezkel Dror. *Israel: High-Pressure Planning*. National Planning Series, no. 5. Syracuse, New York: Syracuse University Press, 1966.

762 Amiran, D. H. K., and A. Shachar. *Development Towns in Israel*. Jerusalem: Hebrew University, 1969.

763 Antonovsky, Aaron, and Alan Arian. *Hopes and Fears of Israelis: Consensus in a New Society*. Jerusalem: Jerusalem Academic, 1972.

764 Bentwick, Joseph S. *Education in Israel.* Philadelphia: Jewish Publication Society of America, 1965.

765 Braham, Randolph L. *Israel, Modern Education System: Report Emphasizing Secondary and Teacher Education.* Washington, D.C.: U.S.G.P.O., n.d.

766 Cohen, E. "Mixed Marriage in an Israeli Town." *Jewish Journal of Sociology* 11:1 (June 1969): 41–50.

767 Cohen, G. "Family Planning in Israel." *Midstream* 12:6 (June–July 1966): 49–54.

768 Eaton, Joseph W. "Gadna: Israel's Youth Corps." *Middle East Journal* 23 (Autumn 1969): 471–83.

769 Eban, A. S. "Some Social and Cultural Problems of the Middle East." *International Affairs* 23 (July 1947): 367–75.

770 Eisenstadt, S. N. "Israeli Society: Major Features and Problems." *Journal of World History* 11:1–2 (1968): 313–28.

771 Elath, Eliahu. "Education in Israel." *Royal Central Asian Journal* 52 (Jan. 1965): 38–41.

772 Elon, Amos. *The Israelis: Founders and Sons.* New York: Holt, Rinehart & Winston, 1971.

773 Fine, Helen. *Behold the Land: Social Studies on the State of Israel.* New York: Union of American Hebrew Congregations, 1968.

774 Marks, A. "Settlement Patterns and Intrasite Variability in the Central Negev, Israel." *American Anthropologist* 73 (Oct. 1971): 1237–44.

775 Oppenheimer, A'haron. *Basic Education in the Army.* Jerusalem: Hebrew University, 1969.

776 Rabi, Z. "Changes in Israel's Population, 1966–70." *Israel Quarterly of Economics* 1:3 (1972): 65–76.

777 Roshwald, Mordecai. "Marginal Jewish Sects in Israel." *International Journal of Middle East Studies* 4 (Apr. 1973): 219-37; 4 (July 1973): 328-54.

778 Russcol, Herbert, and Margalit Banai. *The First Million Sabras: A Portrait of the Native Israeli.* New York: Hart, 1972.

779 Segre, V. D. *Israel: A Society in Transition.* London: Oxford University Press, 1971.

780 Selzer, Michael. *The Aryanization of the Jewish State.* New York: Black Star, 1967.

781 Simon, R. "What Makes a State Jewish." *New Outlook* 15:2 (Feb. 1972): 43-51.

782 Spiegel, Erika. *New Towns in Israel: Urban and Regional Planning and Development.* Translated by Annelie Rookwood. New York: Praeger, 1967.

783 Teller, Judd. *Welfare State and Welfare Society (Israel).* New York: American Histadrut Cultural Exchange Institute, 1967.

784 Weingrod, Alex. *Israel: Group Relations in a New Society.* New York: Praeger, 1965.

785 ———. *Reluctant Pioneers: Village Development in Israel.* Ithaca, New York: Cornell University Press, 1966.

786 Weinryb, Bernard D. "The Impact of Urbanization in Israel." *Middle East Journal* 11 (Winter 1957): 23-36.

787 Wolins, Martin, and Meir Gottesmann. *Group Care: An Israeli Approach, the Educational Path of Youth Aliyah.* New York: Gordon & Breach, 1971.

788 Zahlan, Antoine. *Science and Higher Education in Israel.* Monograph Series, no. 22. Beirut: Institute for Palestine Studies, 1970.

789   Zinger, Z. "Israel's Religious Establishment and Its Critics." *Midstream* 13:3 (Mar. 1967): 50-56.

790   Zohar, Danah. "Israel's Religious Problem." *New Middle East*, no. 45 (June 1972): 17-19.

791   Zucker, Norman L. *The Coming Crisis in Israel: Private Faith and Public Policy.* Cambridge, Massachusetts: M.I.T. Press, 1973.

Arabs in Israel

792   Behrman, Lucy. *Muslim Brotherhoods and Politics in Israel.* Cambridge, Massachusetts: Harvard University Press, 1971.

793   Benor, J. L. "Arab Education in Israel." *Middle Eastern Affairs* 1 (Aug.-Sept. 1950): 224-29.

794   Ben-Porath, Yoram. *The Arab Labor Force in Israel.* Jerusalem: Israel Universities Press, 1966.

795   Berman, M. "Social Change among the Beersheba Bedouin." *Human Organization* 26:1-2 (1967): 69-76.

796   Blanc, H. "The Prospect for Arab-Jewish Coexistence in Israel." *Holy Cross Quarterly* 2 (1972): 24-27.

797   Cohen, Abner. *Arab Border-Villages in Israel: A Study of Continuity and Change in Social Organization.* New York: Humanities Press, 1965.

798   Eyal, E. "The Arab Minority and the Future." *American Zionist* 63:3 (Nov. 1972): 17-20.

799   Goitein, S. D. "The Arab Schools in Israel Revisited." *Middle Eastern Affairs* 3 (Oct. 1952): 272-75.

800   Hadawi, Sami. "Israel and the Arab Minority." Information Paper, no. 7. New York: Arab Information Center, July 1959.

801   Harari, Yechiel, ed. *The Arabs in Israel: Statistics and Facts.* Monograph Series, no. 7. Givat Haviva: Center for Arab and Afro-Asian Studies, 1970.

802 Hofman, John E. "Readiness for Social Relations between Arabs and Jews in Israel." *Journal of Conflict Resolution* 16:2 (June 1972): 241-52.

803 Israel. Ministry for Foreign Affairs. Information Department. *The Arabs in Israel*. Jerusalem: Haaretz, 1961.

804 "Israeli Arabs May Rise to 19.5% by 1990." *Israel Economist* 28:12 (Dec. 1972): 3-6.

805 Jiryis, Sabri. *The Arabs in Israel*. Monograph Series, no. 16. Beirut: Institute for Palestine Studies, 1969.

806 ———. *The Arabs in Israel, 1948-1966*. Beirut: Institute for Palestine Studies, 1968.

807 ———. *Democratic Freedoms in Israel*. Beirut: Institute for Palestine Studies, 1972.

808 ———. "Recent Knesset Legislation and the Arabs in Israel." *Journal of Palestine Studies* 1:1 (1971): 53-67.

809 Khalidi, E. "Palestinian Arab Villages in Israel." *Arab World* 18:5-6 (May-June 1972): 20-26.

810 Landau, Jacob M. *The Arabs in Israel: A Political Study*. New York: Oxford University Press, 1969.

811 Lehrman, Hal. "The Arabs of Israel." *Commentary* 8 (Dec. 1949): 523-33.

812 Marx, E. *Bedouin of the Negev*. Manchester: Manchester University Press, 1967.

813 Mayhew, C. "Israel, Arabs and the Labour Party." *Venture* 23:6 (June 1971): 9-10.

814 Muhsam, H. V. *Bedouin of the Negev: Eight Demographic Studies*. Jerusalem: Jerusalem Academic, 1966.

815 Oded, Yitzhak. "Bedouin Lands Threatened by Takeover." *New Outlook* 7:9 (Nov.-Dec. 1964): 45-52.

816   ———. "Land Losses among Israel's Arab Villagers." *New Outlook* 7:7 (Sept. 1964): 10-25.

817   Peres, Yochanan. "Modernization and Nationalism in the Identity of the Israeli Arab." *Middle East Journal* 24 (Autumn 1970): 479-92.

818   Peretz, Don. "The Arab Minority of Israel." *Middle East Journal* 8 (Spring 1954): 139-54.

819   Pundik, H. "Israel's Arabs Establish Their Identity." *New Middle East*, no. 11 (Aug. 1969): 31-33.

820   Rosen, Harry, M. *The Arabs and Jews in Israel: The Reality, the Dilemma, the Promise*. Jerusalem: Israel Office, Foreign Affairs Department, 1970.

821   Schwarz, C. "Israel and Its Arab Minority." *Swiss Review of World Affairs* 22:7 (Oct. 1972): 6-9.

822   Schwarz, Walter. *The Arabs in Israel*. London: Faber & Faber, 1959.

823   ———. "Israel's Arab Minority." *Commentary* 25 (Jan. 1958): 23-27.

824   Shidlowsky, Benjamin, ed. *Guide to Arab and Druze Settlements in Israel*. Jerusalem: Minister of Arab Affairs of the Office of the Prime Ministers, 1969.

825   Stock, Ernest. *From Conflict to Understanding: Relations between Jews and Arabs in Israel since 1948*. New York: Institute of Human Relations Press, American Jewish Committee, 1968.

826   Suimoni, Jacob. *The Arabs in Israel*. New Haven, Connecticut: Human Relations Area Files, 1956.

827   Toledano, S. "Israel's Arabs: A Unique National Minority." *International Problems* 12:1-2 (June 1973): 39-43.

828   Tuma, Elias H. "The Arabs in Israel: An Impasse." *New Outlook* 9:3 (Mar.-Apr. 1966): 39-46.

829 Vatad, Muhammad. "Arab Youth in Israel: Today and Tomorrow." *New Outlook* 7:5 (June 1964): 22-25.

830 Weigart, Gideon. "Arab-Jewish Economic Cooperation in Israel." *Welt des Islams* 8:4 (1963): 243-51.

831 ———. "Israel's Arabs after 20 Years." *Jewish Observer and Middle East Review* (May 24, 1968): 16-17.

832 Weinryb, Bernard D. "Arabs in Israel." *Palestine Affairs* 3 (Oct. 1948): 113-15.

833 Zaid, K. "Israel's Arabs after Twenty-five Years." *New Outlook* 16:6 (July-Aug. 1973): 11-16.

The Kibbutz

834 Crown, Alan D. "The Changing World of the *Kibbutz*." *Middle East Journal* 19 (Autumn 1965): 422-34.

835 Darin-Drabkin, H. "Whither the Kibbutz." *New Outlook* 15:2 (Feb. 1972): 11-22.

836 Garber-Talmon, Yonina. *Family and Community in the Kibbutz*. Cambridge, Massachusetts: Harvard University Press, 1972.

837 Gorkin, Michael. *Border Kibbutz*. New York: Grosset & Dunlap, 1971.

838 Kanovsky, Eliyahu. *The Economy of the Israeli Kibbutz*. Harvard Middle East Monographs, no. 13. Cambridge, Massachusetts: Harvard University Press, 1966.

839 Klayman, Maxwell I. *The Moshav in Israel: A Case Study of Institution-Building for Agricultural Development*. New York: Praeger, 1969.

840 Nissenson, Hugh. *Notes from the Frontier*. New York: Dial, 1968.

841 Pavel, E. "The Past a Future: Biased Reflections on the Kibbutz." *Midstream* 18:8 (Oct. 1972): 19-32.

842 Schlesinger, B. "Family Life in the Kibbutz of Israel: Utopia Gained or Paradise Lost?" *International Journal of Comparative Sociology* 11 (Dec. 1970): 251-71.

843 Shatil, J. "Development Trends in the Kibbutz." *New Outlook* 14:4 (May 1971): 32-39.

844 Spiro, Melford E. *Kibbutz: Venture in Utopia*. Cambridge, Massachusetts: Harvard University Press, 1956.

845 ———, with Audrey G. Spiro. *Children of the Kibbutz*. New York: Schocken, 1965.

846 Stern, Boris. *The Kibbutz That Was*. Washington, D.C.: Public Affairs, 1965.

Immigration

847 Ash, J. "Planning and Housing for Immigrants in Israel." *Town Planning Review* 37 (July 1966): 117-23.

848 Bruno, M. "The Social Gap [in Israel] Is Not Really Closing." *New Outlook* 16:1 (Jan. 1973): 12-15.

849 Deshen, Shlomo A. *Immigrant Voters in Israel: Parties and Congregations in a Local Campaign*. Manchester: Manchester University Press, n.d.

850 Goldberg, Harvey E. *Cave Dwellers and Citrus Growers: A Jewish Community in Libya and Israel*. New York: Cambridge University Press, 1972.

851 ———. "Culture Change in an Israeli Immigrant Village: The Twist in Even Yosef." *Middle Eastern Studies* 9 (Jan. 1973): 73-80.

852 ———. "Domestic Organization and Wealth in an Israeli Immigrant Village." *Human Organization* 28:1 (1969): 58-62.

853 Harman, Zena. "The Assimilation of Immigrants into Israel." *Middle East Journal* 5 (Summer 1951): 303-18.

854 Jabbour, George. *Settler Colonialism in Southern Africa and the Middle East.* Palestine Books, no. 30. Beirut: Palestine Liberation Organization Research Center, Aug. 1970.

855 Knisbacher, M. "Aliyah of Soviet Jews: Protection of the Right of Immigration under International Law." *Harvard International Law Journal* 14:1 (1973): 89–110.

856 Kushner, Gilbert. *Immigrants from India in Israel.* Tucson: University of Arizona Press, 1973.

857 Sacher, Howard Morely. *Aliyah: The Peoples of Israel.* New York: World, 1962.

858 Shokeid, Moshe. *The Dual Heritage: Immigrants from the Atlas Mountains in an Israeli Village.* Manchester: Manchester University Press, 1971.

859 Shumsky, Abraham. *The Clash of Cultures in Israel: A Problem for Education.* Westport, Connecticut: Greenwood Reprint, 1972.

860 Shuval, Judith T. *Immigrants on the Threshold.* New York: Atherton, 1963.

861 "Twenty Years of Immigration" and "Natural Increase in Israel." *Israel Economist* 25:5–6 (May–June 1969): 130–35.

862 Weinberg, A. "Immigration from Western Countries in Israel." *International Migration* 5:1 (1967): 22–37.

863 Weintraub, Dov. *Immigration and Social Change: Agricultural Settlement of New Immigrants in Israel.* New York: Humanities Press, 1971.

Oriental Jews in Israel

864 Alder, C. "Education and Integration of Immigrants in Israel." *International Migration Review* 3:3 (1969): 3–18.

865 Alport, E. A. "The Integration of Oriental Jews into Israel." *World Today* 23 (Apr. 1967): 153–59.

866 Beller, J. "Israel's North African Jews and Their Origins." *World Jewry* 15:5 (Nov. 1972): 8–11.

867 Cohen, E. "The Black Panthers and Israeli Society." *Jewish Journal of Sociology* 14:1 (June 1972): 93–110.

868 Eisenstadt, S. D., et al., eds. *Integration and Development in Israel*. New York: Praeger, 1970.

869 Frank, M. "Israel's 'Black Panthers': Two Perspectives." *American Zionist* 62:1 (Sept. 1971): 32–37.

870 Hauslich, A. "250,000 Israelis Live in Poverty." *Jewish Observer and Middle East Review* (Feb. 26, 1971): 14–17.

871 "Israel's Oriental Jews: A Statistical Survey." *Journal of Palestine Studies* 1:2 (1972): 144–55.

872 Kanovsky, Eliyahu. "Problems of Integration in Israel." *American Journal of Economics and Sociology* 26 (July 1967): 329–36.

873 Matovu, Benyamin. "Israel Divided: Sephardi vs. Ashkenazi Time-Bomb." *Issues* 19:2 (1965): 25–28.

874 Raphaeli, N. "The Absorption of Orientals into Israeli Bureaucracy." *Middle Eastern Studies* 8 (Jan. 1972): 85–92.

875 Zenner, Walter P. "Ambivalence and Self-Image among Oriental Jews in Israel." *Jewish Journal of Sociology* 5:2 (Dec. 1963): 214–23.

876 ———. "Sephardic Communal Organizations in Israel." *Middle East Journal* 21 (Spring 1967): 173–86.

Economy

877 Berger, L. "Remarks on the Economic Situation of Israel." *International Problems* 9:3–4 (Nov. 1970): 69–77.

878 Bruno, Michael. *Economic Development Problems of Israel, 1970–1980*. Santa Monica, California: RAND, RM–5975, 1970.

879 Davidson, Brian. "Israel Aircraft Industries." *Interavia* (July 1971): 836–37.

880 Doerr, Arthur H., et al. "Agricultural Evolution in Israel in the Two Decades since Independence." *Middle East Journal* 24 (Summer 1970): 319–37.

881 Finger, Nachum. *The Impact of Government Subsidies on Industrial Management: The Israeli Experience.* New York: Praeger, 1971.

882 Halevi, Nadav, and Ruth Lkinov-Malul. *The Economic Development of Israel.* New York: Praeger, 1968.

883 Heth, Meir. *The Flow of Funds in Israel.* New York: Praeger, 1970.

884 Nasmyth, Jenny. "Israel's Distorted Economy." *Middle East Journal* 8 (Autumn 1954): 391–402.

885 Ofer, Gur. *The Service Industries in a Developing Economy: Israel, a Case Study.* New York: Praeger, 1966.

886 Pack, Howard. *Structural Change and Economic Policy in Israel.* New Haven, Connecticut: Yale University Press, 1971.

887 Remba, Oded. "The Ethnography of Rich and Poor in Israel." *New Middle East*, no. 49 (Oct. 1972): 36–39.

888 Sharon, Nahun. "The Histadrut in 1966." *New Outlook* 9:2 (Feb. 1966): 30–35.

889 Shibl, Yusuf, ed. *Essays on the Israeli Economy.* Palestine Books, no. 15. Beirut: Palestine Liberation Organization Research Center, Feb. 1969.

890 Szereszewski, Robert. *Essays on the Structure of the Jewish Economy in Palestine and Israel.* Jerusalem: Maurice Falk Institute, 1968.

891 Wilkenfeld, Harold C. *Taxes and People in Israel.* Cambridge, Massachusetts: Harvard University Press, 1973.

Politics & Government

892 Arian, Alan. *The Elections in Israel, 1969.* Jerusalem: Jerusalem Academic, 1972.

893 ———. "Stability and Change in Israeli Public Opinion and Politics." *Public Opinion Quarterly* 35:1 (1971): 19–35.

894 Badi, Joseph, ed. *The Government of the State of Israel: A Critical Account of Its Parliament, Executive, and Judiciary.* New York: Twayne, 1963.

895 Baker, Henry E. *The Legal System of Israel.* Jerusalem: Israel Universities Press, 1968.

896 Birnbaum, Ervin. *The Politics of Compromise: State and Religion in Israel.* Rutherford, New Jersey: Fairleigh Dickinson University Press, 1970.

897 Czudnowski, Moshe M., and Jacob M. Landau. *The Israeli Communist Party and the Elections for the Fifth Knesset, 1961.* Stanford, California: Hoover Institution Press, 1965.

898 Devlin, K. "Communism in Israel." *Survey* 62 (Jan. 1967): 141–51.

899 Farjo, Ya'akov. "B.G. vs. Eshkol: The Second Round." *New Outlook* 7:4 (May 1964): 6–9.

900 Fein, Leonard J. *Israel: Politics and People.* Boston: Little, Brown, 1968.

901 Geva, Ahron. "The Increasing Moderate Strength of Yigal Allon." *New Middle East,* no. 48 (Sept. 1972): 17–19.

902 Halkin, H. "Dayan as Politician." *Commentary* 55:1 (Jan. 1973): 51–56.

903 Johnston, Scott D. "Election Politics and Social Change in Israel." *Middle East Journal* 16 (Summer 1962): 309–27.

904 Kraines, Oscar. *Government and Politics in Israel.* Boston: Houghton Mifflin, 1961.

905 Leslie, Clement S. *The Rift in Israel: Religious Authority and Secular Democracy.* New York: Schocken, 1971.

906 Likhovski, E. *Israel's Parliament: The Law of the Knesset.* New York: Oxford University Press, 1971.

907 Lissak, M. *Social Mobility and Political Identification in the Israel Consciousness.* Jerusalem: Israel Universities Press, 1969.

908 Medding, Peter Y. *Mapai in Israel: Political Organization and Government in a New Society.* New York: Cambridge University Press, 1972.

909 Nachmias, David. "Status Inconsistency and Political Opposition: A Case Study of an Israeli Minority Group." *Middle East Journal* 27 (Autumn 1973): 456–70.

910 Oren, Stephen. "Continuity and Change in Israel's Religious Parties." *Middle East Journal* 27 (Winter 1973): 36–54.

911 Peretz, Don. "Israel's 1969 Election Issues: The Visible and the Invisible." *Middle East Journal* 24 (Winter 1970): 31–46.

912 Perlmutter, Amos. "The Israeli Army in Politics: The Persistence of the Civilian over the Military." *World Politics* 20 (July 1968): 559–92.

913 ———. *Military and Politics in Israel: Nation-Building and Role Expansion.* New York: Praeger, 1969.

914 Safran, Nadav. "Israeli Politics since the 1967 War." *Current History* 60 (Jan. 1971): 19–25.

915 Sager, S. "Pre-State Influences on Israel's Parliamentary System." *Parliamentary Affairs* 25:1 (1972): 29–50.

916 Seligman, Lester G. *Leadership in a New Nation: Political Development in Israel.* New York: Atherton, 1964.

917 Simon, E. "Israel." *Atlantic Monthly* (Dec. 1969): 18–30.

918   Sowden, L. "The Knesset." *Israel* 8 (1967): 2-8.

919   Stock, E. "Grassroots Politics—Israel Style." *Midstream* 12:6 (June–July 1966): 3-14.

920   Tedeschi, G. *Studies in Israel Private Law*. Jerusalem: Kiryat Sepher, 1966.

921   Zidon, Asher. *Knesset*. New York: Herzl Press, 1967.

Israel & the Arabs

922   Cohen, Geula. "How to Speak to the Arabs: A Maariv Round Table." *Middle East Journal* 18 (Spring 1964): 143-62.

923   Flapan, S. "Resolving the Israeli-Arab Conflict: Some Missed Opportunities." *New Outlook* 16:4 (May 1973): 34-39.

924   "Interview with Prime Minister Levi Eshkol: Troubles for Israel in Hostile Mideast." *U.S. News & World Report* (Apr. 17, 1967): 75-77.

925   Rodinson, M. "Israel: The Arab Options." *Year Book of World Affairs* (1968), pp. 80-92.

926   ———. *Israel and the Arabs*. London: Penguin, 1968.

927   Rowland, Howard. "The Arab-Israeli Conflict as Represented in Arab Fictional Literature." Ph.D. dissertation, University of Michigan, 1971.

Israel's Reprisal Raid Policy

928   Blechman, Barry M. "The Consequences of Israeli Reprisals: An Assessment." Ph.D. dissertation, Georgetown University, 1971.

929   ———. "The Impact of Israel's Reprisals on Behavior of the Bordering Arab Nations Directed at Israel." *Journal of Conflict Resolution* 16:2 (June 1972): 155-82.

930   Brilliant, Moshe. "Israel's Policy of Reprisals." *Harper's* (Mar. 1955): 68-72.

931 Falk, R. D. "The Beirut Raid and International Law of Retaliation." *American Journal of International Law* 63 (July 1969): 415-43.

932 Glubb, Lt. Gen. J. B. "Violence on the Jordan-Israeli Border." *Foreign Affairs* 32 (July 1954): 552-62.

933 Jones, David L. "Reprisal: Israeli Style." *Military Review* 50 (Aug. 1970): 91-96.

934 Khouri, Fred J. "The Policy of Retaliation in Arab-Israeli Relations." *Middle East Journal* 20 (Autumn 1966): 435-55.

935 Mawlawi, F. "The Syrian-Israeli Border Confrontations." *Arab Journal* 4:2-4 (1967): 13-17.

936 Shwadran, Benjamin. "Israel-Jordan Border Tension." *Middle Eastern Affairs* 4 (Dec. 1953): 385-401.

Israel & the World

937 Balabkins, Nicholas. *West German Reparations to Israel.* New Brunswick, New Jersey: Rutgers University Press, 1971.

938 Bentwich, Norman. "Cultural Relations of Israel and Turkey." *Middle Eastern Affairs* 6 (Feb. 1955): 47-51.

939 Day, Alan. "Socialism and the Arab-Israeli Conflict." *New Middle East,* no. 47 (Aug. 1972): 36-38.

940 Draper, Theodore. "Israel and World Politics." *Commentary* 44:2 (Aug. 1967): 19-48.

941 ———. *Israel and World Politics.* New York: Viking, 1968.

942 Eban, Abba. "Reality and Vision in the Middle East: An Israeli View." *Foreign Affairs* 43 (July 1965): 626-38.

943 Herman, Simon N. *American Students in Israel.* Ithaca, New York: Cornell University Press, 1970.

944 "Israel and Europe: Partners in Trade." *Israel Export and Trade Journal* 24 (Nov.-Dec. 1972): 9-11.

945 *Israel and the Geneva Conventions.* Anthology Series, no. 3. Beirut: Institute for Palestine Studies, 1968.

946 Patai, Raphael. *Israel between East and West.* Philadelphia: Jewish Publication Society of America, 1953.

947 Uri, Pierre. "Israel and the EEC." *New Middle East,* nos. 42-43 (Mar.-Apr. 1972): 34-38.

948 Vogel, Rolf, ed. *The German Path to Israel: A Documentation.* Chester Springs, Pennsylvania: Dufour Editions, 1969.

Israel & the Third World

949 Astakhov, S. "Israeli Expansion in the Third World." *International Affairs* (Moscow) (July 1969): 53-58.

950 Bell, J. "Israel's Setbacks in Africa." *Middle East International* (Apr. 1973): 22-24.

951 Comay, M. "Israel's Role in the Developing World." *Commonwealth* 16:3 (June 1972): 77-79.

952 Decalo, S. "Israeli Foreign Policy and the Third World." *Orbis* 11:3 (1967): 724-45.

953 Decraene, P. "Africa and the Middle East Crisis: Is the Romance with Israel Over?" *Africa Report* 18:3 (May-June 1973): 20-23.

954 "For the Record: The Following Is the Full Text of the Secret Memorandum Prepared by the OAU 'Peace Mission' which Visited Both Cairo and Jerusalem Last November in an Effort to Facilitate the Implementation of Security Council Resolution 242." *New Middle East,* no. 41 (Feb. 1972): 38-39.

955 Frank, M. *Cooperative Land Settlements in Israel and Their Relevance to African Countries.* Basel: Kyklos-Verlag, 1968.

956 Froelich, J.-C. "Israel and Black Africa: The Growth of Aid, Trade and Understanding." *Wiener Library Bulletin* 27:1 (1967-1968): 13-20.

957 Gitelson, S. "The OAU Mission and the Middle East Conflict." *International Organization* 27 (1973): 413-20.

958 Israel. Ministry for Foreign Affairs. Division for International Cooperation. *Israel's Programme of International Cooperation.* Jerusalem: Ahvapress, Dec. 1971.

959 Jacob, Abel. "Israel's Military Aid to Africa, 1960-1966." *Journal of Modern African Studies* 9 (Aug. 1971): 165-87.

960 Kashin, Y. "Israeli Designs in Africa." *International Affairs* (Moscow) (Feb. 1972): 62-66.

961 Kochan, R. "An African Peace Mission in the Middle East." *African Affairs* 72:287 (Apr. 1973): 186-96.

962 Kreinin, Mordechai E. *Israel and Africa: A Study in Technical Cooperation.* New York: Praeger, 1964.

963 Laufer, L. *Israel and the Developing Countries: New Approaches to Cooperation.* New York: Twentieth Century Fund, 1967.

964 ———. "Israel and the Third World." *Political Science Quarterly* 87 (Dec. 1972): 615-30.

965 ———. "Israel's Technical Assistance Experts." *International Development Review* 9:1 (Mar. 1967): 9-14.

966 Nahumi, M. "New Directions in Israel-African Relations." *New Outlook* 16:7 (Sept. 1973): 14-21.

967 Peritz, R. "Israel and Asia." *New Outlook* 12:4 (May 1969): 38-43.

968 Schechtman, J. "India and Israel." *Midstream* 12:7 (Aug.-Sept. 1966): 48-61.

969 Segre, D. "Israel and the Third World." *Middle East Information Series* 22 (Feb. 1973): 7-14.

970 Srivastava, R. K. "India-Israel Relations." *Indian Journal of Political Science* 31 (July-Sept. 1970): 238-64.

971 Wellington, S. "Israel, an Agent of Social and Economic Change in Africa." *New Outlook* 16:6 (July-Aug. 1973): 17-27.

Foreign Policy

972 Arnoni, M. "Ideological Myths in Israeli Foreign Policy." *New Outlook* 13:7 (Sept.-Oct. 1970): 25-34.

973 Brecher, M. "A Critique of Israel's Foreign Policy: 'Not Magnanimity but Foresight Missing'." *New Outlook* 16:5 (June 1973): 2-14.

974 ———. *The Foreign Policy System of Israel: Setting, Images, Process.* New Haven, Connecticut: Yale University Press, 1972.

975 Oren, N. "The Origins of the Israel Foreign Ministry." *Public Administration in Israel and Abroad* 9 (1968): 65-71.

976 Roberts, Samuel J. "Israeli Foreign Policy in Historical Perspective." *World Affairs* 135 (Summer 1972): 40-53.

977 Rouleau, E. "Hawks and Doves in Israel's Foreign Policy." *World Today* 24 (Dec. 1968): 496-503.

Israel & the Diaspora

978 Dinur, Ben-Zion. *Israel and the Diaspora.* Philadelphia: Jewish Publication Society of America, 1969.

979 Friedman, George. *The End of the Jewish People?* Translated from the French by Eric Mosbacher. Garden City, New York: Doubleday, 1968.

980 Goldmann, Dr. Nahum. "The Diaspora and Israel: Their Future is Together." *New Middle East,* no. 49 (Oct. 1972): 10-13.

981 Henkin, Louis, ed. *World Politics and the Jewish Condition.* New York: Quadrangle, 1973.

982 Korn, R. "Eshkol's Official Plan for Israel and the Diaspora: Analysis of a Disturbing Earnest of Future Intentions." *Issues* 19:4 (1965): 13-20.

983 Landshut, Siegfried. *Jewish Communities in the Muslim Countries of the Middle East.* London: Jewish Chronicle, 1950.

984 Levi-Valensi, A. "An Israel-Diaspora Dialogue?" *Dispersion & Unity* 11 (1970): 93-100.

985 Peretz, M. "The American Left and Israel." *Commentary* 44:5 (Nov. 1967): 27-34.

986 "The Repercussions of Violence." *Issues* 21:4 (1967); 22:1 (1968): 43-45.

987 "Spotlight on a New Partnership." *Israel Magazine* 1:6 (1968): 9-43. [Special Issue: Israel & World Jewry]

988 Zahlan, A. "Support for Israel: A Legacy." *Middle East Newsletter* 3:1 (Jan.-Feb. 1969): 11-15.

C / Palestinian Arabs

989 Avineri, Shlomo. "The Palestinians and Israel." *Commentary* 49:6 (June 1970): 31-44.

990 ———, ed. *Israel and the Palestinians: Reflections on the Clash of Two National Movements.* New York: St. Martin's Press, 1971.

991 Cattan, Henry. "The Dimensions of the Palestine Problem." *Middle East Forum* 43:2-3 (1967): 35-44.

992 ———. *Palestine, the Arabs and Israel: The Search for Justice.* London: Longmans, 1969.

993 ———. "To Whom Does Palestine Belong?" *Middle East Forum* 45:1-2 (1968): 117-20.

994 *Christians, Zionism, and Palestine*. Anthology Series, no. 4. Beirut: Institute for Palestine Studies, 1970.

995 Green, S. J. "Human Rights and the Palestinian." *Mid East* 7:10 (Dec. 1967): 15-17.

996 Hadawi, Sami. *Palestine Occupied*. New York, Arab Information Center, 1968.

997 Hourani, Albert. "Israel and Palestine." *Middle East Forum* 43:2-3 (1967): 21-28.

998 Hourani, George. "Palestine as a Problem in Ethics." *Arab World* 15:3-4 (Mar.-Apr. 1969): 3-7.

999 *The Palestine Question: Seminar of Arab Jurists on Palestine, Algiers, 22-27 July 1967*. Translated from French by Edward Rizk. Beirut: Institute for Palestine Studies, 1968.

1000 Peretz, Don. *Israel and the Palestine Arabs*. Washington, D.C.: Middle East Institute, 1958.

1001 Quandt, William B.; Fuad Jabber; and Ann Mosely Lesch. *The Politics of Palestinian Nationalism*. Berkeley: University of California Press, 1973.

1002 Rejwan, N. "Who Is a Palestinian?" *Dissent* 20:1 (Winter 1973): 17-21.

1003 Sharabi, Hisham. *Palestine and Israel: The Lethal Dilemma*. New York: Pegasus, 1969.

1004 Stetler, Russell, ed. *Palestine: The Arab-Israeli Conflict*. San Francisco: Ramparts Press, 1972.

D / Palestinian Refugees

1005 *Palestine Refugees: Aid with Justice.* Geneva: World Council of Churches, 1970.

1006 Stevens, R. "The Refugee Problem and American Response." *Arab Journal* 5:4 (1968): 35–41.

1007 Stoessinger, J. G. *The Refugee and the World Community.* Minneapolis: University of Minnesota Press, 1956.

1008 Thicknesse, S. G. "The Arab Refugees: Their Position Today." *Royal Central Asian Journal* 38 (Jan. 1951): 29–30.

1009 Tweedy, Owen. "The Arab Refugees." *International Affairs* 28 (July 1952): 338–43.

1010 Vernant, Jacques. *The Refugee in the Post-War World.* New Haven, Connecticut: Yale University Press, 1953.

1011 Witkamp, F. T. *The Refugee Problem in the Middle East.* The Hague: Research Group for European Migration Problem, 1957.

1012 Wolf, John B. "The Arab Refugee Problem." *Current History* 63 (Dec. 1972): 352.

Origins

1013 Alami, Musa. "The Lesson of Palestine." *Middle East Journal* 3 (Oct. 1949): 373–405.

1014 Childers, E. "The Other Exodus, 1948: Why the Arabs Left Palestine." *Middle East Newsletter* 2:7 (Aug.–Sept. 1968): 3–5.

1015 El-Khalidi, W. "Plan Dalet." *Arab World* 15:10–11 (Oct.–Nov. 1969): 15–20.

1016 ―――. "Why Did the Palestinians Leave?" *Arab Journal* 5:3 (1968): 18–23.

1017 MacInnes, Archdeacon A. C. "The Arab Refugee Problem." *Royal Central Asian Journal* 36 (Apr. 1949): 178–88.

1018 Nevo, Y. "How Many Palestinians?" *New Outlook* 12:4 (May 1969): 28–31.

1019 Parzen, H. "The Arab Refugees: Their Origin and Projection into a Problem (1948–1952)." *Jewish Social Studies* 31:4 (Oct. 1969): 292–323.

1020 Richardson, Channing B. "880,000 Arab Refugees." *Journal of International Affairs* 6:2 (1952): 21–24.

1021 St. Aubin, W. de. "Peace and Refugees in the Middle East." *Middle East Journal* 3 (July 1949): 249–59.

1022 Schechtman, Joseph B. *The Arab Refugee Problem.* New York: Philosophical Library, 1952.

1023 Syrkin, Marie. "The Arab Refugees: A Zionist View." *Commentary* 41:1 (Jan. 1966): 23–30.

Existence & Continuing Problem

1024 Baster, James. "Economic Problems in the Gaza Strip [Economic Review]." *Middle East Journal* 9 (Summer 1955): 323–27.

1025 Bruhns, Fred C. "A Study of Arab Refugee Attitudes." *Middle East Journal* 9 (Spring 1955): 130–38.

1026 Childers, Erskine B. "Palestine: The Broken Triangle." *Journal of International Affairs* 19:1 (1965): 87–99.

1027 Coate, Winifred A. "The Condition of Arab Refugees in Jordan." *International Affairs* 29 (Oct. 1953): 449–56.

1028 Gabbay, Rony E. *A Political Study of the Arab-Jewish Conflict: The Arab Refugee Problem (A Case Study).* Paris: Librairie Minard, 1959.

1029 Hadawi, Sami. *Palestine: Loss of a Heritage.* San Antonio, Texas: Naylor, 1963.

1030 Howard, Harry N. "The Problem of the Arab Refugees: As Yet No Modern Solomon." *Mid East* 7:8 (Oct. 1967): 3–10.

1031 Institute for Mediterranean Affairs. *The Palestine Refugee Problem.* New York: St. Martin's Press, 1958.

1032 Khalidi, U., and A. Majaj. "A Special Report on the Palestine Refugees." *Middle East Forum* 41:2 (1965): 31–39.

1033 Messerschmidt, E. A. "Palestine Refugees: An Arab Propaganda Weapon?" *Orient* (Hamburg) 8:4 (Aug. 1967): 111–14.

1034 Mezerik, A. G., ed. *The Refugee Problem in the Middle East.* New York: International Review Service, 1957.

1035 Peretz, Don. "The Arab Refugee Dilemma." *Foreign Affairs* 33 (Oct. 1954): 134–48.

1036 ———. "The Arab Refugees: A Changing Problem." *Foreign Affairs* 41 (Apr. 1963): 558–70.

1037 Pinner, Walter. *How Many Arab Refugees?* London: MacGibbon & Kee, 1960.

1038 Sayegh, Fayez A. *The Palestine Refugees.* Washington, D.C.: Amara, 1952.

1039 Shlomo, Hilali. "Another Look at the Arab Refugee Problem: Will Everything Change Except This?" *New Outlook* 7:9 (Nov.–Dec. 1964): 19–23.

1040 Shwadran, Benjamin. "Assistance to Arab Refugees." *Middle Eastern Affairs* 1 (Jan. 1950): 2–11.

1041 Stevens, Georgiana G. "Arab Refugees: 1948–1952." *Middle East Journal* 6 (Summer 1952): 281–98.

1042 Stockman, I. "Changing Social Values of the Palestinians: The New Outlook of the Arab Peasant." *New Middle East,* no. 9 (June 1969): 18–21.

1043 Turki, Fawaz. *The Disinherited, Journal of a Palestinian Exile*. New York: Monthly Review Press, 1972.

1044 U.S. Department of State. *The Palestine Refugee Program*. Near and Middle Eastern Series, no. 3. Washington, D.C.: U.S.G.P.O., Publication 3757, Feb. 1950.

Settlement & Compensation

1045 Baster, James. "Economic Aspects of the Settlement of the Palestine Refugees." *Middle East Journal* 8 (Winter 1954): 54–68.

1046 Bergmann, A. "Compensation: Prelude to Peace." *New Outlook* 14:7 (Sept. 1971): 22–25.

1047 Cattan, Henry. "Plunder in the Holy Land." *al-Kulliyah* 30 (Feb. 1955): 10–12.

1048 Hourani, Cecil A. "Experimental Village in the Jordan Valley." *Middle East Journal* 5 (Autumn 1951): 497–501.

1049 Kirk, G. E. "Some Individual Endeavors to Help Arab Refugees." *Royal Central Asian Journal* 40 (Apr. 1953): 117–19.

1050 "The Land Acquisition Law of Israel [Document]." *Middle East Journal* 7 (Summer 1953): 358–60.

1051 Peretz, Don. "Problems of Arab Refugee Compensation." *Middle East Journal* 8 (Autumn 1954): 403–16.

1052 Richardson, J. P. "Dragon's Teeth in a New Field." *Mid East* 7:7 (Aug.–Sept. 1967): 2–6.

1053 Sutcliffe, Claud R. "The East Ghor Canal Project: A Case Study of Refugee Resettlement, 1961–1966." *Middle East Journal* 27 (Autumn 1973): 471–82.

1054 Thicknesse, S. G. *Arab Refugees: A Survey of Resettlement Possibilities*. London: Royal Institute of International Affairs, 1949.

1055   Zarhi, S. "Economics of Refugee Settlement." *New Outlook* 10:9 (Dec. 1967): 31-35.

United Nations Relief & Works Agency (UNRWA)

1056   Buehrig, Edward H. *The UN and the Palestinian Refugees: A Study in Nonterritorial Administration.* Bloomington: Indiana University Press, 1971.

1057   Defrates, J. "UNRWA, the Federal Republic of Germany and the Palestine Refugees." *Orient* (Hamburg) 13:3 (Sept. 1972): 124-26.

1058   Faherty, Robert. *In Human Terms: The 1959 Story of UNRWA and UNESCO Arab Refugee Schools.* Paris: Paul Dupont, 1959.

1059   Fancher, Michael. "Davis, UNRWA and the Palestine Refugees." *Middle East Forum* 40:3 (April 1964): 24-29.

1060   Forsythe, David P. "UNRWA, the Palestine Refugees, and World Politics: 1949-1969." *International Organization* 25 (1971): 26-45.

1061   Howard, Harry N. "UNRWA, the Arab Host Countries and the Arab Refugees." *Middle East Forum* 42:3 (1966): 29-42.

1062   ———. "UNRWA's Technical Assistance Program Among Arab Refugees." *World Affairs* 127:1 (Apr.-June 1964): 23-28.

1063   Perlmutter, A. "Patrons in the Babylonian Captivity of Clients: UNRWA and World Politics." *International Organization* 25 (1971): 306-8.

1064   United Nations. *Report of the Commissioner-General of the United Nations Relief and Works Agency for Palestine Refugees in the Near East, 1 July 1965-30 June 1966.* U.N. General Assembly, Official Records, 21st session. Supplement no. 13. New York, 1966.

1065 ——. *Report of the Commissioner-General of the United Relief and Works Agency for Palestine Refugees in the Near East, 1 July 1967–30 June 1968.* U.N. General Assembly, Official Records, 23d session. Supplement no. 13 (A/7213). New York, 1968.

1066 ——. *Report of the Relief and Works Agency for Palestine Refugees in the Near East, 1970/71.* U.N. General Assembly, Official Records, 26th session. Supplement no. 13. New York, 1971.

1067 ——. *United Nations Relief and Works Agency for Palestine Refugees in the Near East: UNRWA and the Palestine Refugees: In Facts and Figures.* Beirut: UNRWA, 1964.

1068 United Nations Relief and Works Administration. *Twice in a Lifetime.* Beirut: Middle East Export, 1968.

1069 U.S. Congress. House of Representatives. Committee on Foreign Affairs. Subcommittee on the Near East. Hearings: *The United Nations Relief and Works Agency for Palestine Refugees in the Near East (UNRWA).* 92d Cong., 2d sess., Apr. 1972.

1967 Refugees

1070 Astakhov, S. "Israeli Expansionism and the Palestinian Refugees." *International Affairs* (Moscow) (July 1968): 40–45.

1071 Bailey, G. "The Strange World of UNRWA." *Reporter* (Nov. 16, 1967): 20–23.

1072 Barakat, Halim. "1967 Palestinian Refugees: Justice vs. Reality." *Middle East Newsletter* 3:2 (Mar. 1969): 8–13.

1073 ——, and Peter Dodd. *River without Bridges: A Study of the Exodus of the 1967 Palestinian Arab Refugees.* Monograph Series, no. 10. Beirut: Institute for Palestine Studies, 1969.

1074 Bevis, V. "How Israel Forces the Arabs Out." *Middle East Newsletter* 1:3 (Nov. 1967): 1–2.

1075 Davis, J. "UNRWA Effort Continues from Camps to Canvas." *Arab World* 14:1-2 (Jan.-Feb. 1968): 7-9.

1076 Dodd, Peter. "Human Dignity in Exile: The Problem of the Arab Refugees of 1967." *Middle East Forum* 45:1-2 (1968): 91-99.

1077 ———, and Halim Barakat. "Palestinian Refugees of 1967: A Sociological Study." *Muslim World* 60 (Apr. 1970): 123-42.

1078 Gilmour, I., and D. Walters. "The Fate of the Arab Refugees." *Middle East Forum* 45:1-2 (1968): 87-90.

1079 Hadawi, Sami, ed. *The Case of Palestine before the Twenty-third Session of the United Nations, October-December, 1968*. New York: Arab Information Center, Jan. 1969.

1080 Slonim, R. "Why the Arabs Left." *Jewish Spectator* 37:10 (Dec. 1972): 7-10.

1081 Swados, H. "The Bridge on the River Jordan." *New York Times Magazine* (Nov. 26, 1967): 32.

1082 United Nations Relief and Works Administration. *UNRWA and the New Refugees*. Beirut: UNRWA, 1967.

Palestinians & the United Nations

1083 Hadawi, Sami, ed. *United Nations Resolutions on Palestine: 1947-1966*. Basic Documents Series, no. 1. Beirut: Institute for Palestine Studies, 1967.

1084 Hakim, George. "The Palestine Problem at the United Nations." *Middle East Forum* 43:2-3 (1967): 29-34.

1085 Johnson, J. "United Nations Calls for Increased Efforts to Meet Needs of Palestinian Refugees in the Near East." *U.S. Department of State Bulletin* (Jan. 12, 1970): 46-51.

1086 "The Middle East and Palestine Refugees." In *Issues before the Twenty-fifth General Assembly*. International Conciliation, no. 579. New York: Carnegie, Sept. 1970.

1087 "Palestine at the United Nations: 1971." *Arab World* 18:3-4 (Mar.-Apr. 1972): 30-31.

1088 "Palestine Refugees: Assembly Adopts Seven Resolutions." *U.N. Monthly Chronicle* 10 (Jan. 1973): 47.

1089 "Palestine Refugees: Assembly Adopts Six Resolutions." *U.N. Monthly Chronicle* 9 (Jan. 1972): 131-40.

1090 *The Palestinian Refugees: A Collection of United Nations Documents.* Beirut: Institute for Palestine Studies, 1970.

1091 Read, James M. *The United Nations and Refugees: Changing Concepts.* International Conciliation, no. 537. New York: Carnegie, Mar. 1962.

1092 Sayegh, F. "Synopsis of Resolutions on Palestine Adopted by Various Organs of the U.N. since the Cease-Fire of 1967." *Arab World* 17:1-9 (Aug.-Sept. 1971), 19-23.

1093 "The United Nations: Resolutions Affecting Arab Human Rights." *Arab World* 15:12 (Dec. 1969); 16:1 (Jan. 1970): 5-12.

1094 "United Nations General Assembly Fourteenth-Session Proposals for the Continuation of United Nations Assistance to Palestine Refugees [Document]." *Middle East Journal* 13 (Summer 1959): 304-18.

Problem without End? Post-1967

1095 Abu-Lughod, I. "Altered Realities: The Palestinians since 1967." *International Journal* 28:4 (1973): 648-69.

1096 Altoma, Salih J. *Palestinian Themes in Modern Arabic Literature, 1917-1970.* Cairo: Anglo-Egyptian Bookshop, 1972.

1097 Bentov, M. "Israel and the Palestinians." *New Outlook* 13:8 (Nov. 1970): 41-45.

1098 Cooley, John K. "Palestinian 'Boys Town': Where Road Up Starts." *Christian Science Monitor* (May 9, 1973): 11.

1099 Farouki, H. "What Palestinians Want." *New Middle East,* no. 10 (July 1969): 13–15.

1100 Furlonge, Geoffrey. *Palestine Is My Country: The Story of Musa Alami.* London: Murray, 1969.

1101 Gazit, M. "Forgotten Aspects of the Palestine Diaspora." *New Middle East,* no. 10 (July 1969): 11–13.

1102 Holborn, L. "The Palestine Arab Refugee Problem." *International Journal* 23:1 (1967–1968): 82–96.

1103 Kimche, Jon. "Israel and the Palestinians—New Directions." *New Middle East,* no. 35 (Aug. 1971): 3–5.

1104 Kuroda, Y., and A. Kuroda. "Palestinians and World Politics: A Social-Psychological Analysis." *Middle East Forum* 48:1 (1972): 45–58.

1105 Michener, J. "What to Do About the Palestinian Refugees." *New York Times Magazine* (Sept. 27, 1970): 22.

1106 "A People in Crisis: Have the Palestinians a Future?" *Jewish Observer and Middle East Review* (Dec. 22, 1972): 18–20.

1107 Peretz, Don. *The Palestine Arab Refugee Problem.* Santa Monica, California: RAND, RM–5973, 1969.

1108 Stein, Gabriel. "The Refugee Problem." *New Outlook* 11:6 (July–Aug. 1968): 10–17.

1109 Wilson, George C. "Troubled Dreams for Refugees." *Washington Post* (Dec. 16, 1973).

E / Palestine Entity

1110 Anabtawi, S. N. "The Palestinians as a Political Entity." *Muslim World* 60 (Jan. 1970): 47–58.

1111 Hattis, Susan Lee. *The Bi-National Idea in Palestine during Mandatory Times*. Haifa: Shikmona, 1970.

1112 ———. "The Bi-National State and the Challenge of History." *New Middle East*, no. 35 (Aug. 1971): 24-27.

1113 Hertzberg, Arthur. "Palestine: The Logic of Partition Today." *Columbia Forum* 13 (Fall 1970): 17-21.

1114 Hodes, Aubrey. "Martin Buber: Prophet of Co-existence." *New Middle East*, no. 51 (Dec. 1972): 29-31.

1115 Peretz, Don; Evan Wilson; and Richard J. Ward. *A Palestine Entity?* Washington, D.C.: Middle East Institute, 1970.

1116 Radovanovic, L. "The Question of Palestine." *Review of International Affairs* (Belgrade) (Mar. 5, 1971): 13-16.

1117 Rashed, Mohammad. *Towards a Democratic State in Palestine*. Palestine Essays, no. 24. Beirut: Palestine Liberation Organization Research Center, Nov. 1970.

1118 Sha'ath, Nabil. *Palestine-of-Tomorrow for Jews, Christians, and Moslims*. Birmingham, Alabama: Committee for Better American Relations in the Middle East, 1971.

F / Palestinian Arab Solutions

1119 Allon, Yigal. "The Arab-Israeli Conflict: Some Suggested Solutions." *International Affairs* 40 (Apr. 1964): 205-18.

1120 Bentwich, Norman. "The Arab Refugees." *Contemporary Review*, no. 1006 (Aug. 1949): 79-82.

1121 Davis, John H. *The Evasive Peace: A Study of the Zionist Arab Problem*. New York: New World, 1968.

1122 Hilmy, H. "Re-partition of Palestine." *Journal of Peace Research* 9:2 (1972): 133-46.

1123 [Israel]. *Refugees in the Middle East: A Solution in Peace.* Washington, D.C.: Embassy of Israel, 1967.

1124 Johnson, Joseph E. "Proposals on the Arab Refugees." *New Outlook* 7:5 (June 1964): 2,64.

1125 Mansour, A. "The Refugees and What They Want." *New Outlook* 10:9 (Dec. 1967): 25–30.

1126 ———. "Solving the Refugee Problem." *New Outlook* 12:9 (Nov.–Dec. 1969): 44–49.

1127 Reddaway, J. "A European Initiative for the Palestine Refugees." *Middle East International* (July 1972): 11–12.

1128 Robinson, Jacob. *Palestine and the United Nations: Prelude to Solution.* Washington, D.C.: Public Affairs, 1947.

1129 Shlomo, H. "What to Do with Palestine: The Case for Palestinian Self-Determination." *New Outlook* 11:6 (July–Aug. 1968): 34–41.

1130 Tibawi, A. L. "Visions of the Return: The Palestine Arab Refugees in Arabic Poetry and Art." *Middle East Journal* 17 (Autumn 1963): 507–26.

1131 W., D. "Hope for the Arab Refugees: The Yarmuk Project." *World Today* 8 (Dec. 1952): 512–21.

G / Territories Occupied by Israel, 1967

Israeli Administration

1132 Abu-Lughod, I. "Israel's Arab Policy." *Arab World* 14:10–11 (Oct.–Nov. 1968): 31–39.

1133 Al-Abid, Ibrahim. *Human Rights in the Occupied Territories.* Palestine Monographs, no. 73. Beirut: Palestine Liberation Organization Research Center, Sept. 1970.

1134 "The Allon Plan [Document]." *Middle East International* (Jan. 1973): 22.

1135 "Arabs Under Israel." *Economist* (July 24, 1971): 41-43.

1136 *The Arabs under Israeli Occupation*. Palestine Monographs, no. 55. Beirut: Palestine Liberation Organization Research Center, Feb. 1969.

1137 Arab Women's Information Committee. *The Arabs under Israeli Occupation, 1969*. Beirut: Institute for Palestine Studies, 1970.

1138 B'ari, S. "What to Do with the Occupied Territories." *New Outlook* 10:7 (Sept.–Oct. 1967): 5-9.

1139 Becker, Abraham S. *Israel and the Palestinian Occupied Territories: Military-Political Issues in the Debate*. Santa Monica, California: RAND, R-882, Dec. 1971.

1141 Dayan, Moshe. "Spotlight on the Territories." *Israel Magazine* 1:9 (1968): 9-73.

1140 Cooley, John K. "Israelis Put Down Roots in Arab Soil." *Christian Science Monitor* (May 30, 1973): 5.

1142 Dershowitz, A. "Terrorism and Preventive Detention: The Case of Israel." *Commentary* 50:6 (Dec. 1970): 67-78.

1143 Dib, George, and Fuad Jabber. *Israel's Violation of Human Rights in the Occupied Territories: A Documented Report*. 3d ed. Beirut: Institute for Palestine Studies, 1970.

1144 Elazar, D. "Israel and the Territories: Toward a Workable Federal Solution." *Jewish Frontier* 39:8 (Oct. 1972): 17-23.

1145 Elon, Amos. "The Israeli Occupation." *Commentary* 45:3 (Mar. 1968): 41-47.

1146 "Five Years of Israeli Administration in Judea and Samaria." *Israel Economist* 28:11 (Nov. 1972): 266-67.

1147 Foda, Ezzeldin. *Israeli Belligerent Occupation and Palestinian Armed Resistance in International Law.* Palestine Monographs, no. 62. Beirut: Palestine Liberation Organization Research Center, 1970.

1148 Gazit, S. "On the Israel-Administered Areas: Some Problems of a Six Years' Occupation." *International Problems* 11:3-4 (Dec. 1972): 7-24.

1149 Greenspan, Morris. "Human Rights in the Territories Occupied by Israel." *Santa Clara Lawyer* 12:2 (1973): 377-402.

1150 Hammad, M. B. "The Culprit, the Target and the Victims." *Arab World* 15:10-11 (Oct.-Nov. 1969): 3-7.

1151 *The Holy Land under Israeli Occupation, 1967: An Appeal to World Conscience.* Palestine Essays, no. 8. Beirut: Palestine Liberation Organization Research Center, May 1969.

1152 Israel. Central Bureau of Statistics. *Census of Population 1967, Housing Conditions, Household Equipment, Welfare Assistance and Farming in the Administered Areas.* Jerusalem, 1968.

1153 Israel. Ministry for Foreign Affairs. Information Division. *Eye-Witness Reports on the Israel Military Administration from the Foreign Press.* Israel Information Series. Jerusalem: Central Press, Nov. 1970.

1154 ———. *Information Briefing: The Administered Areas, Aspects of Israeli Policy.* Jerusalem: Israel Information Centre, Oct. 1972.

1155 Israel. Ministry of Defense. *The Israel Administration in Judea, Samaria and Gaza: A Record of Progress.* Tel Aviv, 1968.

1156 ———. *The Military Government's Civil Administration: A Concise Comprehensive Survey, June 1967-June 1968.* Tel Aviv, 1968.

1157 ———. Unit for Coordination of Activity in the Administered Areas. *Development and Economic Situation in Judea, Samaria, the Gaza Strip, and North Sinai, 1967–1969: A Summary.* Jerusalem, n.d.

1158 "Israel's Occupation Policies." *New Outlook* 11:6 (July–Aug. 1968): 47–55.

1159 "Israeli Practices Affecting Human Rights in Occupied Territories: Assembly Adopts Resolution." *U.N. Monthly Chronicle* 9 (Jan. 1972): 145–51.

1160 Mallison, W. "The Geneva Convention." *Arab World* 15:6 (June 1969): 3–9.

1161 Mehdi, M. "Israeli Settlements in the Occupied Territories." *Middle East International* (Jan. 1973): 21–26.

1162 Nahumi, Mordechai. "Israel as an Occupying Power." *New Outlook* 15:5 (June 1972): 16–34.

1163 Peretz, Don. "The Arab-Israeli War: Israel's Administration and Arab Refugees." *Foreign Affairs* 46 (Jan. 1968): 336–46.

1164 ———. "Israel's New Arab Dilemma." *Middle East Journal* 22 (Winter 1968): 45–57.

1165 Raphaeli, N. "Military Government in the Occupied Territories: An Israeli View." *Middle East Journal* 23 (Spring 1969): 177–90.

1166 ———. "Problems of Military Administration in the Controlled Territories." *Public Administration in Israel and Abroad* 8 (1967): 48–51.

1167 Rejwan, N. "Palestinians under Israeli Occupation: The Search for Identity." *Midstream* 17:2 (Feb. 1971): 43–52.

1168 Roots, John McCook. "David Ben-Gurion Talks about Israel and the Arabs ... 'Peace Is More Important than Real Estate'." *Saturday Review* (Apr. 3, 1971): 14–16.

1169 Shepherd, Naomi. "Israel's Dilemma." *New Statesman* 80 (Oct. 2, 1970): 404.

1170 Sherman, A. "Israel's Occupation Problems." *World Today* 23 (Nov. 1967): 484–92.

1171 "Two Years of Israeli Administration, 1967–1969, I: Judea and Samaria." *Israel Economist* 25:7 (July 1969): 199–204.

1172 "Two Years of Israeli Administration, 1967–1969, II: Gaza and Northern Sinai." *Israel Economist* 25:8 (Aug. 1969): 223–29.

The West Bank

1173 Farhi, D. "The West Bank, 1948–1971: The Sociological Basis of Israel Occupation Attitudes." *New Middle East*, no. 38 (Nov. 1971): 33–36.

1174 Heruthi, E. "Quiet Co-operation on the West Bank." *New Outlook* 10:9 (Dec. 1967): 52–54.

1175 Nuseibeh, A. "Can We Meet the Challenge?" *New Outlook* 11:2 (Feb. 1968): 3–5, 23.

1176 Oren, Stephen. "Israeli Politics and the West Bank." *Worldview* (Feb. 1973): 28–34.

1177 "Palestinian Trilogy: Views from the West Bank." *New Middle East*, no. 44 (May 1972): 11–13.

1178 *The Resistance of the Western Bank of Jordan to Israeli Occupation 1967.* Beirut: Institute for Palestine Studies, 1967.

1179 Shwadran, Benjamin. "Jordan Annexes Arab Palestine." *Middle Eastern Affairs* 1 (Apr. 1950): 99–111.

1180 Teveth, Shabtai. *The Cursed Blessing: The Story of Israel's Occupation of the West Bank.* New York: Random House, 1971.

1181 "To Vote or Not to Vote: West Bank on the Eve of Crisis." *New Middle East*, no. 40 (Jan. 1972): 34–35.

1182 Zarour, Mariam. "Ramallah: My Home Town." *Middle East Journal* 7 (Autumn 1953): 430–39.

Hussein's Plan

1183 Cygielman, Victor. "Hussein's Proposal and the West Bank Municipal Elections: A Post-Mortem." *New Outlook* 15:3 (Mar.–Apr. 1972): 40–47.

1184 "King Husain's Plan for Federal Kingdom." *New Middle East*, no. 44 (May 1972): 46–50.

1185 Richmond, J. "After the Husain Plan: What Hope for Palestinian Arabs?" *New Middle East*, no. 46 (July 1972): 34–37.

Gaza

1186 Aviram, A. "Behind the Unrest in Gaza." *New Outlook* 12:4 (May 1969): 44–46.

1187 ———. "Civil Administrator for Gaza." *New Outlook* 10:9 (Dec. 1967): 55–60.

1188 Flapan, S. "The Storm over Gaza." *New Outlook* 15:3 (Mar.–Apr. 1972): 19–22.

1189 Raphaeli, N. "Gaza under Four Administrations." *Public Administration in Israel and Abroad* 9 (1968): 40–51.

1190 Tessier, Arlette. *Gaza*. Palestine Essays, no. 27. Beirut: Palestine Liberation Organization Research Center, Aug. 1971.

IV / CLASH OF NATIONALISMS

A / Zionism

1191   Cohen, Israel. *A Short History of Zionism.* London: F. Muller, 1951.

1192   Halpern, Ben. *The Idea of the Jewish State.* Cambridge, Massachusetts: Harvard University Press, 1969.

1193   Heller, Joseph. *The Zionist Idea.* New York: Schocken, 1949.

1194   Hertzberg, Arthur. *The Zionist Idea: An Historical Analysis and Reader from the Writings of Moses Hess, Theodor Herzl, Ahad Ha-am, Martin Buber, Chaim Weizmann, David Ben-Gurion, and Many Others.* New York: Doubleday, 1959.

1195   Laqueur, Walter. *A History of Zionism.* New York: Holt, Rinehart & Winston, 1972.

1196   Taylor, Alan R. "The Zionist Issue in Christian Theology." *Issues* 18:4 (1964): 20–27.

Jewish History in Ancient Times

1197   Dubnov, Semen Markovich. *Jewish History: An Essay in the Philosophy of History.* 1903. Freeport, New York: Books for Libraries Press, 1972.

The Jewish Diaspora

1198   Ben-Gurion, D. "The Facts of Jewish Exile." *Harper's* (Sept. 1965): 47–51.

1199 Castro y Rossi, Adolfo de. *The History of the Jews in Spain, from the Time of Their Settlement in that Country till the Commencement of the Present Century.* Translated by D. G. M. Kirway. London: Cambridge, 1851.

1200 Chouraqui, Andre N. *Between East and West: A History of the Jews of North Africa.* Translated by Michael M. Bernet. Philadelphia: Jewish Publication Society of America, 1968.

1201 Cohen, H. "The Anti-Jewish Farhud in Bagdad, 1941." *Middle Eastern Studies* 3 (Oct. 1966): 2–17.

1202 Eban, Abba. *My People: The Story of the Jews.* New York: Random House, 1968.

1203 Finkelstein, Louis. *Jewish Self-Government in the Middle Ages.* 1924. New York: Greenwood Reprint, 1972.

1204 Frankl, Ludwig August. *The Jews in the East.* 2 vols. Translated from the German by P. Beaton. London, 1859.

1205 Friedman, I. "Lord Palmerston and the Protection of Jews in Palestine, 1839–1851." *Jewish Social Studies* 30:1 (Jan. 1968): 23–41.

1206 Goitein, S. D. *A Mediterranean Society: The Jewish Communities of the Arab World in the Documents of the Cairo Geniza.* Los Angeles: University of California Press, 1967.

1207 Patai, Raphael. *Tents of Jacob—The Diaspora, Yesterday and Today.* Englewood Cliffs, New Jersey: Prentice-Hall, 1971.

1208 Selzer, Michael. *The Wineskin and the Wizard.* New York: Macmillan, 1970.

1209 Sokolow, Nahum. *History of Zionism, 1600–1918.* London: Longmans, Green, 1919.

1210 Swartz, M. "The Position of Jews in Arab Lands Following the Rise of Islam." *Muslim World* 60 (Jan. 1970): 6–24.

The Rise of Zionism: Theory & Environment

1211   Ben-Gurion, David. *Rebirth and Destiny of Israel*. New York: Philosophical Library, 1953.

1212   Buber, Martin. *Israel and Palestine*. New York: Farrar, Straus & Young, 1952.

1213   Cohen, Israel. *Theodor Herzl, Founder of Political Zionism*. New York: Yoseloff, 1959.

1214   Fox, S. "One Man's View of the Soundness of Zionism's Ideology." *Issues* 21:3 (1967): 23-26.

1215   Halbrook, Stephen. "The Class Origins of Zionist Ideology." *Journal of Palestine Studies* 2:1 (1972): 86-110.

1216   Herzl, Theodor. *The Jewish State: An Attempt at a Modern Solution of the Jewish Question*. London: Central Office of Zionist Organization, 1934.

1217   Ivanov, Yuri. *Caution: Zionism! Essays on the Ideology, Organization and Practice of Zionism*. Moscow: Progress, 1970.

1218   Litvinoff, Barnet. *To the House of Their Fathers: A History of Zionism*. New York: Praeger, 1965.

1219   Mallison, W. T., Jr. "The Zionist-Israel Juridical Claims to Constitute 'The Jewish People' Nationality Entity and to Confer Membership in It: An Appraisal in Public International Law." *George Washington Law Review* 32:4 (July 1964): 983-1075.

1220   Patai, Raphael, ed. *Encyclopedia of Zionism and Israel*. 2 vols. New York: McGraw-Hill, 1968.

1221   Selzer, M. "The Jewishness of Zionism: A Continuing Controversy." *Issues* 21:3 (1967): 12-22.

1222   Taylor, A. "Zionism and Jewish History." *Journal of Palestine Studies* 1:2 (1972): 35-51.

1223 Vital, D. "Zionism Revisited: Herzl." *Commentary* 55:5 (May 1973): 69–73.

1224 Vlavianos, Basil J., and Feliks Gross, eds. *Struggle for Tomorrow: Modern Political Ideologies of the Jewish People.* New York: Arts, 1954.

Zionist Political Efforts, 1890–1922

1225 Balfour, Arthur J. *Speeches on Zionism.* London: Arrowsmith, 1928.

1226 Ro'i, Yaacov. "The Zionist Attitude to the Arabs 1908–1914." *Middle Eastern Studies* 4 (Apr. 1968): 198–242.

1227 Sacher, H., ed. *Zionism and the Jewish Future.* London: Murray, 1916.

1228 Stevens, Richard P. *Zionism and Palestine before the Mandate: A Phase of Western Imperialism.* Beirut: Institute for Palestine Studies, 1972.

1229 Sullivan, A. "The Dynamics of French Resistance to Zionism in the 19th and Early 20th Centuries." *Middle East Forum* 44:4 (1968): 45–64.

Zionism under the Mandate, 1922–1948

1230 Carmi, S., and H. Rosenfeld. "Immigration, Urbanization and Crisis: The Process of Jewish Colonization in Palestine during the 1920's." *International Journal of Comparative Sociology* 12 (Mar. 1971): 41–57.

1231 Cohen, Israel. *The Zionist Movement.* New York: Zionist Organization of America, 1946.

1232 *Conquest through Immigration: How Zionism Turned Palestine into a Jewish State.* Pasadena, California: Institute for Special Research, 1968.

1233 Halpern, Ben. "Brandeis' Way to Zionism." *Midstream* 17:8 (Oct. 1971): 3–13.

1234 Jansen, G. H. "The Limits of Lobbying: The Zionist Failure with Mahatma Gandhi." *Middle East Forum* 42:2 (1966): 27-38.

1235 Laqueur, Walter Z. "Zionism and Its Liberal Critics, 1896-1948." *Journal of Contemporary History* 6:4 (Oct. 1971): 161-82.

1236 Lourie, Arthur. "The American Zionist Emergency Council." *Palestine Yearbook* 1 (1944-1945), pp. 368-73.

1237 ———. "The Making of Zionist Diplomacy." *Issues* 21:4 (1967); 22:1 (1968): 95-103.

1238 Naufal, Sayyid. "A Short History of the Arab Opposition to Zionism and Israel." *Islamic Review* 53:2 (Feb. 1965): 4-8; 53:3 (Mar. 1965): 11-14.

1239 Ruppin, Arthur. *Three Decades of Palestine: Speeches and Papers on the Upbuilding of the Jewish National Home.* Jerusalem: Schocken, 1936.

1240 Sayegh, Fayez A. *Zionist Colonialism in Palestine.* Palestine Monographs, no. 1. Beirut: Palestine Liberation Organization Research Center, Sept. 1965.

1241 ———. *The Zionist Diplomacy.* Palestine Monographs, no. 13. Beirut: Palestine Liberation Organization Research Center, June 1969.

Jewish Anti-Zionism

1242 Berger, Elmer. "After Talbot: Zionism on the Defensive." *Issues* 18:4 (1964): 7-19.

1243 ———. *The Jewish Dilemma.* New York: Devin-Adair, 1945.

1244 ———. *Judaism or Jewish Nationalism: The Alternative to Zionism.* New York: Bookman, 1957.

1245 ———. "Prophecy, Zionism and the State of Israel." *Issues* 22:3 (1968); 22:4 (1969): 22-40.

1246 ———. *Who Knows Better Must Say So!* Beirut: Institute for Palestine Studies, 1970.

1247 Bober, Arie, ed. *The Other Israel: The Radical Case Against Zionism.* Garden City, New York: Doubleday, 1972.

1248 Buber, Martin. *Israel and the World: Essays in a Time of Crisis.* New York: Schocken, 1963.

1249 ———; J. L. Magnes; and E. Simon. *Towards Union in Palestine: Essay on Zionism and Jewish-Arab Cooperation.* 1947. New York: Greenwood Reprints, 1972.

1250 Cohen, A. "Buber's Zionism and the Arabs." *New Outlook* 9:7 (Sept. 1966): 5–10.

1251 Davis, U. "Journey Out of Zionism: The Radicalization of an Israeli Pacifist." *Journal of Palestine Studies* 1:4 (1972): 59–72.

Zionism in the United States

1252 Bagrash, G. "The United States and the Zionist Organization. *Arab Journal* 5:1–2 (1968): 43–47.

1253 Batal, James. *Zionist Influence on the American Press.* Beirut: Nasser, 1956.

1254 Berger, Elmer. *Letters and Non-Letters: The White House, Zionism and Israel.* Monograph Series, no. 3. Beirut: Institute for Palestine Studies, 1972.

1255 ———. "The Senate Investigation of the Zionist Structure Operating in the U.S.: What Significance to Arabs?" *Arab Journal* 1:1 (1964): 10–15.

1256 Cooper, B. "American Reform Judaism and Zionism." *Arab World* 16:7–8 (July–Aug. 1970): 3–10.

1257 Gittelson, R., and J. Eisenberg. "American Jews and Israel: Two Views." *Midstream* 18:2 (Feb. 1972): 58–67.

1258 Mallison, W. T. *The Legal Problems Concerning the Juridical Status and Political Activities of the Zionist Organization/ Jewish Agency: A Study in International and U.S. Law.* Monograph Series, no. 14. Beirut: Institute for Palestine Studies, 1968.

1259 Rabinowitz, Ezekiel. *Justice Louis D. Brandeis: The Zionist Chapter of His Life.* New York: Philosophical Library, 1968.

1260 Roucek, J. "Politics vs. Policies and the Problem of American Zionism." *Issues* 20:2 (1966): 42–48.

1261 Shapiro, Yonathan. *Leadership of the American Zionist Organization.* Urbana: University of Illinois Press, 1971.

1262 Stern, Sol. "My Jewish Problem—and Ours." *Ramparts* (Aug. 1971): 31–40.

1263 U.S. Congress. Senate. Committee on Foreign Relations. Hearings: *Activities of Nondiplomatic Representatives of Foreign Principals in the United States* (13 parts) 88th Cong., 1st sess., 1963.

Zionism after Israel

1264 Alter, R. "Zionism for the 70's." *Commentary* 49:2 (Feb. 1970): 47–57.

1265 Avnery, Uri. *Israel without Zionists: A Plea for Peace in the Middle East.* New York: Macmillan, 1968.

1266 Bardin, Shlomo. *Self-Fulfillment through Zionism.* Freeport, New York: Books for Libraries, 1971.

1267 Ben-Gurion, David. *The Jews in Their Land.* London: Aldus, 1966.

1268 Blumber, H. "The Congress: Can Israel Survive without Zionism?" *New Middle East,* no. 41 (Feb. 1972): 9–12.

1269 Bolshakov, V. "Zionism: Playing International Reactions Game." *International Affairs* (Moscow) (Jan. 1973): 51–55.

1270 ———. "The Zionists' Profession—Anti-Sovietism." *International Affairs* (Moscow) (Apr. 1971): 55–59.

1271 Goldmann, Nahum. "World Jewry and the Middle East." *New Outlook* 7:4 (May 1964): 11–13.

1272 Halkin, H. "Zionism Revisited: The Historic Enterprise." *Commentary* 55:5 (May 1973): 74–78.

1273 Harris, Mervyn. "From Nile to Euphrates: The Evolution of a Myth." *New Middle East,* nos. 42–43 (Mar.–Apr. 1972): 46–48.

1274 Kaplan, Mordecai Menahem. *New Zionism.* Rev. ed. New York: Herzl Press, 1959.

1275 Laptev, V. "Zionists Undermine World Peace and Security." *International Affairs* (Moscow) (July 1971): 56–62.

1276 Laqueur, Walter Z. "The Jewish Question: Zionism and New Anti-Semitism." *Encounter* 37:2 (Aug. 1971): 43–52.

1277 ———. "Zionism: The Marxist Critique and the Left." *Dissent* 18:6 (Dec. 1971): 560–74.

1278 Lobel, Eli. "Palestine and the Jews." In *The Arab World and Israel.* Edited by Kodsy and Lobel. New York: Monthly Review Press, 1970.

1279 Lumer, Human. "The Reactionary Role of Zionism." *Political Affairs* 50 (Aug. 1971): 39–55.

1280 ———. *Zionism: Its Role in World Politics.* New York: International Publishers, 1972.

1281 Medvedko, L. "Zionism and Israel." *International Affairs* (Moscow) (Jan. 1971): 60–65.

1282 Menuhin, Moshe. *The Decadence of Judaism in Our Time.* New York: Exposition Press, 1965.

1283 Petuchowski, Jakob J. *Zion Reconsidered.* New York: Twayne, 1966.

1284   Prahye, B. *Deceived by Zionism*. Moscow: Novosti, 1971.

1285   Rabinowicz, Oscar K. *Fifty Years of Zionism*. London: Anscome, 1952.

1286   Razzuq, As'ad. *Greater Israel: A Study in Zionist Expansionist Thought*. Beirut: Palestine Liberation Organization Research Center, 1970.

1287   "Resolutions of the Twenty-eighth Zionist Congress, 1972." *Journal of Palestine Studies* 1:3 (1972): 175–202.

1288   Sayegh, Fayez A. "The 'Non-Colonial' Zionism of Mr. Abba Eban." *Middle East Forum* 42:4 (1966): 43–74.

1289   Schechtman, Joseph B. *Zionism and Zionists in Soviet Russia: Greatness and Drama*. New York: World Zionist Organization, 1966.

1290   Selzer, M. "Zionism and the Middle Eastern Imbroglio." *Antioch Review* 27 (1967–1968): 515–32.

1291   Shapiro, J. "Dezionizing the Jewish Agency." *New Middle East*, no. 11 (Aug. 1969): 33–35.

1292   Taylor, Alan R. "Zionist Ideology: An Interpretive Analysis." *Middle East Journal* 18 (Autumn 1964): 431–42.

1293   'Uthmani, S. "The Relationship between World Imperialism and World Zionism." *Islamic Review* 58:4 (Apr. 1970): 19–27.

1294   World Zionist Organization. Information Department. *Zionism, the Force of Change: History, Organization, Facts and Figures, Tasks and Problems*. Jerusalem: World Zionist Organization, 1968.

1295   *Zionism: Instrument of Imperialist Reaction*. Moscow: Novosti, 1971.

B / Arab Nationalism

Origins

1296 Dawn, C. Ernest. *From Ottomanism to Arabism.* Urbana: University of Illinois Press, 1973.

1297 ———. "The Rise of Arabism in Syria." *Middle East Journal* 16 (Spring 1962): 145-68.

1298 Haim, Sylvia G., ed. *Arab Nationalism: An Anthology.* Los Angeles: University of California Press, 1962.

1299 Khan, Rasheeduddin. "The Rise of Arab Nationalism and European Diplomacy: 1908-1916." *Islamic Culture* 36 (July 1962): 196-206; 36 (Oct. 1962): 244-55.

1300 Tibawi, A. L. "Greater Syria, 1876-1890: Divided Loyalties: Ottoman, Muslim, or Arab." *Islamic Quarterly* 11 (Jan.-June 1967): 8-33.

1301 Young, G. *Nationalism and War in the Near East.* 1915. New York: Johnson Reprint, 1968.

1302 Zeine, Zeine N. *Arab-Turkish Relations and the Emergence of Arab Nationalism.* Beirut: Khayats, 1958.

Islam & Nationalism

1303 Al-Bazzaz, A. R. "Islam and Arab Nationalism." *Welt des Islams* 3:3-4 (1954): 201-18.

1304 Ansari, Zafar Ishaq. "Contemporary Islam and Nationalism: A Case Study of Egypt." *Welt des Islams* 7:1-4 (1961): 3-38.

1305 Badeau, John S. "Islam and the Modern Middle East." *Foreign Affairs* 38 (Oct. 1959): 61-74.

1306 Baly, Dennis. *Multitudes in the Valley: Church and Crisis in the Middle East.* Greenwich, Connecticut: Seabury, 1957.

1307 Dawn, C. Ernest. "Arab Islam in the Modern Age." *Middle East Journal* 19 (Autumn 1965): 435-46.

1308 Haim, Sylvia G. "Islam and the Theory of Arab Nationalism." *Welt des Islams* 4:2–3 (1955): 124–49.

1309 Morrison, S. A. "Arab Nationalism and Islam." *Middle East Journal* 2 (Apr. 1948): 147–59.

1310 Salem, Elie. "Nationalism and Islam." *Muslim World* 52 (Oct. 1962): 277–87.

1311 Samra, M. "Islam and Arab Nationalism: Complementary or Competitive?" *Middle East Forum* 42:2 (1966): 11–16.

1312 Tibawi, A. L. "English-Speaking Orientalists: A Critique of Their Approach to Islam and Arab Nationalism." *Muslim World* 53 (July 1963): 185–204.

1313 Wynn, C. Wilton. "The Latest Revival of Islamic Nationalism." *Muslim World* 38 (Jan. 1948): 11–16.

Nationalism under the Mandates

1314 Antonius, George. *The Arab Awakening: The Story of the Arab National Movement.* New York: Putnam, 1965.

1315 Barbour, Nevill. "Britain and the Rise of Arab Nationalism." *Fortnightly Review* (July 1951): 438–45.

1316 Bentwich, Norman. *England in Palestine.* London: Kegan Paul, Trench & Trubner, 1932.

1317 Haim, Sylvia G. "The Arab Awakening: A Source for the Historian?" *Welt des Islams* 2:1 (1953): 237–50.

1318 Kimche, Jon. *The Second Arab Awakening: The Middle East, 1914–1970.* New York: Holt, Rinehart & Winston, 1970.

1319 Marlowe, John. *Arab Nationalism and British Imperialism.* New York: Praeger, 1961.

Post–World War II Arab Nationalism

1320 Ahmed, Jamal Mohammed. *The Intellectual Origins of Egyptian Nationalism.* London: Oxford University Press, 1960.

ZIONISM / 113

1321 Beling, Willard. *Pan-Arabism and Labor.* Cambridge, Massachusetts: Harvard University Press, 1960.

1322 Bethmann, E. "The Arabs' Search for Intellectual Identity." *Mid East* 7:9 (Nov. 1967): 26-27.

1323 Farah, Caesar E. "The Dilemma of Arab Nationalism." *Welt des Islams* 8:3 (1963): 140-64.

1324 Faris, N. A., and M. T. Husayn. *The Crescent in Crisis.* Lawrence: University of Kansas Press, 1955.

1325 Fatemi, Nasrollah S. "The Roots of Arab Nationalism." *Orbis* 2:4 (1959): 437-56.

1326 Finer, Herman. "Reflections on the Nature of Arab Nationalism." *Middle Eastern Affairs* 9 (Oct. 1958): 302-12.

1327 Haim, Sylvia G., et al. *Arab Nationalism and a Wider World.* Middle East Area Studies, series 5. New York: American Academic Association for Peace in the Middle East, 1971.

1328 Jabara, Abdeen, and Janice Terry, eds. *The Arab World: From Nationalism to Revolution.* Wilmette, Illinois: Medina University Press, 1971.

1329 Kenny, L. M. "Sati' al-Husri's Views on Arab Nationalism." *Middle East Journal* 17 (Summer 1963): 231-56.

1330 Lenczowski, G. "Arab Radicalism: Problems and Prospects." *Current History* 60 (Jan. 1971): 32-37.

1331 Nolte, Richard H. "Arab Nationalism and the Cold War." *Yale Review* 49 (Autumn 1959): 1-19.

1332 Nuseibeh, Hazem Saki. *The Ideas of Arab Nationalism.* Ithaca, New York: Cornell University Press, 1956.

1333 Peabody, Lt. Col. James B. "Nationalism: Curse or Cure for the Middle East?" *Military Review* 52 (Nov. 1972): 12-21.

1334 Pfaff, Richard H. "The Function of Arab Nationalism." *Comparative Politics* 2:2 (Jan. 1970): 167.

1335 Sayegh, Fayez A. "Arab Nationalism Today." *Current History* 33 (Nov. 1957): 283–87.

1336 Scott, Alan. "Arab Nationalism." *Contemporary Review,* no. 970 (Oct. 1946): 208–11.

1337 Tutsch, Hans E. *Facets of Arab Nationalism.* Detroit: Wayne State University Press, 1965.

1338 Von Grunebaum, Gustave. "Nationalism and Cultural Trends in the Arab Near East." *Studia Islamica* 14 (1961): 123–53.

1339 Walker D. "The Origins of Arab Nationalism in Algeria." *Islamic Culture* 46 (Oct. 1972): 285–92.

V / WORLD WARS & MANDATE

A / Palestine: Pre-World War I Period

1340 Bevis, R. "Making the Desert Bloom: An Historical Picture of Pre-Zionist Palestine." *Middle East Newsletter* 5:2 (Feb.–Mar. 1971): 2–7.

1341 Golomb, Eliyahu. *The History of Jewish Self-Defence in Palestine, 1878–1921*. Tel Aviv: Lion, 1947.

1342 Mandel, Neville. "Attempts at an Arab-Zionist Entente, 1913–1914." *Middle Eastern Studies* 1 (Apr. 1965): 238–67.

1343 ———. "Ottoman Policy and Restrictions on Jewish Settlement in Palestine: 1881–1908—Part I." *Middle Eastern Studies* 10 (Oct. 1974): 321–32.

B / Middle East: World War I Period

1344 Bell, Gertrude M. L. *Amurath to Amurath*. London: Heinemann, 1911.

1345 Bowman-Manifold, Michael G. E. *An Outline of the Egyptian and Palestine Campaigns, 1914–1918*. Chatham: Mackay, 1922.

1346 Burgoyne, Elizabeth. *Gertrude Bell: From Her Personal Papers, 1914–1926*. London: Ernest Benn, 1961.

1347   Busch, Briton Cooper. *Britain, India, and the Arabs, 1914–1921*. Berkeley: University of California Press, 1971.

1348   Courtney, Lord, ed. *Nationalism and War in the Near East. 1915*. New York: Arno, 1971.

1349   Gardner, Brian. *Allenby of Arabia*. New York: Coward-McCann, 1966.

1350   McMunn, Sir G., and C. Falls. *Military Operations: Egypt and Palestine*. London: H.M.S.O., 1928.

1351   Patterson, J. H. *With the Zionists in Gallipoli*. New York: Doran, 1916.

1352   Storrs, Sir Ronald. *Memoirs Orientations*. London: William Blackwood, 1938.

1353   Tibawi, A. L. "Syria in War-Time Agreements and Disagreements." *Middle East Forum* 43:2–3 (1967): 77–109.

1354   Wavell, Sir Archibald P. *Allenby: A Study in Greatness*. London: Harrap, 1940.

1355   ———. *The Palestine Campaigns*. 1928. London: Constable, 1941.

1356   Werfel, Franz V. *The Forty Days of Musa Dagh*. Translated from the German by Geoffrey Dunlop. New York: Viking, 1967.

Sykes-Picot Agreement

1357   Kedourie, E. "Sir Mark Sykes and Palestine, 1915–16." *Middle Eastern Studies* 6 (Oct. 1970): 340–45.

1358   Klieman, A. "Britain's War Aims in the Middle East in 1915." *Journal of Contemporary History* 3:3 (July 1968): 237–51.

1359   Nevakivi, Jukka. "Anglo-French Rivalry in the Making of the Sykes-Picot Agreement." *New Middle East*, no. 5 (Feb. 1969): 32–37.

1360 ———. *Britain, France and the Arab Middle East, 1914–1920.* New York: Oxford University Press, 1969.

Hussein-McMahon Correspondence

1361 Friedman, Isaiah. "The McMahon-Hussein Correspondence and the Question of Palestine." *Journal of Contemporary History* 5:2 (Apr. 1970): 83–122.

1362 Great Britain. Colonial Office. *Correspondence between Sir Henry McMahon and the Sharif of Mecca, July, 1915–March, 1916.* Cmnd. 5957. London: H.M.S.O., 1939.

1363 ———. *Report of a Committee Set Up to Consider Certain Correspondence between Sir Henry McMahon and the Sharif of Mecca in 1915 and 1916.* Cmnd. 5974. London: H.M.S.O., 1939.

1364 "The McMahon-Hussein Correspondence: Comments by Arnold Toynbee and a Reply by Isaiah Friedman." *Journal of Contemporary History* 5:4 (Oct. 1970): 184–201.

1365 Tibawi, A. L. "Syria in the McMahon Correspondence: Fresh Evidence from the British Foreign Office Records." *Middle East Forum* 42:4 (1966): 5–32.

Balfour Declaration

1366 "The Balfour Declaration: An Anniversary Remembered." *New Middle East,* no. 50 (Nov. 1972): 11–12.

1367 *Edwin Montagu and the Balfour Declaration.* New York: Arab League Office, n.d.

1368 Grieb, Conrad K. *The Balfour Declaration: Warrant for Genocide.* New York: Examiner Books, 1972.

1369 Herrmann, Klaus J. "Political Response to the Balfour Declaration in Imperial Germany: German Judaism." *Middle East Journal* 19 (Summer 1965): 303–20.

1370 Howard, Norman. "The Balfour Declaration in American Foreign Policy." *Middle East Forum* 38:9 (Dec. 1962): 25–31.

1371   Ingrams, D. "Balfour Defeated by the House of Lords." *Middle East International* (Mar. 1972): 36-40.

1372   Jeffries, J. "The Balfour Declaration." *Middle East Forum* 45:1-2 (1968): 9-23.

1373   Judd, Denis. *Balfour and the British Empire: A Study In Imperial Evolution, 1874-1932*. New York: St. Martin's Press, 1968.

1374   Kimche, Jon. *The Unromantics: The Great Powers and the Balfour Declaration*. London: Weidenfeld & Nicolson, 1968.

1375   Lebow, R. "Woodrow Wilson and the Balfour Declaration." *Journal of Modern History* 40 (Dec. 1968): 501-23.

1376   "Lord Balfour's Personal Position on the Balfour Declaration." *Middle East Journal* 22 (Summer 1968): 340-49.

1377   Mallison, W. T. "The Balfour Declaration." In *The Transformation of Palestine*. Edited by Ibrahim Abu-Lughod. Evanston, Illinois: Northwestern University Press, 1971.

1378   Stein, Leonard Jacques. *The Balfour Declaration*. New York: Simon & Schuster, 1961.

1379   Sykes, Christopher. *Two Studies in Virtue*. New York: Knopf, 1953.

1380   Verete, M. "The Balfour Declaration and Its Makers." *Middle Eastern Studies* 6 (Jan. 1970): 48-76.

1381   Zebel, Sydney H. *Balfour: A Political Biography*. Cambridge: Cambridge University Press, 1973.

The Arab Revolt

1382   Aldington, Richard. *Lawrence of Arabia: A Biographical Enquiry*. London: Collins, 1955.

1383 Dawn, C. Ernest. "The Amir of Mecca al-Husayn ibn 'Ali and the Origin of the Arab Revolt." *Proceedings of the American Philosophical Society* 104 (Feb. 1960): 11–34.

1384 Graves, Robert. *Lawrence and the Arabs.* London: Jonathan Cape, 1927.

1385 Knightly, Philip, and Colin Simpson. *The Secret Lives of Lawrence of Arabia.* New York: McGraw-Hill, 1970.

1386 Lawrence, T. E. *Seven Pillars of Wisdom.* Garden City, New York: Doubleday, 1951.

1387 Liddell Hart, Basil H. *Colonel Lawrence (of Arabia): The Man Behind the Legend.* New York: Halcyon, 1937.

1388 Mousa, Suleiman. *T. E. Lawrence: An Arab View.* Translated by Albert Butros. New York: Oxford University Press, 1966.

1389 Thomas, Lowell. *With Lawrence in Arabia.* New York: Grosset, 1955.

The Kingdom of Greater Syria

1390 al-Husri, Sati. *The Day of Maysalun: A Page from the Modern History of the Arabs.* Translated by Sidney Glazer. Washington, D.C.: Middle East Institute, 1966.

1391 Tibawi, A. L. "Syria from the Peace Conference to the Fall of Damascus." *Islamic Quarterly* 11 (July–Dec. 1967): 77–122.

1392 ———. "T. E. Lawrence, Faisal and Weizmann: The 1919 Attempt to Secure an Arab Balfour Declaration." *Royal Central Asian Journal* 56 (June 1969): 156–63.

1393 Wright, Quincy. "The Bombardment of Damascus." *American Journal of International Law* 20 (Apr. 1926): 263–80.

1394 Zeine, Zeine N. *The Struggle for Arab Independence: Western Diplomacy and the Rise and Fall of Faisal's Kingdom in Syria.* Beirut: Khayats, 1960.

Paris Peace Conference

1395 Ingrams, Doreen. *Palestine Papers, 1917-1922: Seeds of Conflict.* New York: Braziller, 1973.

1396 Manuel, Frank E. "The Palestine Question in Italian Diplomacy 1917-1920." *Journal of Modern History* 27 (Sept. 1955): 263-80.

1397 Perlmann, M. "Chapters of Arab-Jewish Diplomacy, 1918-22." *Jewish Social Studies* 6:2 (Apr. 1944): 123-54.

1398 Shotwell, J. T. *At the Paris Conference.* New York: Macmillan, 1937.

1399 Stern, G. "The Weizmann-Feisal Agreement." *New Outlook* 12:3 (Mar.-Apr. 1969): 20-25.

1400 Temperly, H. W., ed. *A History of the Peace Conference of Paris.* 6 vols. London: Henry Frowde; Hodder & Stoughton, 1920-1924.

Partition of the Ottoman Empire

1401 Evans, Laurence. *United States Policy and the Partition of Turkey, 1914-1924.* Baltimore: Johns Hopkins Press, 1965.

1402 Gidney, James B. "The King-Crane Commission." *Middle East Forum* 37:8 (Oct. 1961): 26-33.

1403 Hadawi, S. "The Arab States: Why Won't They Negotiate?" *Arab World* 14:5-6 (May-June 1968): 10.

1404 Howard, Harry N. "An American Experiment in Peace-Making: The King-Crane Commission." *Moslem World* 32 (Apr. 1942): 122-46.

1405 ———. *The King-Crane Commission: An American Inquiry in the Middle East.* Beirut: Khayats, 1963.

1406 ———. *The Partition of Turkey: A Diplomatic History, 1913-1923.* New York: H. Fertig, 1966.

1407 ———. "Postscript to the King-Crane Commission." *Middle East Forum* 40:6 (Summer 1964): 29–32.

1408 Loder, J. de V. *The Truth about Mesopotamia, Palestine and Syria*. London: Allen & Unwin, 1923.

1409 Mejcher, Helmut. "British Middle East Policy 1917–1921: The Inter-Departmental Level." *Journal of Contemporary History* 8:4 (Oct. 1973): 81–101.

1410 Yale, William. "Ambassador Morgenthau's Special Mission of 1917." *World Politics* 1 (Apr. 1949): 308–20.

C / Mandate Period, 1922–1948

Immediate Postwar Rule in Palestine

1411 Great Britain. Colonial Office. *Correspondence with the Palestine Arab Delegation and the Zionist Organization.* [Churchill] Parliamentary Papers, Cmd. 1700. London: H.M.S.O., 1922.

1412 ———. *An Interim Report on the Civil Administration of Palestine During the Period 1st July, 1920–30th June, 1921.* Parliamentary Papers, Cmd. 1499. London: H.M.S.O., 1921.

1413 ———. *Palestine Disturbances of May, 1921: Reports of the Commissioners of Inquiry* . . . [Haycraft] Parliamentary Papers, Cmd. 1540. London: H.M.S.O., 1921.

1414 Harrison, P. W. "The Situation in Arabia." *Atlantic Monthly* (Dec. 1920): 49–55.

1415 Klieman, Aaron. *Foundations of British Policy in the Arab World: The Cairo Conference of 1921*. Baltimore: Johns Hopkins Press, 1971.

Establishment of the Mandates in the Middle East

1416 Aston, Major General Sir George. "The British Middle-East Mandates." *Outlook* (July 12, 1922): 448.

1417 Bentwich, Norman. *The Mandates System*. London: Longmans, Green, 1930.

1418 Chowdhuri, R. N. *International Mandates and Trusteeship Systems*. The Hague: Nijhoff, 1955.

1419 Cumming, H. H. *Franco-British Rivalry in the Post-War Near East: The Decline of French Influence*. London: Oxford University Press, 1938.

1420 Hill, Duncan H. *Mandates, Dependencies, and Trusteeships*. Washington, D.C.: Carnegie Foundation for International Peace, 1948.

1421 Khan, R. "Mandate and Monarch in 'Iraq'." *Islamic Culture* 43 (Oct. 1969): 255-76.

1422 Rohf, S. "The Zionists and St. John Philby." *Jewish Social Studies* 34:2 (Apr. 1972): 107-21.

1423 Shorrock, W. "The Origin of the French Mandate in Syria and Lebanon: The Railroad Question, 1901-1914." *International Journal of Middle East Studies* 1 (Apr. 1970): 133-53.

1424 Twitchett, K. J. "The Intellectual Genesis of the League of Nations Mandates System." *International Relations* 3:13 (Apr. 1966): 16-39.

1425 Wright, Quincy. *Mandates under the League of Nations*. Chicago: University of Chicago Press, 1930.

Britain & the Arabs

1426 Porath, Yehoshua. "The Palestinians and the Negotiations for the British-Hijazi Treaty, 1920-1925." *Asian and African Studies* 8 (1972): 20-48.

1427 Seton-Williams, M. N. *Britain and the Arab States: A Survey of Anglo-Arab Relations, 1920–1948*. London: Luzac, 1948.

D / Mandate for Palestine

1428 Beatty, Ilene. *Arab and Jew in the Land of Canaan*. Chicago: Regnery, 1957.

1429 Boustany, Wedi Fr. *The Palestine Mandate: Invalid and Impracticable*. Beirut: American Press, 1936.

1430 *Christians, Zionism and Palestine: A Selection of Articles and Statements on the Religious Aspects of the Palestine Problem*. Beirut: Institute for Palestine Studies, 1970.

1431 Cohen, M. "British Strategy and the Palestine Question: 1936–1939." *Journal of Contemporary History* 7:3–4 (July–Oct. 1972): 157–84.

1432 Graves, Philip. *Palestine, the Land of the Three Faiths*. London: Jonathan Cape, 1923.

1433 Graves, R. M. *Experiment in Anarchy*. London: Gollancz, 1949.

1434 Hadawi, Sami. *Bitter Harvest: Palestine between 1914–1967*. New York: New World, 1967.

1435 ———, and Robert John. *The Palestine Diary*. Vol. 1. *British Involvement, 1914–1945;* Vol. 2. *United States, United Nations Intervention, 1945*–1948. New York: New World, 1970.

1436 Hopkins, Lister G. "Population." In *Economic Organization of Palestine*. Edited by Said B. Himadeh. Beirut: American Press, 1938.

1437 "The International Status of Palestine." *Journal du Droit Internationale* 90:4 (Oct.–Nov. 1963): 4–11.

1438 Katz, Samuel. *Days of Fire*. Garden City, New York: Doubleday, 1968.

1439 Kedourie, Elie. *The Chatham House Version and other Middle Eastern Studies*. New York: Praeger, 1970.

1440 Khalidi, Walid, ed. *From Haven to Conquest: Readings in Zionism and the Palestine Problem until 1948*. Beirut: Institute for Palestine Studies, 1971.

1441 Koestler, Arthur. *Promise and Fulfillment: Palestine 1917–1949*. New York: Macmillan, 1949.

1442 Luke, Harry C., and Edward Keith-Roach. *The Handbook of Palestine and Trans-Jordan*. London: Macmillan, 1930.

1443 Matthews, Charles D. "Palestine—Mohammedan Holy Land." *Moslem World* 33 (Oct. 1943): 239–53.

1444 Newton, Frances. *Fifty Years in Palestine*. London: Coldharbour, 1948.

1445 *Palestine: A Study of Jewish, Arab, and British Policies*. 2 vols. 1947. New York: Kraus Reprint, 1970.

1446 Parkes, James William. *A History of Palestine from 135 A.D. to Modern Times*. New York: Oxford University Press, 1949.

1447 ———. "The Palestinian Jews: Did Someone Forget?" *New Middle East*, no. 13 (Oct. 1969): 29–34.

1448 ———. *Whose Land? A History of the Peoples of Palestine*. Baltimore: Penguin, 1970.

1449 Tolkowsky, Samuel. *The Gateway to Palestine: A History of Jaffa*. London: Routledge & Sons, 1924.

1450 Ulitzur, Abraham. *Foundations: A Survey of Twenty-Five Years of Activity of the Palestine Foundation Fund*. Jerusalem: Karen Hayesod, 1946.

1451 Waines, David. *The Unholy War: Israel and Palestine, 1897–1971*. Wilmette, Illinois: Medina University Press International, 1971.

1452 Ziff, William Bernard. *The Rape of Palestine*. 1938. New York: Greenwood Reprint, 1971.

Britain Mandatory Power

1453 Abu-Jaber, F. S. "The British in Palestine." *Middle East Forum* 45:3 (1969): 29–44.

1454 Andrews, Fannie F. *The Holy Land under Mandate*. 2 vols. Boston: Houghton Mifflin, 1931.

1455 Bentwich, Norman. "The Legal System of Palestine under the Mandate." *Middle East Journal* 2 (Jan. 1948): 33–46.

1456 ———, and H. Bentwich. *Mandate Memoirs, 1918–1948*. London: Hogarth Press, 1965.

1457 Fitzsimons, Matthew A. *Empire by Treaty: Britain and the Middle East in the Twentieth Century*. Notre Dame: University of Notre Dame Press, 1964.

1458 Frischwasser Ra'anan, H. F. *Frontiers of a Nation: A Reexamination of the Forces which Created the Palestine Mandate and Determined Its Territorial Shape*. London: Batchworth, 1955.

1459 Great Britain. Colonial Office. *Mandate for Palestine (and Note on Application to Transjordan)*. Parliamentary Papers, Cmd. 1785. London: H.M.S.O., July 1922.

1460 ———. *Mandates, Final Drafts*. Parliamentary Papers, Cmd. 1500. London: H.M.S.O., 1921.

1461 Hanna, Paul. *British Policy in Palestine*. Washington, D.C.: American Council on Public Affairs, 1942.

1462 Hyamson, Albert. *Palestine under the Mandate, 1920–1948*. London: Methuen, 1950.

1463 Joseph, Bernard. *British Rule in Palestine*. Washington, D.C.: Public Affairs, 1948.

1464 Kendall, Henry, and K. H. Baruth. *Village Development in Palestine during the British Mandate*. London: Crown Agents for the Colonies, 1949.

1465 Lengyel, Emil. "Great Britain's Palestine Mandate Policy in a New Light." *Middle Eastern Affairs* 6 (Mar. 1955): 91-95.

1466 Marlowe, John. *The Seat of Pilate: An Account of the Palestine Mandate*. London: Cresset, 1959.

1467 Meinertzhagen, Richard. *Middle East Diary, 1917-1956*. London: Cresset, 1959.

1468 Polk, William R.; David M. Stamler; and Edmund Asfour. *Backdrop to Tragedy: The Struggle for Palestine*. Boston: Beacon, 1957.

1469 Royal Institute of International Affairs. *Great Britain and Palestine, 1915-1945*. 3d ed. London: Royal Institute of International Affairs, 1946.

1470 Sidebotham, Herbert. *Great Britain and Palestine*. London: Macmillan, 1937.

1471 Upthegrove, Campbell L. *Empire by Mandate: A History of the Relations of Great Britain with the Permanent Mandates Commission of the League of Nations*. New York: Bookman, 1954.

Mandate in the 1920s

1472 Bowle, John. *Viscount Samuel: A Biography*. London: Gollancz, 1957.

1473 Great Britain. Colonial Office. *Papers Relating to the Elections for the Palestine Legislative Council*. Parliamentary Papers, Cmd. 1889. London: H.M.S.O., 1923.

1474 ———. *Proposed Formation of an Arab Agency.* Parliamentary Papers, Cmd. 1989. London: H.M.S.O., Nov. 1923. [Correspondence with High Commissioner for Palestine]

1475 ———. *Report of the Commission.* [Shaw] Parliamentary Papers, Cmd. 3530. London: H.M.S.O., 1930. [Palestine disturbances of Aug. 1929]

1476 ———. *Report of the High Commissioner on the Administration of Palestine, 1920–1925.* Parliamentary Papers, Colonial Number 15. London: H.M.S.O., 1925.

1477 Kedourie, E. "Sir Herbert Samuel and the Government of Palestine." *Middle Eastern Studies* 5 (Jan. 1969): 44–68.

1478 "Report of the Commission Appointed by His Majesty's Government in United Kingdom of Great Britain and Northern Ireland, December 1930." In *The Rights and Claims of Moslems and Jews in Connection with the Wailing Wall at Jerusalem.* Basic Documents Series, no. 4. Beirut: Institute for Palestine Studies, 1968.

1479 Samuel, Horace. *Unholy Memories of the Holy Land.* London: Hogarth Press, 1930.

1480 Samuel, Viscount Herbert. *Memoirs.* London: Cresset, 1945.

Arab Society in Mandatory Palestine

1481 Abu-Ghazaleh, Adnan M. "Arab Cultural Nationalism in Palestine during the British Mandate." *Journal of Palestine Studies* 1:3 (1972): 37–63.

1482 Asfour, John. "Arab Labour in Palestine." *Journal of the Royal Central Asian Society* 32 (May 1945): 201–5.

1483 Granatt, A. *Land System in Palestine.* New York: British Book Centre, 1952.

1484 Granqvist, Hilma. *Birth and Childhood Among the Arabs: Studies in a Muhammadan Village in Palestine.* Helsinki: Soderstrom, 1947.

1485 Himadeh, Sa'id, ed. *Economic Organization of Palestine.* Beirut: American Press, 1938.

1486 Husseini, Mohammed Y. al. *Social and Economic Changes in Arab Palestine.* Jerusalem: Beit al-Makdis, 1947.

1487 Tibawi, A. L. *Arab Education in Mandatory Palestine.* London: Luzac, 1956.

1488 Weinryb, Bernard D. "The Arab Economy of Palestine." *Palestine Affairs* 3 (Jan. 1948): 1–4.

Jewish Immigration

1489 Boehm, Adolf, and Adolf Pollak. *The Jewish National Fund: Its History, Function and Activity.* Jerusalem: Jewish National Fund, 1939.

1490 Cohen, Michael. "Direction of Policy in Palestine 1939–45." *Middle Eastern Studies* 11 (Oct. 1975): 237–57.

1491 Kimche, Jon, and David Kimche. *The Secret Roads: The "Illegal" Migration of a People, 1938–1948.* London: Secker & Warburg, 1955.

1492 Kushnir, S. *The Village Builder: A Biography of Abraham Harzfeld.* New York: Herzl Press, 1967.

1493 Lewisohn, Ludwig. *Israel.* 1925. New York: Greenwood Reprint, 1971.

1494 Muenzner, G. *Jewish Labour Economy in Palestine.* London: Gollancz, 1945.

1495 Nardi, Noach. *Zionism and Education in Palestine.* New York: Teachers College, Columbia University, 1934.

1496 Weinstock, Nathan. "The Impact of Zionist Colonization on Palestinian Arab Society before 1948." *Journal of Palestine Studies* 2:2 (1973): 49–63.

1497 Wilhelm, Kurt. *Roads to Zion: Four Centuries of Travelers' Reports.* New York: Schocken Library, 1948.

1498   Ziman, Joshua. *The Revival of Palestine.* New York: Sharon, 1946.

Mandate in the 1930s

1499   Abbass, Abdul Majid. "Palestine (1933–39)." In *Challenge and Response in Internal Conflict.* Edited by D. M. Condit and Bert H. Cooper, Jr. Washington, D.C.: Center for Research in Social Systems, American University, 1967.

1500   Barbour, Nevill. "Some Less Familiar Aspects of the Palestine Problem." *Journal of the Royal Central Asian Society* 25 (Oct. 1938): 554–70.

1501   Borochow, Baer. *Nationalism and the Class Struggle: A Marxian Approach to the Jewish Problem.* 1937. New York: Greenwood Reprint, 1972.

1502   Cust, Archer. "Cantonization: A Plan for Palestine." *Journal of the Royal Central Asian Society* 23 (Apr. 1936): 194–220.

1503   Gibb, H. A. R. "The Islamic Congress at Jerusalem in December 1931." In *Survey of International Affairs, 1934.* London: Oxford University Press, 1935.

1504   Great Britain. Colonial Office. *Palestine, Statement with Regard to British Policy.* Parliamentary Papers, Cmd. 3582. London: H.M.S.O., May 1930.

1505   ———. *Report on Immigration, Land Settlement and Development by Sir John Hope Simpson* . . . Parliamentary Papers, Cmd. 3683–3687. London: H.M.S.O., 1930.

1506   ———. *Statement of Policy by His Majesty's Government in the United Kingdom Presented by the Secretary of State for the Colonies to Parliament by Command of His Majesty.* [Passfield] Parliamentary Papers, Cmd. 3692. London: H.M.S.O., 1930.

1507   Horowitz, David, and Rita Hinden. *Economic Survey of Palestine (with Special Reference to 1936 and 1937).* Tel Aviv: Jewish Agency, 1938.

1508   Jewish Agency for Palestine. *Memorandum Submitted to the Palestine Royal Commission on Behalf of the Jewish Agency for Palestine.* London: Jewish Agency for Palestine, 1936.

1509   Kisch, Frederick H. *Palestine Diary.* London: Gollancz, 1938.

1510   Rose, Norman A. "The Debate on Partition, 1937–38: The Anglo-Zionist Aspect—The Proposal." *Middle Eastern Studies* 6 (Oct. 1970): 297–318.

1511   ———. "The Debate on Partition, 1937–38: The Anglo-Zionist Aspect—II. The Withdrawal." *Middle Eastern Studies* 7 (Jan. 1971): 3–24.

1512   Schmidt, H. D. "The Nazi Party in Palestine and the Levant, 1932–39." *International Affairs* 28 (Oct. 1952): 460–69.

1513   Sheffer, G. "Intentions and Results of British Policy in Palestine: Passfield's White Paper." *Middle Eastern Studies* 9 (Jan. 1973): 43–60.

1514   Stein, Leonard. *Memorandum on "Report of the Commission on Palestine Disturbances of August 1929."* London: Jewish Agency, 1930.

Arab Revolt in Palestine, 1936–1939

1515   Bauer, Y. "The Arab Revolt of 1936." *New Outlook* 9:6 (July–Aug. 1966): 49–57.

1516   ———. "The Arab Revolt of 1936, II." *New Outlook* 9:7 (Sept. 1966): 21–28.

1517   Canaan, Muhammad Tawfiq. *The Palestine Arab Cause.* Jerusalem: Modern, 1936.

1518   Cohen, M. "British Strategy and the Palestine Question: 1936–1939." *Journal of Contemporary History* 7:3–4 (July–Oct. 1972): 157–84.

1519 ———. "Sir Arthur Wauchope, the Army, and the Rebellion in Palestine, 1936." *Middle Eastern Studies* 9 (Jan. 1973): 19–34.

1520 Feiwel, T. R. *No Ease in Zion*. London: Secker & Warburg, 1938.

1521 Great Britain. Colonial Office. *Proposed New Constitution for Palestine*. Parliamentary Papers, Cmd. 5119. London: H.M.S.O., Mar. 1936.

1522 ———. *Report of the Palestine Partition Commission*. [Woodhead] Parliamentary Papers, Cmd. 5854. London: H.M.S.O., 1938.

1523 ———. *Report of the Palestine Royal Commission . . .* [Peel] Parliamentary Papers, Cmd. 5479. London: H.M.S.O., 1937.

1524 ———. *Statement of Policy . . .* Presented by the Secretary of State for the Colonies. . . . Parliamentary Papers, Cmd. 5513. London: H.M.S.O., 1937.

1525 ———. *Statement of Policy . . .* Presented by the Secretary of State for the Colonies. . . . Parliamentary Papers, Cmd. 5893. London: H.M.S.O., 1938.

1526 Jeffries, Joseph M. N. *Palestine: The Reality*. London: Longmans, Green, 1939.

1527 Main, Ernest. *Palestine at the Crossroads*. London: George Allen, 1937.

1528 Mansur, George. *The Arab Worker under the Palestine Mandate*. Jerusalem: Commercial, 1937.

1529 Marlowe, John. *Rebellion in Palestine*. London: Cresset, 1946.

1530 Mogannam, Matiel. *The Arab Woman and the Palestine Problem*. London: Herbert Joseph, 1937.

1531 Mosley, Leonard. *Gideon Goes to War*. New York: Scribners, 1956. [Biography of General Orde C. Wingate]

1532 Rose, Norman Anthony. "The Arab Rulers and Palestine, 1936: The British Reaction." *Journal of Modern History* 44 (June 1972): 312–31.

1533 Simson, H. J. *British Rule and Rebellion*. London: William Blackwood, 1938.

1534 Woolbert, Robert Gale. "Pan-Arabism and the Palestine Problem." *Foreign Affairs* 16 (Jan. 1938): 309–22.

1939 White Paper

1535 Great Britain. Colonial Office. *Statement of Policy* ... Presented by the Secretary of State for the Colonies. ... [MacDonald] Parliamentary Papers, Cmd. 6019. London: H.M.S.O., 1939.

1536 Mason, C. "White Paper: An Anti-British Riot in Jerusalem in 1939." *Blackwood's* 259 (Mar. 1946): 153–58.

United States & Palestine

1537 Burrows, Millar. *Palestine Is Our Business*. Philadelphia: Westminster, 1949.

1538 Byrnes, James F. *Speaking Frankly*. New York: Harper, 1947.

1539 Fink, Reuben. *America and Palestine*. New York: American Zionist Emergency Council, 1944.

1540 Friedrich, Carl J. *American Policy toward Palestine*. 1944. New York: Greenwood Reprint, 1971.

1541 Jansen, Michael E. *The Three Basic American Decisions on Palestine*. Palestine Essays, no. 25. Beirut: Palestine Liberation Organization Research Center, Mar. 1971.

1542 ———. *The United States and the Palestinian People*. Monograph Series, no. 23. Beirut: Institute for Palestine Studies, 1970.

1543   Manuel, Frank E. *The Realities of American-Palestine Relations.* Washington, D.C.: Public Affairs, 1949.

1544   "U.S.-Arab Views on the Palestine Problem [Exchange of Messages between King Ibn Saud and President Truman]." *U.S. Department of State Bulletin* (Nov. 10, 1946): 848–51.

1545   Wilson, Evan M. "The American Interest in the Palestine Question and the Establishment of Israel." *Annals of the American Academy of Political and Social Science* 401 (May 1972): 64–73.

E / World War II in Palestine & the Middle East

1546   Babcock, F. Lawrence. "The Explosive Middle East." *Fortune* (Oct. 1944): 113.

1547   Hirszowicz, Lukasz. *The Third Reich and the Arab East.* London: Routledge & Kegan Paul, 1966.

1548   Kahn, A. E. "Palestine: A Problem in Economic Evaluation." *American Economic Review* 34 (Sept. 1944): 538–60.

1549   Knatchbull-Hugessen, Hughe (Brabourne). *Diplomat in Peace and War.* London: Murray, 1949.

1550   MacIntyre, Donald. *The Battle for the Mediterranean.* London: Batsford, 1964.

1551   Moorehead, Alan. *The March to Tunis: The North African War, 1940–1943.* New York: Dell, 1968.

1552   Schechtman, Joseph B. *The Mufti and the Fuehrer: The Rise and Fall of Haj Amin el-Husseini.* New York: Yoseloff, 1965.

1553 Stark, Freya. *Dust in the Lion's Paw*. New York: Harcourt, Brace, 1961. [Autobiography 1939-1946]

1554 Sulzberger, Cyrus L. "German Preparations in the Middle East." *Foreign Affairs* 20 (July 1942): 663-78.

1555 Swaminathan, V. S. "Palestine and the War." *Spectator* (Dec. 26, 1941): 594.

1556 Yisraeli, D. "The Third Reich and Palestine." *Middle Eastern Studies* 7 (Oct. 1971): 343-54.

Jewish Terrorism in Palestine during World War II

1557 Bauer, Yehuda. "From Cooperation to Resistance: The Haganah, 1938-1946." *Middle Eastern Studies* 2 (Apr. 1966): 182-210.

1558 ———. *From Diplomacy to Resistance: A History of Jewish Palestine, 1939-1945*. Translated by Alton Winters. Philadelphia: Jewish Publication Society of America, 1970.

1559 Begin, Menachem. "Our Fight for Freedom (Irgun)." *Israel Magazine* 5:3-4 (1973): 47-51.

1560 ———. *The Revolt: Story of the Irgun*. New York: Schuman, 1951.

1561 Brenner, Y. "The 'Stern Gang', 1940-1948." *Middle Eastern Studies* 2 (Oct. 1965): 2-30.

1562 Cohen, Geula. *Woman of Violence: Memoirs of a Young Terrorist*. Translated by Hillel Halkin. New York: Holt, Rinehart & Winston, 1966.

1563 Frank, Gerold. *The Deed: The Assassination of Lord Moyne*. London: Jonathan Cape, 1964.

1564 ———. "The Truth about the Terrorists." *Nation* (Dec. 2, 1944): 685-86.

1565   Gerling, Shalom. *Adventures of a Jewish Fighter, 1939-45.* Tel Aviv: Hakibbutz Hameuchad, 1968.

1566   Gervasi, Frank. "Terror in Palestine." *Collier's* (Aug. 11, 1945): 24.

1567   Lurie, Jesse. "Guns in Palestine." *Nation* (Jan. 22, 1944): 92-94.

1568   Partridge, Burgo. *Memoirs of an Assassin: Confessions of a Stern Gang Killer.* New York: Yoseloff, 1959.

1569   Wallace-Clarke, G. "Terrorism under the Mandate." *New Middle East,* no. 10 (July 1969): 16.

1570   Wilson, Major R. D. *Cordon and Search with the Airborne Division in Palestine, 1945-1948.* Aldershot: Gale & Polden, 1949.

1571   Yalin-Mor, N. "The British Called Us the Stern Gang." *Israel Magazine* 5:2 (1973): 76-84.

1572   Zhabotinskii, Vladimir Evgan'evich. *The Jewish War Front.* London: Allen & Unwin, 1940.

F / The Destruction of Jews in Europe

1573   Arendt, Hannah. *Eichmann in Jerusalem.* New York: Viking, 1965.

1574   Levin, Nora. *The Holocaust: The Destruction of European Jewry, 1933-1945.* New York: Schocken, 1973.

1575   Parkes, James. *The Emergence of the Jewish Problem, 1878-1939.* New York: Oxford University Press, 1946.

1576   Poliakov, Leon. *Harvest of Hate: The Nazi Program for the Destruction of the Jews of Europe.* 1954. New York: Greenwood Reprint, 1971.

1577 Reichmann, Eva G. *Hostages of Civilisation: The Social Sources of National Socialist Anti-Semitism.* Boston: Beacon Press, 1951.

1578 Weizmann, Chaim. "Palestine's Role in the Solution of the Jewish Problem." *Foreign Affairs* 20 (Jan. 1942): 324–38.

G / End of the Mandate, 1940–1948

Palestine Question, 1940–1948

1579 Abcarius, M. F. *Palestine through the Fog of Propaganda.* London: Hutchinson, 1946.

1580 Anglo-American Committee of Inquiry. *Survey of Palestine.* Jerusalem: Government Printer, 1946.

1581 Barbour, Nevill N. *Nisi Dominus: A Survey of the Palestine Controversy.* London: Harrap, 1946.

1582 Chase, Francis. "Palestine Today." *National Geographic* (Oct. 1946): 501–16.

1583 Fielding, George. *Hate, Hope and High Explosives: A Report on the Middle East.* Indianapolis: Bobbs-Merrill, 1948.

1584 Hurewitz, J. C. *The Struggle for Palestine.* New York: Norton, 1950.

1585 Jabotinsky, Vladimir. *An Answer to Ernest Bevin: Evidence Submitted to the Palestine Royal Commission, House of Lords.* New York: Jabotinsky Foundation, 1946.

1586 Kirk, George E. *The Middle East, 1945–1950.* London: Oxford University Press, 1954.

1587 Lazar, David. *L'opinion française et la naissance de l'état d'Israël: 1945–1949.* Paris: Calmann-Levy, 1972.

1588 Lowdermilk, Walter C. *Palestine, Land of Promise.* New York: Harper, 1944.

1589 Maugham, Robin C. R. *Approach to Palestine.* London: Falcon, 1947.

1590 Nathan, Robert R.; Oscar Gass; and Daniel Creamer. *Palestine: Problem and Promise, an Economic Study.* Washington, D.C.: Public Affairs, 1946.

1591 *Palestine: A Study of Jewish, Arab, and British Policies.* 2 vols. New Haven, Connecticut: Yale University Press, for Esco Foundation, 1947.

1592 Patai, Raphael. "On Culture Contact and Its Working in Modern Palestine." *American Anthropologist* 49 (Oct. 1947): 1–48.

1593 Sakran, Frank C. *Palestine Dilemma: Arab Rights versus Zionist Aspirations.* Washington, D.C.: Public Affairs, 1948.

1594 Sinai, Anne, and I. Robert Sinai. *Israel and the Arabs: Prelude to the Jewish State.* New York: Facts on File, 1972.

British Palestine Policy

1595 Charteris, M. M. C. "A Year as an Intelligence Officer in Palestine." *Journal of the Middle East Society* 1 (Oct.–Dec. 1946): 15–23.

1596 Crossman, Richard H. S. *Palestine Mission: A Personal Record.* New York: Harper, 1947.

1597 ———. "The Role Britain Hopes to Play." *Commentary* 5 (June 1948): 493–97.

1598 Cunningham, Sir Alan. "Palestine: The Last Days of the Mandate." *International Affairs* 24 (Oct. 1948): 481–90.

1599 Deighton, H. S. "Policy in the Middle East." *Fortnightly Review* (Nov. 1949): 307–14.

1600 "The Empire and the Middle East." *Round Table* 146 (Mar. 1947): 103–11.

1601 Granovsky (Granott), Abraham. *The Land System in Palestine.* London: Eyre & Spottiswoode, 1952.

1602 Hanna, Paul L. *British Policy in Palestine.* Washington, D.C.: Public Affairs, 1942.

1603 Mayhew, C. "The View from the Foreign Office, 1946/7." *Middle East International* (Nov. 1972): 23-25.

Zionism in Palestine

1604 Cadett, Thomas. "The Exodus 1947: The British Case." *New York Herald-Tribune* (Sept. 17, 1947).

1605 Gruber, Ruth. *Destination Palestine: The Story of Haganah Ship Exodus, 1947.* New York: Current Books [A. A. Wyn], 1948.

1606 Gruenbaum, Ludwig. *Outlines of a Development Plan for Jewish Palestine.* Jerusalem: Economic Research Institute of the Jewish Agency for Palestine, 1946.

1607 Hirschmann, Ira A. *Life Line to a Promised Land.* New York: Vanguard, 1946.

1608 Stevens, R. "Colonization by Proxy: Two Franchising Ventures of the Home Office." *Arab World* 18:3-4 (Mar.-Apr. 1972): 18-25.

1609 Syrkin, Marie. *Blessed Is the Match.* New York: Knopf, 1947.

1610 Thorbecke, Ellen. *Promised Land.* New York: Harper, 1947.

Arab Society, 1940-1948

1611 "Arab Education in Palestine." *Palestine Affairs* 1 (Oct. 1946): 3-5.

1612 Berger, Elmer. *The Jewish Dilemma.* New York: Devin-Adair, 1945.

1613 Dajani, Burhan. "National Movement for Freedom in Syria and Palestine." *India Quarterly* 3 (June 1947): 135-43.

1614 *The Future of Palestine.* Beirut: Hermon, 1970.

1615 Hadawi, Sami. *Village Statistics, 1945: A Classification of Land and Area Ownership in Palestine.* Facts and Figures, no. 34. Beirut: Palestine Liberation Organization Research Center, Sept. 1970.

1616 Henricus [pseud.]. "Patterns of Power in the Arab Middle East." *Political Quarterly* 17 (Apr.–June 1946): 93–122.

1617 Pearlman, Maurice. *Mufti of Jerusalem: The Story of Haj Amin el-Husseini.* London: Gollancz, 1947.

1618 Perlmann, M. "Political Organization of the Arabs of Palestine." *Palestine Affairs* 2 (May 1947): 53–55.

1619 Porath, Y. "al-Hajj Amin al-Husayni, Mufti of Jerusalem: His Rise to Power and the Consolidation of His Position." *Asian and African Studies* 7 (1971): 121–56.

United States & Zionism after World War II

1620 Arnold, G. L. "Lessons of Palestine." *Nineteenth Century and After* 144 (Oct. 1948): 192–201.

1621 Crum, Bartley C. *Behind the Silken Curtain: A Personal Account of Anglo-American Diplomacy in Palestine and the Middle East.* New York: Simon & Schuster, 1947.

1622 Hare, Raymond A. "The Great Divide: World War II." *Annals of the American Academy of Political and Social Science* 401 (May 1972): 23–30.

1623 McClellan, Grant S. "Palestine and America's Role in the Middle East." *Foreign Policy Reports* (July 1, 1945): 98–107.

1624 Millis, Walter, ed. *The Forrestal Diaries.* New York: Viking, 1951.

1625 Schectman, Joseph B. *The United States and the Jewish State Movement: The Crucial Decade, 1939–1949.* New York: Herzl Press, 1966.

1626 Taylor, Alan R. "The Crucial Years of Zionist Diplomacy, 1939–1948." *Middle East International* (Dec. 1972): 13–16.

1627 ———. *Prelude to Israel: An Analysis of Jewish Diplomacy, 1897–1947.* New York: Philosophical Library, 1959.

Solutions Never Tested

1628 Azcarate, Pablo de. *Mission in Palestine, 1948–1952.* Washington, D.C.: Middle East Institute, 1966.

1629 Barbour, Nevill. *Palestine: Star or Crescent?* New York: Odyssey, 1947.

1630 Buber, Martin; Judah L. Magnes; and Moshe Smilansky. *Palestine: A Bi-National State.* New York: Ihud (Union) Association of Palestine, Aug. 1946.

1631 Forsythe, David P. *United Nations Peacemaking: The Conciliation Commission for Palestine.* Baltimore: Johns Hopkins Press, 1972.

1632 Kaznelson, Siegmund. *The Palestine Problem and Its Solution: A New Scheme.* Jerusalem: Jewish Publishing House, 1946.

1633 Magnes, Judah L., and Martin Buber. *Arab-Jewish Unity: Testimony before the Ihud (Union) Association.* London: Gollancz, 1947.

H / Partition of Palestine

1634 Acheson, Dean G. *The Pattern of Responsibility.* Edited by McGeorge Bundy from the record of Secretary of State Dean Acheson. Clifton, New Jersey: Kelley, 1972.

1635 Atiyah, Edward. *The Palestine Question.* London: Diplomatic, 1948.

1636 *Book of Documents Submitted to the General Assembly of the United Nations Relating to the Establishment of the National Home for the Jewish People.* New York: Jewish Agency for Palestine, 1947.

1637 Cobban, Alfred. *National Self-Determination.* Chicago: University of Chicago Press, 1948.

1638 Cohn, David. "Can Israel Help the Arabs?" *Atlantic Monthly* (Aug. 1948): 34–35.

1639 Fay, Sidney. "Arabs, Zionists, and Oil." *Current History* 14 (May 1948): 270–76.

1640 Glick, Edward B. *Latin America and the Palestine Problem.* New York: Herzl Foundation, 1958.

1641 *The Jewish Plan for Palestine: Memoranda and Statements Presented by the Jewish Agency for Palestine to the United Nations Special Committee on Palestine.* Jerusalem. Jewish Agency, 1947.

1642 Krammer, A. "Soviet Motives in the Partition of Palestine, 1947–8." *Journal of Palestine Studies* 2:2 (1973): 102–19.

1643 Levitch, Joel, and Laurel Vlock. "The Diary of Eddie Jacobson." *Washington Post* (May 6, 1973).

1644 Lumer, H. "On the Origins of the State of Israel." *Political Affairs* 49 (Dec. 1970): 52–56.

1645 Magnes, Judah Leon. *Palestine—Divided or United? The Case for a Bi-National Palestine before the United Nations.* 1947. New York: Greenwood Reprint, 1972.

1646 *The Partition of Palestine.* Beirut: Institute for Palestine Studies, 1968.

1647 Robinson, Jacob. *Palestine and the United Nations.* Washington, D.C.: Public Affairs, 1947.

1648 Roosevelt, Kermit. "The Partition of Palestine: A Lesson in Pressure Politics." *Middle East Journal* 2 (Jan. 1948): 1–16.

1649 Trevor, Daphne. *Under the White Paper*. Jerusalem: Jerusalem Press, 1948.

1650 Truman, Harry. *Memoirs*. Garden City, New York: Doubleday, 1956.

I / The Palestine War, 1948

1651 Arsenian, Seth. "Wartime Propaganda in the Middle East." *Middle East Journal* 2 (Oct. 1948): 417–29.

1652 Bar-Yaacov, N. *The Israeli-Syrian Armistice: Problems of Implementation, 1949–1966*. Jerusalem: Magnes, 1967.

1653 Ebon, Martin. "Communist Tactics in Palestine." *Middle East Journal* 2 (July 1948): 255–69.

1654 Garcia-Granados, Jorge. *The Birth of Israel: The Drama as I Saw It*. New York: Knopf, 1948.

1655 Kimche, Jon. *Seven Fallen Pillars*. New York: Praeger, 1953.

1656 Kimche, Jon, and David Kimche. *Both Sides of the Hill: Britain and the Palestine War*. London: Secker & Warburg, 1960.

1657 ———. *A Clash of Destinies: The Arab-Jewish War and the Founding of the State of Israel*. New York: Praeger, 1960.

1658 Kurzman, Dan. *Genesis 1948: The First Arab-Israeli War*. New York: World, 1970.

1659 Lorch, N. "Code Name: The Aunt." *Israel Magazine* 5:5 (1973): 69–76.

1660 O'Ballance, Edgar. *The Arab-Israeli War, 1948.* New York: Praeger, 1957.

1661 Schultz, Lillie. "The Palestine Fight:—An Inside Story." *Nation* (Dec. 20, 1947): 675–78.

Israeli Views of the 1948 War

1662 Eban, Aubrey S. "The Future of Arab-Jewish Relations." *Commentary* 6 (Sept. 1948): 199–206.

1663 Kimche, Jon, and David Kimche. "Ben Gurion Reconsiders 1948: An Interview with Some Surprising Conclusions." *New Middle East,* no. 9 (June 1969): 14–17.

1664 Knohl, Dov, ed. *Siege in the Hills of Hebron: The Battle of the Etzion Bloc.* New York: Yoseloff, 1958.

1665 Larkin, Margaret. *The Hand of Mordechai.* New York: Yoseloff, 1968.

1666 Levin, Harry. *I Saw the Battle of Jerusalem.* New York: Schocken, 1950.

1667 Lorch, Netanel. *The Edge of the Sword: Israel's War of Independence, 1947–1949.* New York: Putnam, 1961.

1668 Waters, M. P. *Haganah: The Story of Jewish Self-Defense in Palestine.* London: Wolsey, 1947.

Arab Views of the 1948 War

1669 Al-Qawuqji, Fauzi. "Memoirs, 1948: I." *Journal of Palestine Studies* 1:4 (1972): 27–58.

1670 ———. "Memoirs 1948: II." *Journal of Palestine Studies* 2:1 (1972): 3–33.

1671 The American Christian Palestine Committee. *The Arab War Effort: A Documented Account.* New York: American Christian Palestine Committee, 1946.

1672 Nasser, A. G. "Nasser's Memoirs of the First Palestinian War." Translated by Walid Khalidi. *Journal of Palestine Studies* 2:2 (1973): 3–32.

1673 Roosevelt, Kermit. "The Puzzle of Jerusalem's Mufti." *Saturday Evening Post* (June 12, 1948): 26.

1674 ———. "Will the Arabs Fight?" *Saturday Evening Post* (Dec. 27, 1947): 20.

1675 Teller, J. L. "Behind Palestine's Arab 'Armies'." *Commentary* 3 (Mar. 1947): 243–49.

1676 Zimmerman, J. "The 1948 War: Who Was for the Palestinians?" *New Middle East,* no. 44 (May 1972): 42–43.

1677 Zurayk, Constantine N. *Palestine: The Meaning of the Disaster.* Beirut: Khayats, 1956.

Count Folke Bernadotte & Conciliation

1678 Bell, J. Bowyer. "Assassination in International Politics: Lord Moyne, Count Bernadotte, and the Lehi." *International Studies Quarterly* 16:1 (1972): 59–82.

1679 Bernadotte, Count Folke. *Instead of Arms.* New York: Bonniers, 1948.

1680 ———. *To Jerusalem.* London: Hodder & Stoughton, 1951.

1681 Hamzeh, Fuad S. "The U.N. Conciliation Commission for Palestine." *Middle East Forum* 40:2 (Feb.–Mar. 1964): 35–36.

1682 ———. *United Nations Conciliation Commission for Palestine, 1949–1967.* Beirut: Institute for Palestine Studies, 1968.

1683 Hewins, Ralph. *Count Folke Bernadotte: His Life and Works.* Minneapolis, Minnesota: Denison, 1950.

1684 "A Tribute to Count Folke Bernadotte: Special Memorial Issue." *Arab World* 14:9 (Sept. 1968): 1–12.

Armistice

1685 Haupert, J. S. "Political Geography of the Israeli-Syrian Boundary Dispute, 1949–1967." *Professional Geographer* 21:3 (May 1969): 163–71.

1686 Jabbarah, 'Abidin. *The Armistice in International Law*. Beirut: Palestine Liberation Organization Research Center, 1965.

J / British Policies: An Overview

Britain in the Middle East

1687 Barman, T. "Britain—The Middle East Scapegoat?" *World Today* 23 (July 1967): 275–78.

1688 *British Interests in the Mediterranean and the Middle East.* New York: Oxford University Press, 1958.

1689 Buchan, A. "A Sea of Troubles." *Round Table* 243 (July 1971): 329–46.

1690 Bullard, Sir Reader. *Britain and the Middle East.* London: Longmans, Green, 1951.

1691 ———. "Britain and the Middle East." *Yale Review* 41 (Summer 1952): 539–49.

1692 Busch, Briton Cooper. *Britain and the Persian Gulf, 1894–1914.* Los Angeles: University of California Press, 1967.

1693 Hamlett, Bruce D. "A Comparative Analysis of British Foreign Relations: The Palestine War, 1947–1949, the Suez Crisis, 1956, the Arab-Israeli Crisis, 1967." Ph.D. dissertation, Claremont College and Graduate School, 1971.

1694 Hodson, H. V. "British Interests in the Middle East." *Listener* (Jan. 20, 1949): 85–86.

1695 Johns, R. "Britain and the Middle East." *Middle East International* (Jan. 1973): 10–11.

1696 Liddell Hart, B. H. "Can We Defend the Middle East?" *Military Review* 31 (Dec. 1951): 30–36.

1697 MacLean, Donald. *British Foreign Policy: The Years since Suez.* New York: Stein & Day, 1970.

1698 Mansfield, P. "Britain and the Middle East." *Venture* 20:9 (Oct. 1968): 14–16.

1699 Marriott, J. A. R. *The Eastern Question: An Historical Study in European Diplomacy.* Oxford: Oxford University Press, 1917.

1700 Medlicott, William Norton. *Bismarck, Gladstone, and the Concert of Europe.* London: Athlone Press, 1956.

1701 Monroe, Elizabeth. *Britain's Moment in the Middle East, 1914–1956.* Baltimore: Johns Hopkins Press, 1963.

1702 ———. "British Interests in the Middle East." *Middle East Journal* 2 (Apr. 1948): 129–46.

1703 Saundby, Robert. "Britain and the Middle East." *Military Review* 33 (Sept. 1953): 106–9.

1704 Searight, Sarah. *The British in the Middle East.* New York: Atheneum, 1970.

1705 Spears, Sir E. L. "The Middle East and our Policy There." *Royal Central Asian Journal* 32 (May 1945): 156–65.

1706 Williams, Ann. *Britain and France in the Middle East and North Africa, 1914–1967.* New York: St. Martin's Press, 1968.

1707 Wilmington, Martin W. *The Middle East Supply Center.* Albany: State University of New York Press, 1971.

1708 ———. "The Middle East Supply Center: A Reappraisal." *Middle East Journal* 6 (Spring 1952): 144–66.

Britain & Palestine

1709 Buzzard, A. "Israel, the Arabs, and British Responsibilities." *World Today* 27 (July 1971): 310–18.

1710 Kimche, Jon. "What Is a Pro-Arab Policy?" *Asian Affairs* 58 (June 1971): 140–46.

1711 Nutting, A. "Britain and Palestine: A Crime or a Blunder?" *Middle East International* (Nov. 1972): 20–22.

1712 Parkinson, Sir Cosmo. *The Colonial Office from Within: 1909–1945.* London: Faber & Faber, 1947.

1713 Simonhoff, Harry. *Under Strange Skies.* New York: Philosophical Library, 1953.

1714 Sousa, N. *British Interests in Palestine, 1800–1901.* London: Oxford University Press, 1961.

1715 Sykes, Christopher. *Cross Roads to Israel: Palestine from Balfour to Bevin.* London: New English Library, 1967.

1716 Tibawi, A. L. "British Interests in Palestine." *Royal Central Asian Journal* 42 (Jan. 1955): 70–79.

Britain & the Arabs

1717 Barbour, Nevill. "England and the Arabs." *Royal Central Asian Journal* 52 (Apr. 1965): 102–15.

1718 Glubb, John. "Britain and the Arabs." *Royal Central Asian Journal* 46 (July–Oct. 1959): 232–41.

1719 Harrigan, Anthony. "Aden: Strategic Crossroads." *Military Review* 47 (Oct. 1967): 42–47.

1720 King, Gillian. *Imperial Outpost—Aden: Its Place in British Strategic Policy.* London: Oxford University Press, 1964.

1721 Seton-Williams, M. V. *Britain and the Arab States.* London: Luzac, 1948.

1722 Toynbee, Arnold. "Britain and the Arabs: The Need for a New Start." *International Affairs* 40 (Oct. 1964): 638–45.

1723 "Treaty of Alliance between His Majesty in Respect of the United Kingdom of Great Britain and Northern Ireland and His Majesty the King of the Hashimite Kingdom of Trans-Jordan [Document]." *Middle East Journal* 2 (Oct. 1948): 469–73.

VI / ARAB-ISRAELI WARS

A / Military Developments, 1948–1955

1724 Abu-Jaber, F. S. "The Egyptian Revolution and the Middle East Defense, 1952–1955." *Middle East Forum* 45:4 (1969): 25–56.

1725 Allon, Yigal. *The Making of Israel's Army.* London: Vallentine, Mitchell, 1970.

1726 Barnes, Wyatt E. "Changing Trends in the Mediterranean Balance of Power, 1935–1957." *U.S. Naval Institute Proceedings* 84 (Mar. 1958): 53–61.

1727 Falls, Cyril. "Communist Arms for Egypt." *Illustrated London News* (Oct. 15, 1955): 652.

1728 Hoskins, Halford L. "Some Aspects of the Security Problem in the Middle East." *American Political Science Review* 47 (Mar. 1953): 188–98.

1729 Kagan, Col. Benjamin. *The Secret Battle for Israel.* Cleveland, Ohio: World, 1966.

1730 Lehrman, Hal. "The Arabs, Israel, and Near East Defense." *Commentary* 14 (Dec. 1952): 563–74.

1731 ———. "Western Self-Interest and Israeli Self-Defense." *Commentary* 21 (May 1956): 401–8.

1732 Leopold, Louis E., Jr. "The Cyprus Bastion." *U.S. Naval Institute Proceedings* 78 (Mar. 1952): 257–63.

150 / ARAB-ISRAELI WARS

1733   Lias, Godfrey. *Glubb's Legion*. London: Evans, 1956.

1734   "New Egypt Displays Its Power." *Life* (Apr. 16, 1956): 29–34.

1735   Raleigh, J. S. "The West and the Defense of the Middle East." *Middle Eastern Affairs* 6 (June–July 1955): 177–84.

1736   Rivlin, Lt. Col. Gershon. *Israel Defense Army, 1948–1958: A Pictorial Review*. New York: Taplinger, 1963.

1737   Safran, Nadav. *From War to War: The Arab-Israeli Confrontation, 1948–1967*. New York: Pegasus, 1969.

1738   Slater, Leonard. *The Pledge*. New York: Simon & Schuster, 1970.

1739   Spain, James W. "Middle East Defense: A New Approach." *Middle East Journal* 8 (Summer 1954): 251–66.

B / Suez-Sinai War, 1956

History of Suez Canal

1740   Avram, Benno. *The Evolution of the Suez Canal Status from 1869 up to 1956, a Historico-Juridical Study*. Paris: Librairie Minard, 1958.

1741   Baxter, R. R. *The Law of International Waterways, with Particular Regard to Interoceanic Canals*. Cambridge, Massachusetts: Harvard University Press, 1964.

1742   El-Behairy, M. "The Suez Canal: A Symbol of Power." *Arab World* 15:6 (June 1969): 19–23.

1743   Farnie, D. A. *East and West of Suez: The Suez Canal in History, 1854–1956*. Oxford: Clarendon Press, 1969.

1744   Fletcher, M. E. "The Suez Canal and World Shipping, 1869–1914." *Journal of Economic History* 18 (Dec. 1958): 556–73.

1745   Hallberg, Charles. *The Suez Canal*. New York: Columbia University Press, 1931.

1746 Kinross, Lord. *Between Two Seas: The Creation of the Suez Canal*. New York: Morrow, 1969.

1747 Marlowe, John. *World Ditch: The Making of the Suez Canal*. New York: Macmillan, 1964.

1748 Mezerik, A. G. *The Suez Canal: 1956 Crisis–1967 War*. New York: International Review Service, 1969.

1749 Obieta, J. A. *The International Status of the Suez Canal*. The Hague: Nijhoff, 1960.

1750 Pudney, John. *Suez: De Lesseps' Canal*. New York: Praeger, 1969.

1751 Schonfield, Hugh J. *The Suez Canal: In Peace and War, 1869–1969*. Coral Gables, Florida: University of Miami Press, 1969.

1752 ———. *The Suez Canal in World Affairs*. New York: Constellation, 1952.

1753 Society of Comparative Legislation and International Law. *The Suez Canal: A Selection of Documents Relating to the International Status of the Suez Canal and the Position of the Suez Canal Company, 30 November 1854–26 July 1956*. London, 1956.

1754 "The Suez Canal." *Overseas Review* 62 (May 1971): 10–13.

1755 Watt, D. C. *Britain and the Suez Canal*. London: Oxford University Press, 1956.

1756 Wilson, Arnold. *The Suez Canal: Its Past, Present and Future*. London: Oxford University Press, 1939.

Aswan Dam

1757 "Aswan High Dam—Statement by the United States, July 19, 1956 [Document]." *Middle Eastern Affairs* 7 (Aug.–Sept. 1956): 298–99.

1758 "Beyond Aswan." *Economist* (May 21, 1960): 762–65.

1759   "The Dam U.S. Wouldn't Build." *U.S. News & World Report* (Dec. 29, 1969): 66–68.

1760   "Egypt's Hopes Rise with the Aswan Dam." *Fortune* (Jan. 1967): 128–35.

1761   El Sabban, Gamil. "The Aswan High Dam." *Middle Eastern Affairs* 6 (Dec. 1955): 383–89.

1762   Feiner, Leon. "Economic Review: The Aswan Dam Development Project." *Middle East Journal* 6 (Autumn 1952): 464–67.

1763   Greener, Leslie. *High Dam over Nubia.* New York: Viking, 1962.

1764   "The High Dam Project." *Economist* (July 28, 1956): 295.

1765   Joesten, Joachim. "Nasser's Daring Dream: The Aswan High Dam." *World Today* 16 (Feb. 1960): 55–63.

1766   Little, Tom. "The High Dam." *Middle East Forum* 39:5 (May 1963): 17–21.

1767   ———. *High Dam at Aswan: The Subjugation of the Nile.* New York: John Day, 1965.

1768   Nasser, Abdul. "Speech at Alexandria, July 26, 1956." *U.S. News & World Report* (Aug. 17, 1956): 75–77.

1769   Shibl, Yusuf. *The Aswan High Dam.* Beirut: Arab Institute for Research and Publishing, 1971.

1770   "Soviet-Egyptian Pact on Aswan Dam, December 27, 1958 [Text]." *Middle Eastern Affairs* 10 (Feb. 1959): 78–79.

1771   Stewart, Desmond. "New Wonder of the Nile." *Nation* (June 27, 1959): 573–74.

Suez Canal Nationalization

1772   "Anglo-Egyptian Agreement Regarding the Suez Canal Base [Document]." *Middle East Journal* 8 (Autumn 1954): 460.

1773 Berding, Andrew H. *Dulles on Diplomacy*. Princeton, New Jersey: Van Nostrand, 1965.

1774 "A Challenge to Law." *Round Table* 184 (Sept. 1956): 307–11.

1775 Cherson, Randolph. "The Anglo-Egyptian Question." *Middle East Journal* 7 (Autumn 1953): 456–83.

1776 Comstock, Alzada. "Egypt: Nationalism Threatens the Canal." *Current History* 21 (July 1951): 24–27.

1777 "The Future of the Suez Canal Zone." *Round Table* 171 (June 1953): 220–27.

1778 Hanna, Paul H. "The Anglo-Egyptian Negotiations of 1950–1952." *Middle Eastern Affairs* 3 (Aug. 1952): 213–40.

1779 Horrocks, Gen. Brian. "Middle East Defense—A British View." *Middle Eastern Affairs* 6 (Feb. 1955): 33–41.

1780 Hoskins, Halford L. "The Guardianship of the Suez Canal: A View of Anglo-Egyptian Relations." *Middle East Journal* 4 (Apr. 1950): 143–54.

1781 Hourani, Albert. "The Anglo-Egyptian Agreement: Some Causes and Implications." *Middle East Journal* 9 (Summer 1955): 239–55.

1782 Koburger, Charles W., Jr. "The Legal Background to the Suez Crisis." *U.S. Naval Institute Proceedings* 83 (Mar. 1957): 315–20.

1783 L., T. R. "Britain, Egypt, and the Canal Zone since July 1952." *World Today* 10 (May 1954): 186–97.

1784 Longgood, William F. *The Suez Story: Key to the Middle East*. New York: Greenberg, 1957.

1785 Robertson, Terrence. *Crisis: The Inside Story of the Suez Conspiracy*. New York: Atheneum, 1965.

1786 Shwadran, Benjamin. "Egypt before the Security Council." *Middle Eastern Affairs* 2 (Dec. 1951): 383–400.

1787   Siegfried, Andre. "The Suez: International Roadway." *Foreign Affairs* 31 (July 1953): 605–18.

1788   U.S. Department of State. *The Suez Canal Problem: July 26–September 22, 1956.* Washington, D.C.: U.S.G.P.O., Oct. 1956.

1956 Suez Crisis

1789   Adams, Michael. *Suez and After: Year of Crisis.* Boston: Beacon, 1958.

1790   Azar, Edward E. "Conflict Escalation and Conflict Reduction in an International Crisis: Suez, 1956." *Journal of Conflict Resolution* 16:2 (June 1972): 183–201.

1791   Barker, A. J. *Suez: The Seven Day War.* New York: Praeger, 1964.

1792   Childers, Erskine B. *The Road to Suez: A Study of Western-Arab Relations.* London: Macgibbon & Kee, 1962.

1793   Eayrs, James. *The Commonwealth and Suez: A Documentary Survey.* London: Oxford University Press, 1964.

1794   Finer, Herman. *Dulles Over Suez: The Theory and Practice of His Diplomacy.* Chicago: Quadrangle, 1964.

1795   Love, Kennett. *Suez: The Twice Fought War: A History.* New York: McGraw-Hill, 1969.

1796   Nutting, Anthony. *No End of a Lesson.* New York: Potter, 1967.

1797   Perlmann, M. "Between the Devil and the Deep Red Sea." *Middle Eastern Affairs* 7 (Dec. 1956): 425–35.

1798   Shepilov, D. T. *The Suez Problem.* Moscow: Foreign Languages Publishing House, 1956.

1799   Suleiman, M. "An Evaluation of Middle East News Coverage in Seven American News-Magazines, July–December 1956." *Arab Journal* 4:2–4 (1967): 63–75.

1800 Thomas, Hugh. *Suez*. New York: Harper & Row, 1969.

1801 U.S. Department of State. *The Suez Problem, July 26-September 22, 1956: A Documentary Publication*. Washington, D.C.: U.S.G.P.O., 1956.

1802 ———. *United States Policy in the Middle East, September 1954-June 1957: Documents*. Washington, D.C.: U.S.G.P.O., 1957.

1803 ———. *United States Policy in the Middle East, September 1956-June 1957: Documents*. Washington, D.C.: U.S.G.P.O., 1957.

1804 Wint, Guy, and Peter Calvocoressi. *Middle East Crisis*. Baltimore: Penguin, 1957.

Prelude to November 1956

1805 Abuetan, Barid. "East-West Middle East Policies." *Middle Eastern Affairs* 7 (Aug.-Sept. 1956): 269-85.

1806 Dayan, Maj. Gen. Moshe. "Israel's Border and Security Problem." *Foreign Affairs* 33 (Jan. 1955): 250-67.

1807 Glubb, John Bagot. "Glubb Tells How Our Mid-East Enemies Work." *Life* (Feb. 16, 1956): 145-56.

1808 Hutchison, Cmdr. E. H. *Violent Truce*. New York: Devin-Adair, 1956.

1809 Tsur, Jacob. *Prélude à Suez: Journal d'une Ambassade, 1953-1956*. Paris: Presses de la Cité, 1968.

1810 Weinberger, Siegbert J. "The Suez Canal in Anglo-Egyptian Relations." *Middle Eastern Affairs* 1 (Dec. 1950): 347-56.

Israel's Sinai Campaign

1811 Abi Mershed, Walid. *Israeli Withdrawal from Sinai*. Beirut: Institute for Palestine Studies, 1966.

1812 Childers, Erskine B. "The Sinai War, 1956." *Arab Journal* 1:2-3 (1964): 68-82.

1813 Dayan, Moshe. *Diary of the Sinai Campaign.* New York: Schocken, 1967.

1814 Eban, Abba. *The Voice of Israel.* New York: Horizon, 1957.

1815 Ereli, Eliezer. "The Bat Galim Case before the Security Council." *Middle Eastern Affairs* 6 (Apr. 1955): 108–17.

1816 Fall, Bernard B. "The Two Sides of the Sinai Campaign." *Military Review* 37 (July 1957): 3–23.

1817 Gordon, Cyrus H. "The Problem of Israel." *Current History* 30 (June 1956): 347–52.

1818 Henriques, Robert. *100 Hours to Suez.* New York: Viking, 1957.

1819 Israel. Army. General Headquarters. Historical Branch. *The Sinai Campaign.* Tel Aviv, n.d.

1820 Marshall, S. L. A. *Sinai Victory.* New York: Morrow, 1967.

1821 O'Ballance, Edgar. *The Sinai Campaign, 1956.* London: Faber & Faber, 1959.

1822 Stock, Ernest. *Israel on the Road to Sinai 1949–1956.* Ithaca, New York: Cornell University Press, 1967.

British & French Intervention

1823 "After the Cease-Fire." *Round Table* 185 (Dec. 1956): 3–7.

1824 Barjot, P. "Réflexions sur les opérations de Suez 1956." *Revue de défense nationale* 22 (Dec. 1966): 1911–24.

1825 Beaufre, Andre. *The Suez Expedition, 1956.* New York: Praeger, 1970.

1826 Bernard, Edward Fergusson. *The Watery Maze: The Story of Combined Operations.* London: Collins, 1961.

1827 Bess, Demaree. "How Our Allies Tricked Us." *Saturday Evening Post* (Apr. 20, 1957): 23.

1828   Bromberger, M. and S. *Secrets of Suez*. London, 1957.

1829   Byford-Jones, W. *Oil on Troubled Waters*. Hollywood-by-the-Sea, Florida: Transatlantic Arts, 1957.

1830   Cavanaugh, Sandy. *Airborne to Suez*. London: Kimber, 1965.

1831   Clark, D. M. J. *Suez Touchdown: A Soldier's Tale*. London: Davies, 1964.

1832   Eden, Sir Anthony. *Full Circle: The Memoirs of Anthony Eden*. Boston: Houghton Mifflin, 1960.

1833   ———. *The Suez Crisis of 1956*. Boston: Beacon, 1968.

1834   Epstein, Leon D. *British Politics in the Suez Crisis*. Urbana: University of Illinois Press, 1964.

1835   Glubb, John. "Anglo-Arab Relations." *Arab World* 2:8 (July 1956): 7–10.

1836   Johnson, Paul. *The Suez War*. New York: Greenberg, 1957.

1837   "The Jordan coup d'etat: March 1st, 1956." *History Today* (London) 7 (Jan. 1957): 3–10.

1838   Knight, M. M. "The Algerian Revolt: Some Underlying Factors." *Middle East Journal* 10 (Autumn 1956): 355–67.

1839   Leulliette, Pierre. *St. Michael and the Dragon: Memoirs of a Paratrooper*. Boston: Houghton Mifflin, 1964.

1840   Lichtheim, George. "Why England and France Intervened." *Commentary* 22 (Dec. 1956): 507–11.

1841   Macmillan, Harold. *Riding the Storm, 1956–1959*. New York: Harper & Row, 1971.

1842   Nutting, Anthony. *I Saw for Myself*. New York: Doubleday, 1958.

1843 Schramm, Wilbur, ed. *One Day in the World's Press: Fourteen Great Newspapers on a Day of Crisis.* Stanford: Stanford University Press, 1959. [Nov. 2, 1956]

1844 Soustelle, Jacques. "France Looks at Her Alliances." *Foreign Affairs* 35 (Oct. 1956): 116–30.

1845 Stewart, James. "The Suez Operation." *U.S. Naval Institute Proceedings* 90 (Apr. 1964): 37–47.

United States, U.S.S.R., & Evacuation

1846 Adams, Sherman. *First Hand Report.* New York: Harper & Row, 1961.

1847 Eisenhower, Dwight D. *Waging Peace: 1956–1961.* Garden City, New York: Doubleday, 1965.

1848 Garrett, W. B. "The U.S. Navy's Role in the 1956 Suez Crisis." *Naval War College Review* 22:7 (Mar. 1970): 66–79.

1849 McSherry, James E. "Soviet Diplomacy from Stalin to Suez." *U.S. Naval Institute Proceedings* 83 (Dec. 1957): 1298–1307.

1850 Mones, Hussein. "Our Foreign Policy (U.S.): An Egyptian View." *Current History* 31 (Dec. 1956): 357–69.

1851 Murphy, Charles J. V. "Washington and the World." *Fortune* (Jan. 1957): 78–83.

1852 "United Nations General Assembly Resolution on the Recent Hostilities in Egypt." *Middle East Journal* 11 (Winter 1957): 92–94.

Aftermath

1853 Aldrich, Winthrop W. "The Suez Crisis: A Footnote to History." *Foreign Affairs* 45 (Apr. 1967): 541–52.

1854 Atyeo, Henry C. "Egypt since the Suez Crisis." *Middle Eastern Affairs* 9 (June–July 1958): 197–208.

1855 Baldwin, Hanson W. "Strategy of the Middle East." *Foreign Affairs* 35 (July 1957): 655–65.

1856 Bustani, Emile. *Doubts and Dynamite: The Middle East Today*. London: Allan Wingate, 1958.

1857 Calvocoressi, Peter. *Suez: Ten Years After*. New York: Pantheon, 1967.

1858 Childers, Erskine. "Notes on a Road Past Suez." *Middle East Forum* 39:3 (Mar. 1963): 15–18.

1859 Edgerton, Glen E. "An Engineer's View of the Suez Canal." *National Geographic* (Jan. 1957): 123–40.

1860 El Mallakh, Ragaei, and Carl McGuire. "The Economics of the Suez Canal under UAR Management." *Middle East Journal* 14 (Spring 1960): 125–40.

1861 Feis, Herbert. "Suez Scenario: A Lamentable Tale." *Foreign Affairs* 38 (July 1960): 598–612.

1862 Harlech, L. "Suez SNAFU, Skybolt SABU." *Foreign Policy* 2 (1971): 38–50.

1863 Hessler, William H. "There's No Substitute for Diplomacy or for Power." *U.S. Naval Institute Proceedings* 83 (July 1957): 691–97.

1864 Hinteroff, E. "The Middle East in the Perspective of a Decade." *Revue militaire générale* 3 (Mar. 1967): 379–92.

1865 Hoskins, Halford L. "The Suez Canal." *Current History* 33 (Nov. 1957): 257–62.

1866 Howard, H. N. "Postmortems on the Suez Conflict of 1956." *Orbis* 11:3 (1967): 903–7.

1867 Issawi, Charles. "Crusades and Current Crises in the Near East." *International Affairs* 33 (July 1957): 269–79.

1868 Lauterpacht, E., ed. *The Suez Canal Settlement*. New York: Praeger, 1960.

1869 Lewis, Bernard. "The Middle Eastern Reaction to Soviet Pressures." *Middle East Journal* 10 (Spring 1956): 125–37.

1870 Malone, Joseph J. "Germany and the Suez Crisis." *Middle East Journal* 20 (Winter 1966): 20–30.

1871 Nasser, Gamel Abdul. "Nasser Describes 'Failing' of Israel." *New York Times* (Dec. 5, 1956).

1872 Nolte, Richard H. "Year of Decision in the Middle East." *Yale Review* 46 (Dec. 1956): 228–44.

1873 Perlmann, M. "New Doctrine, Old Realities." *Middle Eastern Affairs* 8 (Mar. 1957): 97–107.

1874 "Report of Secretary General Hammarskjold on the Clearing of the Suez Canal [Document]." *Middle East Journal* 11 (Autumn 1957): 432–35.

1875 Sullivan, M. B. "Suez Ten Years After: Running Fine without the British." *Mid East* 6:8 (Oct. 1966): 6–9.

1876 Thayer, Philip W., ed. *Tension in the Middle East*. Baltimore: Johns Hopkins Press, 1958.

1877 "U.S. Senator Hubert H. Humphrey Talks with Nasser." *U.S. News & World Report* (May 17, 1957): 37–40.

C / Military Evolution to 1967

1878 Barkes, G., and J. Hutton. "Camouflage of Middle East Airfields." *Military Review* 33 (Jan. 1954): 99–107.

1879 Bell, J. Bowyer. *The Long War: Israel and the Arabs since 1946*. Englewood Cliffs, New Jersey: Prentice-Hall, 1969.

1880 Dayan, Moshe. "The Supreme Weapon." *Israel Magazine* 1:1 (1967): 5–13.

1881 Doty, L. L. "Jordan's Purchase of F-104 Adds to Jumble of Arab Arms Buildup." *Aviation Week & Space Technology* (May 23, 1966): 34.

1882 "Egypt's Aviation Industry." *Interavia* 21:11 (Nov. 1966): 1796-98.

1883 Elkashef, Ahmed R. *United States Policy towards the Arab-Israeli Arms Race, 1950-1966*. Palestine Monographs, no. 64. Beirut: Palestine Liberation Organization Research Center, Sept. 1969.

1884 Heiman, Leo. "Israel's Nahal Corps." *Military Review* 47 (July 1967): 65-70.

D / Six-Day War, 1967

1885 Abu-Lughod, Ibrahim, ed. *The Arab-Israeli Confrontation of June 1967: An Arab Perspective*. Evanston, Illinois: Northwestern University Press, 1970.

1886 Anabtawi, S. "The United Nations and the Middle East Conflict of 1967." *Arab World* 14:10-11 (Oct.-Nov. 1968): 53-58.

1887 Badeau, J. S. "The Arabs, 1967." *Atlantic Monthly* (Dec. 1967): 102-10.

1888 Bar-Zohar, Michael. *Embassies in Crisis: Diplomats and Demagogues behind the Six-Day War*. Englewood Cliffs, New Jersey: Prentice-Hall, 1971.

1889 Belyayev, I.; T. Kolesnichenko; and Y. Primakov. *The "Dove" Has Been Released*. JPRS 45, 468. Washington, D.C.: Joint Publications Research Service, 1968.

1890 Burrowes, R., and D. Muzzio. "The Road to the Six Day War: Aspects of an Enumerative History of Four Arab States and Israel, 1965–1967." *Journal of Conflict Resolution* 16:2 (June 1972): 211–26.

1891 Chesnoff, Richard; Edward Klein; and Robert Littell. *If Israel Lost the War*. New York: Coward-McCann, 1969.

1892 Gervasi, Frank. *The Case for Israel*. New York: Viking, 1967.

1893 Glubb, Sir John B. *The Middle East in Crisis: A Personal Interpretation*. London: Hodder & Stoughton, 1967.

1894 Harris, Frank. "The Arab People and the Arab-Israeli Conflict." *Middle East Forum* 43:2–3 (1967): 57–64.

1895 Howard, M., and R. E. Hunter. *Israel and the Arab World: The Crisis of 1967*. Adelphi Papers, no. 41. London: Institute for Strategic Studies, Oct. 1967.

1896 Johnson, Lyndon Baines. *The Vantage Point: Perspectives of the Presidency, 1963–1969*. New York: Holt, Rinehart & Winston, 1971.

1897 Lall, Arthur. *The UN and the Middle East Crisis, 1967*. New York: Columbia University Press, 1968.

1898 Laqueur, Walter Z. *The Road to Jerusalem: The Origins of the Arab-Israeli Conflict, 1967*. New York: Macmillan, 1968.

1899 Monroe, E. "British Bases in the Middle East: Assets or Liabilities?" *International Affairs* 42 (Jan. 1966): 24–34.

1900 Rosenaft, Menachem Z. *Not Backward to Belligerency: A Study of Events Surrounding the Six-Day War of June, 1967*. New York: Yoseloff, 1969.

1901 Safran, Nadav. "The Arab-Israeli Dispute in Perspective." *Current History* 53 (Dec. 1967): 261.

1902 Samo, Elias. *The June 1967 Arab-Israeli War: Miscalculation or Conspiracy*. Wilmette, Illinois: Medina University Press, 1971.

1903 Young, O. "Intermediaries and Interventionists: Third Parties in the Middle East Crisis." *International Journal* 23:1 (1967-1968): 52-73.

The Buildup, May 1967

1904 Alexander, Yonah, and Miriam L. Sweet. "The 'Just War' Concept and Its Application to the 1967 Arab-Israeli War." *International Problems* 9:3-4 (Nov. 1970): 34-39.

1905 Clark, Senator Joseph S. *War or Peace in the Middle East?* Report to the Committee on Foreign Relations, Senate, by Senator Joseph S. Clark, on a Study Mission to Greece, the United Arab Republic, Jordan and Israel. Washington, D.C.: U.S.G.P.O., 1967.

1906 "Countdown in the Middle East." *National Review* (May 30, 1967): 562-71.

1907 Dawn, C. Ernest. "The Egyptian Remilitarization of Sinai." *Journal of Contemporary History* 3:3 (July 1968): 201-24.

1908 Higgins, R. "The June War: The United Nations and Legal Background." *Journal of Contemporary History* 3:3 (July 1968): 253-73.

1909 "If Egypt Does Fight Israel—Who Wins?" *U.S. News & World Report* (June 12, 1967): 32-35.

1910 "Israel's War Motives in Serious Doubt." *Middle East International* (July 1972): 21-22.

1911 Kosut, Hal, ed. *Israel and the Arabs: The June 1967 War*. New York: Facts on File, 1968.

1912 Kraft, E. "New Light on the Six Day War: Judge Fortas' Secret Tip-off to Israel." *Jewish Observer and Middle East Review* (May 26, 1972): 14.

1913 Levenberg, A. "When War Is in the Air." *New Outlook* 10:5 (June 1967): 11-14.

1914 Nes, D. "American Policy in the Middle East: Before and After the June War." *Middle East Newsletter* 2:8 (Oct. 1968): 10–13.

1915 Schiff, Z. "The Dispute on the Syrian-Israeli Border." *New Outlook* 10:2 (Feb. 1967): 6–16.

1916 Sharabi, Hisham. "Prelude to War: The Crisis of May–June 1967." *Arab World* 14:10–11 (Oct.–Nov. 1968): 23–29.

1917 United Nations. *Report of the Secretary-General on the United Nations Emergency Force.* A/6672. July 12, 1967.

1918 ———. *Report of the Secretary-General on the Withdrawal of the United Nations Emergency Forces.* A/6730/Add.3. July 26, 1967.

1919 Yost, C. W. "The Arab-Israeli War: How It Began." *Foreign Affairs* 46:2 (Jan. 1968): 304–20.

United Nations Emergency Force (UNEF)

1920 Armstrong, Hamilton Fish. "The U.N. Experience in Gaza." *Foreign Affairs* 35 (July 1957): 600–619.

1921 Boyd, James. *United Nations Peace-Keeping Operations: A Military and Political Appraisal.* New York: Praeger, 1971.

1922 Burns, E. L. M. "The Withdrawal of UNEF and the Future of Peacekeeping." *International Journal* 23:1 (1967–1968): 1–17.

1923 Cohen, M. "The Demise of UNEF." *International Journal* 23:1 (1967–1968): 18–51.

1924 Darwish, I. "The United Nations Emergency Force: An Analysis of the Theory and Practice." *L'Egypte contemporaine* 63:349 (July 1972): 53–100.

1925 Gagnon, M. H. "Peace Forces and the Veto: The Relevance of Consent." *International Organization* 21 (1967): 812–36.

1926 Lauterpacht, E., ed. *The United Nations Emergency Force: Basic Documents.* New York: Praeger, 1960.

1927 "Why Did U Thant Pull Out?" *Reporter* (June 15, 1967): 18–23.

Straits of Tiran & Gulf of Aqaba

1928 Bloomfield, L. M. *Egypt, Israel and the Gulf of Aqaba in International Law.* Toronto: Carswell, 1957.

1929 Cagle, Malcolm W. "The Gulf of Aqaba: Trigger of Conflict." *U.S. Naval Institute Proceedings* 85 (Jan. 1959): 75–81.

1930 Colombos, C. John. *The International Law of the Sea.* London: Longmans, Green, 1954.

1931 Elath, E. *Israel and Elath: The Political Struggle for the Inclusion of Elath in the Jewish State.* London: Weidenfeld & Nicolson, 1967.

1932 Evron, Y. "Sharm-al-Shaikh." *Survival* 12 (Jan. 1970): 2–6.

1933 Halderman, John W., ed. "The Middle East Crisis: Test of International Law." *Law and Contemporary Problems* 33:1 (1968): 1–193.

1934 Hindle, P. "Aqaba: An Old Port Revived." *Geographical Journal* 132 (Mar. 1966): 64–67.

1935 Porter, Paul A. *The Gulf of Aqaba: An International Waterway. Its Significance to International Trade.* Washington, D.C.: Public Affairs, 1957.

1936 Reyner, Anthony S. "The Strait of Tiran and the Sovereignty of the Sea: A Geographical Review." *Middle East Journal* 21 (Summer 1967): 403–8.

1937 Salans, C. "Gulf of Aqaba and Strait of Tiran: Troubled Waters." *U.S. Naval Institute Proceedings* 94 (Dec. 1968): 54–62.

1938 Yaari, D. "Why Sharm el Sheikh Is Necessary." *New Middle East,* nos. 42–43 (Mar.–Apr. 1972): 26.

The War

1939 Atallah, R. "Six Jours d'irresponsabilité." *Jeune Afrique* (Aug. 6, 1967): 13–15.

1940 Barclay, Brig. Cyril N. "Israel at War." *Army* 21:9 (Sept. 1971): 40–45.

1941 Barer, S. *Israel's Six-Day War.* Tel Aviv: Israel University Press, 1967.

1942 Bar-on, Mordechai. *Israel Defense Forces: The Six-Day War.* New York: Chilton, 1971.

1943 Bashan, Raphael. *The Victory: Six Days in 1967.* Edited by O. Zmora. Chicago: Quadrangle, 1968.

1944 Beaufre, Gen. A. "Les enseignements opérationnels de la guerre isráelo-arabe." *Stratégie* (July–Sept. 1967): 27–36.

1945 Berkman, Ted. *Sabra: Israeli Portraits from the Six-Day War.* New York: Harper & Row, 1969.

1946 Blanchard, Allan E. "The 6 Day War." *Army* 17:8 (Aug. 1967): 24–26.

1947 Buchan, Alastair. "The Great Contingency." *Encounter* 29 (Aug. 1967): 3–6.

1948 Churchill, R. S. and W. S. *The Six Day War.* Boston: Houghton Mifflin, 1967.

1949 Dayan, David. *Strike First! A Battle History of Israel's Six-Day War.* New York: Pitman, 1968.

1950 Dayan, Yael. *Yael Dayan: Israel Journal, 1967.* New York: McGraw-Hill, 1967.

1951 Donovan, R. J. *Six Days in June (June 5–10, 1967): Israel's Fight for Survival.* New York: New American Library, 1967.

1952 Elon, Amos. "Letter from the Sinai Front." *Commentary* 44:2 (Aug. 1967): 60–68.

1953 Harbutt, C. "Eyewitness to War in the Holy Land." *National Geographic* (Dec. 1967): 782–97.

1954 Harkabi, Y. "Basic Factors in the Arab Collapse During the Six-Day War." *Orbis* 11:3 (1967): 677–91.

1955 Heiman, Leo. "War in the Middle East: An Israeli View." *Military Review* 47 (Sept. 1967): 56–66.

1956 Herzog, C., ed. *Six Day War.* Tel Aviv: Sifriat Maariv, 1967.

1957 Israel Ministry for Foreign Affairs. "Israel's War for Peace." *Israel* 9 (1967): 2–31.

1958 *Israel's Swift Victory.* Chicago: Time, June 1967. [Special *Life* edition]

1959 Keesing's Research Report. *The Arab-Israeli Conflict: The 1967 Campaign.* New York: Scribners, 1968.

1960 Kimche, David, and Dan Bawly. *The Sandstorm: The Arab-Israeli War of 1967: Prelude and Aftermath.* New York: Stein & Day, 1968.

1961 Koch, H. "June 1967: The Question of Aggression." *Arab World* 15:6 (June 1969): 10–13.

1962 Kotch, W. J. "The Six-Day War of 1967." *U.S. Naval Institute Proceedings* 94 (June 1968): 72–81.

1963 Liddell Hart, B. H. "Strategy of a War." *Military Review* 48 (Nov. 1968): 80–85.

1964 Marshall, S. L. A. *Swift Sword: The Historical Record of Israel's Victory, June 1967.* New York: American Heritage, 1967.

1965   O'Ballance, Edgar. *The Third Arab-Israeli War*. Hamden, Connecticut: Archon, 1972.

1966   Paz, Ury. *The Shortest War: Israel Fights for Survival*. Tel Aviv: Ramdor, 1967.

1967   Pepper, Curtis G. "Hawk of Israel." *New York Times Magazine* (July 9, 1967): 5.

1968   Shoemaker, R. "The Arab-Israeli War." *Military Review* 48 (Aug. 1968): 56–69.

1969   Stevenson, W. *Strike Zion!* New York: Bantam, 1967.

1970   Teveth, Shabtai. *The Tanks of Tammuz*. New York: Viking, 1969.

1971   Young, Peter. *The Israeli Campaign 1967*. London: Kimber, 1967.

Aftermath

1972   "The ABC's of Middle East Crisis. Arabs and Israel: The Case for Each Side." *U.S. News & World Report* (Oct. 30, 1967): 90–95.

1973   Abdel-Malik, A. "The Crisis in Nasser's Egypt." *New Left Review* 45 (Sept.–Oct. 1967): 67–81.

1974   Brown, Neville. *Has Israel Really Won?* London: Fabian Society, 1967.

1975   Carthew, Anthony. "Double-Think Egyptian Style." *New York Times Magazine* (Aug. 20, 1967): 19.

1976   ———. "There Is No False Courage Left in Egypt." *New York Times Magazine* (Dec. 3, 1967): 45.

1977   Carvely, A. "The Aftermath of the Six-Day War." *Arab World* 15:7–8 (July–Aug. 1969): 8–12.

1978   Cleveland, R. "The Arab-Israeli Problem as Compounded by the June '67 War." *Issues* 21:3 (1967): 31–35.

1979   Corditz, D. "But What Do We Do About the Arabs?" *Fortune* (Sept. 1, 1967): 75–79.

1980   Ginay, E. "Khartoum and Peace." *New Outlook* 10:7 (Sept.–Oct. 1967): 3–5.

1981   Hourani, C. "The Moment of Truth: Towards a Middle Eastern Dialogue—An Arab Speaks to the Arab World." *Encounter* 29:5 (Nov. 1967): 3–14.

1982   Israel. Ministry for Foreign Affairs. Division of Information. *Back to Normal Life: Israel Lays the Hopeful Foundations of an Era of Lasting Peace and Prosperity throughout the Middle East*. Jerusalem, 1967.

1983   Jalis, A. "Thoughts on Arab Defeat." *Islamic Literature* 13:10 (Oct. 1967): 53–60.

1984   Kanovsky, Eliyahu. "The Economic Aftermath of the Six Day War: UAR, Jordan and Syria." *Middle East Journal* 22 (Summer 1968): 278–96.

1985   ———. *The Economic Impact of the Six-Day War: Israel, the Occupied Territories, Egypt, Jordan*. New York: Praeger, 1970.

1986   Kazin, A. "In Israel: After the Triumph." *Harper's* (Nov. 1967): 72–85.

1987   Kenny, L. "The Aftermath of Defeat in Egypt." *International Journal* 23:1 (1967–1968): 97–108.

1988   Le Gassick, T. "Some Recent War-Related Arabic Fiction." *Middle East Journal* 25 (Autumn 1971): 491–505.

1989   "The Lesson of Suez Is Paying Off." *Business Week* (June 10, 1967): 37–38.

1990   Levenberg, Aliza. "Volunteers to Israel." *New Outlook* 10:7 (Sept.–Oct. 1967): 29–32.

1991   Lewis, B. "The Arab-Israeli War: The Consequences of Defeat." *Foreign Affairs* 46 (Jan. 1968): 321–35.

1992 Medzini, M. "Israel Five Years after the Six Day War." *Holy Cross Quarterly* 2 (1972): 34-36.

1993 "Middle East: After the Arab Defeat." *Atlantic Monthly* (Oct. 1967): 38.

1994 "The Oil Keeps Flowing." *Business Week* (July 8, 1967): 32.

1995 Perlmutter, A. "Assessing the Six-Day War." *Commentary* 49:1 (Jan. 1970): 71-75.

1996 Rejwan, N. "Impact of the June War on Arab Intellectuals." *New Outlook* 14:8 (Oct.-Nov. 1971): 25-34.

1997 Rovere, Richard H. "Letter from the United Nations." *New Yorker* (July 8, 1967): 67-73.

1998 Shapira, Avraham. *The Seventh Day: Soldiers' Talk about the Six-Day War.* New York: Scribners, 1970.

1999 Simpson, D. J. "Israel after Victory." *Current History* 53 (Dec. 1967): 341.

2000 "Situation in the Middle East." *U.N. Monthly Chronicle* 4 (July 1967): 3-80.

2001 Talmon, Jacob. *The Six Day War in Historical Perspective: Reflections on Jewish Statehood.* Rehovot: Weizmann, 1971.

2002 "U.N. Security Council Continues Consideration of the Crisis in the Near East." *U.S. Department of State Bulletin* (June 19, 1967): 920-29.

2003 U.S. Congress. House of Representatives. Committee on Foreign Affairs. Subcommittee on the Near East. Report: *The Continuing Near East Crisis.* 91st Cong., 1st sess., 1969.

Six-Day War: World Effects

2004 Dessouki, A. "Canadian Foreign Policy and the June War." *Middle East Forum* 45:3 (1969): 61-74.

2005 Deutscher, I. "On the Israeli-Arab War." *New Left Review* 44 (July–Aug. 1967,): 30–45.

2006 Laqueur, Walter Z. "Israel, the Arabs, and World Opinion." *Commentary* 44:2 (Aug. 1967): 49–59.

2007 Mates, L. "The War and the Palestine Problem." *Review of International Affairs* (Belgrade) (Nov. 20, 1970): 8–11.

2008 Roughton, Richard A. "Algeria and the June 1967 Arab-Israeli War." *Middle East Journal* 23 (Autumn 1969): 433–44.

The Great Powers & the Six-Day War

2009 Abu-Jaber, F. "United States Policy toward the June Conflict." *Arab World* 14:10–11 (Oct.–Nov. 1968): 67–71.

2010 Astakhov, S. "More about the Secret Springs of the Israeli Aggression." *International Affairs* (Moscow) (Oct. 1967): 33–40.

2011 Beaton, Leonard. "The Great Powers Abdicate." *International Journal* 23:1 (1967–1968): 74–81.

2012 Farbenstein, Leonard, and William S. Broomfield. *Report of Special Factfinding Mission to Israel.* Pursuant to H. Res. 179; Nov. 7, 1967. Washington, D.C., 1967.

2013 Howard, Harry N. "The U.S. in the 1967 Middle East Crisis." *Current History* 53 (Dec. 1967): 337.

2014 Jabara, A. "The American Left and the June Conflict." *Arab World* 14:10–11 (Oct.–Nov. 1968): 73–80.

2015 Landis, Lincoln. "Middle East Crises and the USSR." *World Affairs* 130:1 (Apr.–June 1967): 13–16.

E / Palestinian Resistance

2016 "ABC of the Palestine Question." *Arab Palestinian Resistance* 3:9 (Sept. 1971): 48–54.

2017 Abu-Lughod, Ibrahim. "Educating a Community in Exile: The Palestinian Experience." *Journal of Palestine Studies* 2:3 (1973): 94–111.

2018 Aruri, Naseer, ed. *The Palestinian Resistance to Israeli Occupation.* Monograph Series, no. 2. Wilmette, Illinois: Medina University Press, 1970.

2019 Bell, J. Bowyer. *The Myth of the Guerrilla: Revolutionary Theory and Malpractice.* New York: Knopf, 1971.

2020 Borodin, Nikolai. "The Palestinian Resistance Movement: A Soviet View." *New Middle East,* no. 51 (Dec. 1972): 27–28.

2021 Chaliand, Gerard. *The Palestinian Resistance.* Middlesex: Penguin, 1972.

2022 Cooley, John K. *Green March, Black September: The Story of the Palestinian Arabs.* London: Cass, 1973.

2023 Dinstein, Yoram. "The Legal Causes of 'Para-War' and Peace in the Middle East." *St. John's Law Review* 44 (Jan. 1970): 466–82.

2024 Friendly, A., Sr. "The Middle East: The Fedayeen." *Atlantic Monthly* (Sept. 1969): 12–20.

2025 Gendzier, I. "The Palestinian Revolution, Palestine, Fatah, the Jews, and Other Matters." *New Middle East,* no. 28 (Jan. 1971): 38–41.

2026 Harkabi, Y. "Scope and Limit of a Fedayeen Consensus." *Wiener Library Bulletin* 24:4 (1970–1971): 1–7.

2027 "How American Radicals See the Resistance Dilemma: A Discussion." *Journal of Palestine Studies* 1:4 (1972): 3–26.

2028 Hudson, Michael. "The Palestinian Resistance: Developments and Setbacks, 1967-71." *Journal of Palestine Studies* 1:3 (1972): 64-84.

2029 Ismael, Tareq Y. "The Palestinian Emergence and U.S. Foreign Policy." *Middle East Forum* 46:2-3 (1970): 65-71.

2030 Israel. Ministry for Foreign Affairs. Division of Information. Israel Information Center. *Accessories to Terror: The Responsibility of Arab Governments for the Organization of Terrorist Activities*. Middle East Information Series. Jerusalem, 1973.

2031 Jabber, Fuad. "The Arab Regimes and the Palestinian Revolution, 1967-71." *Journal of Palestine Studies* 2:2 (1973): 79-101.

2032 Mallison, W. T. and S. V. "The Juridical Characteristics of Palestinian Resistance: An Appraisal in International Law." *Journal of Palestine Studies* 2:2 (1973): 66-78.

2033 Mroue, Karim. "Arab National Liberation Movement." *World Marxist Review* 16 (Feb. 1973): 65-72.

2034 Mruhe, Kerim. "The Arab Liberation Movement." *World Marxist Review* 15 (Oct. 1972): 44.

2035 "The Palestinian Resistance Movement and the Arab-Israeli Conflict in Arabic Periodicals." *Journal of Palestine Studies* 1:2 (1972): 120-32.

2036 Quandt, William B. *Palestinian Nationalism: Its Political and Military Dimensions*. Santa Monica, California: RAND, R-782, 1971.

2037 Sharabi, H. "Palestinian Radicals and Political Settlement." *Middle East Newsletter* 5:5 (Aug.-Sept. 1971): 13-14.

2038 Sirhan, Bassem. *Palestinian Children: The Generation of Liberation*. Palestine Essays, no. 23. Beirut: Palestine Liberation Organization Research Center, Sept. 1970.

2039 Yodfat, A. "The Soviet Union and the Palestine Guerrillas." *Mizan* 11:1 (Jan.-Feb. 1969): 8-17.

Palestine Liberation Organization (PLO) to 1968

2040 Hasan, Saadat. "Why the Palestine Liberation Organization." *Arab Journal* 2:3 (1965): 3–7.

2041 Tannous, E. "The Palestine Liberation Organization." *Arab Journal* 3:3 (1966): 8–14.

Origins & Rise of Resistance, 1964–1970

2042 Al-Fattal, R. K. "Palestine Liberation Movement." *Islamic Review* 57:6 (June 1969): 33–36.

2043 "Arab Commandos: Growing Power in the Middle East." *U.S. News & World Report* (Nov. 24, 1969): 82–84.

2044 Denoyan, Gilbert. *El Fath Parle: Les Palestiniens contre Israël*. Paris: Editions Albin Michel, 1970.

2045 Dorsey, W. H., Jr. "Arab Commandos." *New Republic* (Nov. 22, 1969): 19–22.

2046 Gaspard, J. "Palestine: Who's Who Among the Guerrillas." *New Middle East*, no. 18 (Mar. 1970): 12–17.

2047 Grant, Z. B. "Commando Revolution: A Hundred Years' War in the Middle East?" *New Republic* (Jan. 24, 1970): 9–11.

2048 Harkabi, Yehoshafat. *Fedayeen Action and Arab Strategy*. Adelphi Papers, no. 53. London: Institute for Strategic Studies, Dec. 1968.

2049 ———. "The Position of the Palestinians in the Arab-Israeli Conflict and Their National Covenant (1968)." *Journal of International Law and Politics* 3:1 (Spring 1970).

2050 Hirst, D. "Force: The Faith of al Fatah." *Middle East Forum* 45:1–2 (1968): 113–16.

2051 Hudson, Michael. "The Palestinian Arab Resistance Movement: Its Significance in the Middle East Crisis." *Middle East Journal* 23 (Summer 1969): 291-307.

2052 Jargy, S. "War and Peace in Palestine." *International Affairs* (Moscow) (Mar. 1970): 114-21.

2053 Little, Shelby. "Fedayeen: Palestinian Commandos." *Military Review* 50 (Nov. 1970): 49-55.

2054 Little, Tom. "The Nature of the Palestine Resistance Movement." *Royal Central Asian Journal* 57 (June 1970): 157-69.

2055 Mertz, Robert Anton. "Why George Habash Turned Marxist." *Mid East* 11:4 (Aug. 1970): 31-36.

2056 Peretz, D. "Arab Palestine: Phoenix or Phantom?" *Foreign Affairs* 48 (Jan. 1970): 322-33.

2057 Schleifer, Abdullah. "Al Fatah Speaks: A Conversation with 'Abu Amar'." *Evergreen Review* (July 1968): 45.

2058 ———. "The Emergence of Fatah." *Arab World* 15:5 (May 1969): 16-20.

2059 Sharabi, Hisham. "Liberation or Settlement: The Dialectics of Palestinian Struggle." *Journal of Palestine Studies* 2:2 (1973): 33-48.

2060 ———. "Palestine Guerrillas: Their Credibility and Effectiveness." *Middle East Forum* 46:2-3 (1970): 19-64.

2061 Wren, C. "Revolt of the Arab Refugees: 'We'll Meet in Tel Aviv'." *Look* (May 13, 1969): 27-36.

2062 Yaari, Ehud. "Al-Fatah's Political Thinking." *New Outlook* 11:9 (Nov.-Dec. 1968): 20-33.

Jordanian Civil War, 1970-1971

2063 Antic, P. "Showdown with al Fatah." *Review of International Affairs* (Belgrade) (Mar. 5-20, 1972): 16-17.

2064 Brown, Neville. "After the Showdown: Jordan Is On the Move." *New Middle East*, no. 48 (Sept. 1972): 20–24.

2065 ———. "Jordanian Civil War." *Military Review* 51 (Sept. 1971): 38–48.

2066 ———. "Palestinian Nationalism and the Jordanian State." *World Today* 26 (Sept. 1970): 370–78.

2067 "Civil War in Jordan." *Mid East* 10:6 (Dec. 1970): 21–24.

2068 Haddad, W. "Jordan's Civil War of 1970–71 in Historical Perspective." *Illinois Quarterly* 34:1 (Sept. 1971): 43–53.

2069 Howard, H. N. "Jordan in Turmoil." *Current History* 62 (Jan. 1972): 14–19.

2070 Howard, N. F. "Jordan: The Commando State." *Current History* 58 (Jan. 1970): 16–20.

2071 Malawer, Stuart S. "United States Foreign Policy and International Law: The Jordanian Civil War and Air Piracy." *International Problems* 10:1–2 (June 1971): 31–40.

2072 Prlja, A. "The Jordanian Crisis and Intra-Arab Relations." *Review of International Affairs* (Belgrade) (July 5–20, 1970): 31–32.

2073 Sharabi, Hisham. "Palestine Resistance: Crisis and Reassessment." *Middle East Newsletter* 5:1 (Jan. 1971): 11–14.

2074 Sheehan, E. "In the Flaming Streets of Amman." *New York Times Magazine* (Sept. 27, 1970): 26.

Lebanon, the Resistance, & Israel

2075 Barakat, H. "Social Factors Influencing Attitudes of University Students in Lebanon towards the Palestinian Resistance Movement." *Journal of Palestine Studies* 1:1 (1971): 87–112.

2076 Buffum, W. "US Abstains on UN Resolution on Lebanese Complaint against Israel." *U.S. Department of State Bulletin* (Oct. 5, 1970): 402–3.

2077 Entelis, J. "Palestinian Revolutionism in Lebanese Politics: The Christian Response." *Muslim World* 62 (Oct. 1972): 335-51.

2078 Gendzier, I. "Lebanon and the Palestinians." *New Outlook* 12:2 (Feb. 1969): 2-27.

2079 Hudson, M. "Fedayeen Are Forcing Lebanon's Hand." *Mid East* 10:1 (Feb. 1970): 7-15.

2080 "The Hundred Years' War."*Economist* (Nov. 1, 1969): 14-16.

2081 Muftic, M. "A Background Study of the Recent Lebanese Tussle with the Fath Organization."*Islamic Review* 57:10 (Oct. 1969): 14-17.

2082 "Security Council Calls on Israel to Refrain from Military Acts against Lebanon." *U.N. Monthly Chronicle* 9 (July 1972): 10-33.

2083 "Security Council Demands Israel Halt Military Action against Lebanon and Withdraw Forces." *U.N. Monthly Chronicle* 9 (Mar. 1972 : 65-86.

2084 Stevens, G. "Beirut." *Atlantic Monthly* (Feb. 1970): 2-32.

2085 Suleiman, Michael W. "Crisis and Revolution in Lebanon." *Middle East Journal* 26 (Winter 1972): 11-24.

2086 "U.S. Calls for End to Cycle of Violence on Israel-Lebanon Border." *U.S. Department of State Bulletin* (June 8, 1970): 726-30.

2087 Wolf, John B. "Shadow on Lebanon." *Current History* 58 (Jan. 1970): 21-26.

Guerrillas to World Terrorism

2088 Arafat, Y. "The Struggle in Palestine." *Review of International Affairs* (Belgrade) (Apr. 5, 1972): 4-5.

2089 Ashhab, N. "To Overcome Crisis of Palestine Resistance Movement." *World Marxist Review* 15 (May 1972): 71-78.

2090 Boskovic, M. "What is Going On in the Palestine Resistance Movement?" *Review of International Affairs* (Belgrade) (May 20, 1972): 14–19.

2091 Evans, A. "Aircraft Hijacking: What Is Being Done." *American Journal of International Law* 67 (Oct. 1973): 641–71.

2092 ———. "Aircraft Hijacking: What Is To Be Done?" *American Journal of International Law* 66 (Oct. 1972): 819–22.

2093 Franjieh, S. "How Revolutionary Is the Palestinian Resistance? A Marxist Interpretation." *Journal of Palestine Studies* 1:2 (1972): 52–60.

2094 Heradstveit, D. "A Profile of the Palestine Guerrillas." *Cooperation and Conflict* 7:1 (1972): 13–36.

2095 Kuroda, Yasumasa. "Young Palestinian Commandos in Political Socialization Perspective." *Middle East Journal* 26 (Summer 1972): 253–70.

2096 Lehm, W. "The Palestinians: Refugees to Guerrillas." *Middle East Forum* 48:1 (1972): 27–44.

2097 Nakhleh, Emile A. "The Anatomy of Violence: Theoretical Reflections on Palestinian Resistance." *Middle East Journal* 25 (Spring 1971): 180–200.

2098 O'Ballance, Edgar. "Some Arab Guerrilla Problems." *Military Review* 52 (Oct. 1972): 27–34.

2099 Pryce-Jones, David. *The Face of Defeat: Palestinian Refugees and Guerrillas*. London: Weidenfeld & Nicolson, 1972.

2100 "Resistance Operations During August 1971." *Arab Palestinian Resistance* 3:9 (Sept. 1971): 54–58.

2101 Rouleau, E. "The Wandering Palestinians: Conflict, Terror, Disarray." *New Outlook* 16:2 (Feb. 1973): 2–8.

2102 Weller, Jac. "Military Aspects of the Palestinian Collapse." *Military Review* 53 (July 1973): 56–67.

2103 Wolf, John B. "The Palestinian Resistance Movement." *Current History* 60 (Jan. 1971): 26–31.

2104 Yaari, Ehud. "The Decline of al-Fatah." *Midstream* 17:5 (May 1971): 3–12.

Israeli Counteractions

2105 "Attacks on Palestinians." *Middle East International* (Feb. 1973): 20–23.

2106 Hochman, L. "Israel and the Arab Revolution." *Arab World* 15:6 (June 1969): 14–17.

2107 "Israel's Counter-Terror." *Israel and Palestine* 19 (Mar. 1973): 1–9.

2108 Lamar, Lt. Col. Kirby. "R & D for Counterinsurgency in the Middle East." *Military Review* 47 (Mar. 1967): 35–40.

2109 O'Ballance, Edgar. "Israeli Counter-Guerrilla Measures." *Journal of the Royal United Services Institute for Defense Studies* 117 (Mar. 1972): 47–52.

2110 Razzouk, Ass'ad; Ezzeldin Foda; and Elias W. Hanna. *Zionism and Arab Resistance*. Palestine Monographs, no. 54. Beirut: Palestine Liberation Organization Research Center, Feb. 1969.

2111 "Security Council Condemns Israel for Diversion of Civilian Airliner." *U.S. Department of State Bulletin* (Sept. 10, 1973): 356–58.

2112 Silverburg, S. "The Israeli Reaction to Terrorism." *New Outlook* 12:1 (Jan. 1969): 41–43.

2113 *Who Are the Terrorists? Aspects of Zionist Israeli Terrorism*. Monograph Series, no. 33. Beirut: Institute for Palestine Studies and the Arab Women's Information Committee, 1972.

Black September

2114 Graham, R. "The Effect of Munich on the Palestinian Dilemma." *Middle East International* (Nov. 1972): 8-10.

2115 Hottinger, A. "Black September." *Swiss Review of World Affairs* 22:7 (Aug. 1972): 5.

2116 Wolf, John B. "Black September: Militant Palestinianism." *Current History* 64 (Jan. 1973): 5-8.

2117 Yahalom, Dan. *File on Arab Terrorism*. Jerusalem: Carta, 1973.

F / Military Evolution Since the Six-Day War

The Arms Balance

2118 Brown, Neville. "The Real Capabilities of Soviet and U.S. Weapons in the Middle East and How the Two Sides Use Them." *New Middle East,* no. 20 (May 1970): 11-14.

2119 Cottrell, Alvin J. "The Role of Air Power in the Military Balance of the Middle East: The Function of the Phantom." *New Middle East,* no. 19 (Apr. 1970): 12-16.

2120 DeVore, Ronald M. "The Arab-Israeli Military Balance: New Perspectives." *Military Review* 53 (Nov. 1973): 65-71.

2121 Douglas-Home, C. "The Balance of Power." *Middle East International* (Jan. 1972): 7-11.

2122 Duchene, François. "The Arms Trade and the Middle East." *Political Quarterly* 44 (Oct.-Dec. 1973): 453-65.

2123 Evron, Y. "French Arms Policy in the Middle East." *World Today* 26 (Feb. 1970): 82-90.

2124 ——, and N. Safran. "Consequences of War on the Indian Sub-Continent." *New Middle East,* no. 40 (Jan. 1972): 15–19.

2125 Heiman, L. "Armored Forces in the Middle East." *Military Review* 48 (Nov. 1968): 11–19.

2126 Hishmeh, G. "The Military Balance of Power in the Middle East: An American View." *Journal of Palestine Studies* 1:3 (1972): 3–16.

2127 Hurewitz, J. C. *Changing Military Perspectives in the Middle East.* Santa Monica, California: RAND, RM–6355, 1970.

2128 ——. *Middle East Politics: The Military Dimension.* New York: Praeger, 1968.

2129 Kemp, Geoffrey. "Arms Sales and Arms Control in the Developing Countries." *World Today* 22 (Sept. 1966): 386–95.

2130 ——. *Arms and Security: The Egypt-Israel Case.* Adelphi Papers, no. 52. London: Institute for Strategic Studies, Sept. 1969.

2131 ——. *Arms Traffic and Third World Conflicts.* International Conciliation, no. 577. New York: Carnegie, Mar. 1970.

2132 ——. "Controlling Arms in the Middle East: Some Preliminary Observations." *World Today* 23 (July 1967): 285–92.

2133 Kirshner, S. "Report on Israel's Budding Arms Industry." *New Outlook* 16:7 (Sept. 1973): 43–49.

2134 "Middle East Crisis: Arms for Arabs." *Gallup Opinion Index.* Report 103 (Jan. 1974): 15.

2135 "Middle East Crisis: Arms for Israel." *Gallup Opinion Index,* Report 103 (Jan. 1974): 14.

2136 Milstein, Jeffrey S. *Soviet and American Influences on the Arab-Israeli Arms Race: A Quantitative Analysis.* New Haven, Connecticut: Yale University Press, 1970.

2137 Newcombe, Hanna. "The Case for an Arms Embargo." *War/Peace Report* 11 (Mar. 1971): 17–19.

2138 O'Ballance, Edgar. "Some Israeli Defense Problems." *Army Quarterly and Defence Journal* 103 (Jan. 1973): 152–81.

2139 Pa'il, Meir. "The Moral Use of Arms." *New Outlook* 16:2 (Feb. 1973): 30–41.

2140 Reese, H. "The Search for Equilibrium in the Middle East." *Military Review* 48 (Apr. 1968): 29–40.

2141 Slonim, S. "U.S., the Indian-Pakistani War and the Middle East." *Midstream* 18:3 (Mar. 1972): 3–7.

2142 Stockholm International Peace Research Institute [SIPRI]. *The Arms Trade with the Third World.* New York: Humanities Press, 1971.

2143 Tahitnen, Dale R. *The Arab-Israeli Military Balance Today.* A.E.I. Foreign Affairs Studies, no. 9. Washington, D.C.: American Enterprise Institute for Public Policy Research, Nov. 1973.

2144 Whetten, L. "Sadat's Strategic Options in the Canal War." *World Today* 29 (Feb. 1973): 58–67.

2145 ———. "Strategic Parity in the Middle East." *Military Review* 50 (Sept. 1970): 24–31.

2146 Zahlan, A. "The Science and Technology Gap in the Arab-Israeli Conflict." *Journal of Palestine Studies* 1:3 (1972): 17–36.

Israel Defense Forces (IDF)

Doctrine & Tactics

2147 Chapra, M. "Israel Beyond Cease-Fire." *Military Review* 51 (Feb. 1971): 12–19.

2148   Dayan, Moshe. "Israel: Military Strength and Political Confidence." *Survival* 14 (Nov.–Dec. 1972): 280–83.

2149   Heymont, Irving. "Israeli Career Officer Corps." *Military Review* 48 (Oct. 1968): 13–19.

2150   ———. "Israeli Defense Forces." *Military Review* 47 (Feb. 1967): 37–47.

2151   ———. "The Israeli Naval Program." *Middle East Journal* 21 (Summer 1967): 314–24.

2152   ———. "The Israeli Reserves: Minutemen of the Desert." *Army* 23:6 (July 1973): 14–19.

2153   Lowenstein, R. "Military Press Censorship in Israel." *Military Review* 50 (Feb. 1970): 3–9.

2154   Marshall, S. L. A. "The Army of Israel." *Military Review* 48 (Apr. 1968): 3–9.

2155   Pearlman, Lt. Col. Moshe. *The Army of Israel.* New York: Philosophical Library, 1950.

2156   Peres, Shimon. *David's Sling.* London: Weidenfeld & Nicolson, 1970.

2157   Porath, Reuben. "The Israeli Navy." *U.S. Naval Institute Proceedings* 97 (Sept. 1971): 33–39.

2158   Portal, R. "Les forces armées israéliennes." *Europe Sud Est* 81 (Sept. 1970): 13–18.

2159   Reese, H. "Arab-Israeli Interval of Uncertainty." *Military Review* 49 (June 1969): 3–13.

2160   Reich, B. "Israel's Quest for Security." *Current History* 62 (Jan. 1972): 1–5.

2161   Rolbant, Samuel. *The Israeli Soldier: Profile of an Army.* Cranbury, New Jersey: Yoseloff, 1970.

2162 Toma, E. "Israel's Military Doctrine and Reality." *International Affairs* (Moscow) (Mar. 1972): 68–72.

2163 "Ups and Downs in Israel Strategy Since 1967." *New Middle East*, no. 18 (Mar. 1970): 17–20.

2164 Weller, Jac. "Israeli Armour: Lesson from the Six-Day War." *Military Review* 51 (Nov. 1971): 44–50.

2165 ———. "Israeli Paratroopers." *Military Review* 53 (Mar. 1973): 49–59.

2166 ———. "Mechanized Infantry in Israel." *Infantry* 62:5 (Sept.–Oct. 1972): 32–38.

2167 ———. "Sir Basil Liddell Hart's Disciples in Israel." *Military Review* 54 (Jan. 1974): 13–23.

2168 ———. "Soldiers for a Lifetime." *National Guardsmen* (Dec. 1972): 2–7.

Air Force

2169 Jackson, Robert. *The Israeli Air Force Story*. London: Tandem, 1972.

2170 Leavitt, William. "Israel's Air Force—In a Class by Itself." *Air Force Magazine* 54 (June 1971): 36–42.

2171 Marshall, Thomas. "Israeli Helicopter Forces: Organization and Tactics." *Military Review* 52 (July 1972): 94–99.

2172 Miller, Martin J. "The Israeli Air Force." *Ordnance* 57 (Sept.–Oct. 1972): 124–29.

2173 Stevenson, William. *Zanek! A Chronicle of the Israeli Air Force*. New York: Viking, 1971.

2174 Wetmore, Warren C. "Israeli Airlines Mobilized for Mideast War." *Aviation Week & Space Technology* (July 31, 1967): 26–28.

2175 ———. "Israelis Relied on Helicopters for Movement of Troops, Logistics Support, Pilot Rescue." *Aviation Week & Space Technology* (Aug. 7, 1967): 90–91.

Weapons

2176 Ashkar, Riad, and Ahmed Khalidi. *Weapons and Equipment of the Israeli Armed Forces*. Monograph Series, no. 27. Beirut: Institute for Palestine Studies, 1971.

2177 Carr, J. "U.S. Army Buys Israeli Electronics." *Jewish Observer and Middle East Review* (Mar. 10, 1972): 19.

2178 Carrol, R. "FOB Cherbourg: Israel Gets Its Boats." *Newsweek* (Jan. 12, 1970): 27–29.

2179 "Israeli Firm Seeking Broader Market through Collaboration." *Aviation Week & Space Technology* (June 4, 1973): 55–67.

2180 "Israel Shows Off a New Rifle That She Says Rates with Best [Galil assault rifle]." *New York Times* (Apr. 15, 1973).

2181 Lockwood, L. "Israel's Expanding Arms Industry." *Journal of Palestine Studies* 1:4 (1972): 73–91.

2182 Miller, Martin J. "Israel's Quest for Military Self-Sufficiency." *Military Review* 51 (Mar. 1971): 67–73.

2183 ———, and Konrad F. Schreier. "Revolution in Tank Armament." *Army* 21:3 (Mar. 1971): 49–53.

2184 Nihart, Brooke. "Israel Aerial Refueling Capability Blow to Arab Strategy." *Armed Forces Journal* 108 (Feb. 1, 1971): 15–16.

2185 Owen, Henry. "The Weapons Debate." *Atlantic Monthly* (June 1972): 6–12.

2186 Ropelewski, Robert. "Israel to Get 50 to 100 New A-4N's." *Aviation Week & Space Technology* (June 19, 1972): 19–20.

2187 Stanley, John. "The International Arms Trade—Controlled or Uncontrolled?" *Political Quarterly* 43 (Apr.–June 1972): 155–68.

2188 Weller, Jac. "Israeli Arms Production." *Ordnance* 55 (May–June 1971): 540–44.

War of Attrition (Suez Canal), 1969–1970

2189 Avnery, U. "The Third Year of the Six Day War." *Muslim World* 60 (Jan. 1970): 59–73.

2190 "Confrontation Across the Canal." *New Middle East*, no. 25 (Oct. 1970): 26–29.

2191 Heymont, I. "Israeli Defense of the Suez Canal." *Military Review* 51 (Jan. 1971): 3–11.

2192 "Israel Downs 145 Aircraft Since War." *Israel Economist* 28:11 (Nov. 1972): 262.

2193 "Israel Gets Set for Prolonged War." *U.S. News & World Report* (Oct. 20, 1969): 50–60.

2194 Luttwak, Edward. "(MIG-21+MIG-23+SAM-3)−(F-4+A-4+AGM)=? The Canal Front." *New Middle East*, no. 39 (Dec. 1971): 10–12.

2195 ———. "The Military Balance: Moscow Notwithstanding." *New Middle East*, no. 48 (Sept. 1972): 15–16.

2196 Mok, M. "Dug In for an Undeclared War." *Life* (Oct. 3, 1969): 26–31.

2197 O'Ballance, Edgar. "A Military Solution to the Suez Canal Impasse." *Military Review* (July 1971): 84–89.

2198 Rouleau, Eric. "Reprieve from Attrition: Tacit Israeli-Egyptian Truce." *LeMonde* [Weekly English Edition] (Nov. 11, 1970).

2199 Wakebridge, Charles. "Electrons Over Suez." *Ordnance* 56 (May–June 1972): 473–77.

2200 Whetten, Lawrence L. "June 1967 to June 1971: Four Years of Canal War Reconsidered." *New Middle East*, no. 33 (June 1971): 15-25.

Arab Armed Forces

2201 Colvin, Robert D. "Aftermath of the Elath." *Survival* 12 (Jan. 1970): 7-12.

2202 Cox, Frederick J. "The Russian Presence in Egypt." *Naval War College Review* 22:6 (Feb. 1970): 44-53.

2203 Frank, L. A. "Nasser's Missile Program." *Orbis* 11:3 (1967): 746-57.

2204 Johnson, Maj. Thomas M. "The AK47." *Army* 20:6 (June 1970): 40-45.

2205 Lanteri, R. "Nasser arme le fellah." *L'Express* (Feb. 2-8, 1970): 20-22.

2206 Mezerette, Jean. "Où sont les Mirages de Khadafi?" *Paris Match* (May 5, 1973): 38-41.

2207 O'Ballance, Edgar. "Problems of the Egyptian Phoenix." *Army Quarterly and Defence Journal* 102 (July 1972): 451-57.

2208 Shafei, H. "Fighting Readiness and Arab Countries." *Review of International Affairs* (Belgrade) (Jan. 5, 1971): 8-9.

2209 Sheehan, E. "The Way Egyptians See Israel, Uncle Sam, the SAM's." *New York Times Magazine* (Sept. 20, 1970): 28-29.

2210 Wetmore, Warren C. "Israelis Class MIG-21C as Efficient, High Altitude Fighter." *Aviation Week & Space Technology* (July 31, 1967): 50-51.

2211 Yodfat, A. "Arms and Influence in Egypt: The Record of Soviet Military Assistance since 1967." *New Middle East*, no. 10 (July 1969): 27-32.

Nuclear Weapons

2212 Beaton, Leonard. "Why Israel Does *Not* Need the Bomb: A Report on the Real Nuclear Standing of Egypt, India and Israel." *New Middle East,* no. 7 (Apr. 1969): 7–11.

2213 Beaufre, A. "Les armes nucléaires et l'Asie." *Stratégie* (July–Sept. 1969): 5–22.

2214 Bell, J. Bowyer. "Israel's Nuclear Option." *Middle East Journal* 26 (Autumn 1972): 379–88.

2215 Harkabi, Yehoshafat. *Nuclear War and Nuclear Peace.* Jerusalem: Israel Universities Press, 1966.

2216 ———, et al. *The Bomb in the Middle East.* New York: Friendship, 1969.

2217 Hodes, Aubrey. "Implications of Israel's Nuclear Capability." *Wiener Library Bulletin* 22 (1968): 6.

2218 Jabber, Fuad. "Israel's Nuclear Options." *Journal of Palestine Studies* 1:1 (1971): 21–38.

2219 ———. *Israel and Nuclear Weapons: Present Option and Future Strategies.* London: Chatto & Windus, 1971.

2220 Nimrod, Y., and A. Korczyn. "Suggested Patterns for Israeli-Egyptian Agreement to Avoid Nuclear Proliferation." *New Outlook* 10:1 (Jan. 1967): 9–20.

2221 Quester, George H. "Israel and the Nuclear Non-Proliferation Treaty." *Bulletin of the Atomic Scientists* 25:6 (July 1969): 7–10.

2222 Smith, Hedrick. "U.S. Assumes the Israelis Have a Bomb or Its Parts." *New York Times* [Late City Edition] (July 18, 1970): 1, 8.

Soviets Out of Egypt, 1972

2223 Eran, Oded, and Jerome Singer. "Exodus from Egypt and the Threat to Kremlin Leadership." *New Middle East,* no. 50 (Nov. 1972): 21–25.

2224   Gabelic, A. "The Knowns and Unknowns of Sadat's Decision." *Review of International Affairs* (Belgrade) (Aug. 5–20, 1972): 26–29.

2225   Laqueur, Walter Z. "On the Soviet Departure from Egypt." *Commentary* 54:6 (Dec. 1972): 61–68.

2226   Lenczowski, George. "Egypt and the Soviet Exodus." *Current History* 64 (Jan. 1973): 13–16.

2227   Luchsinger, F. "Expulsion from Egypt." *Swiss Review of World Affairs* 22:5 (Aug. 1972): 2–3.

2228   McDermott, Anthony. "A Russian Withdrawal: Or Divorce, Egyptian Style." *New Middle East*, no. 47 (Aug. 1972): 4–6.

2229   ———. "Sadat and the Soviet Union." *World Today* 28 (Sept. 1972): 404–10.

2230   "The Moscow Communique between Egypt and the USSR." *Orient* (Hamburg) 13:2 (July 1972): 88.

2231   Smolansky, Oles. "The Soviet Setback in the Middle East." *Current History* 64 (Jan. 1973): 17–20.

2232   ———, and B. Smolansky. "Soviet Policy in Egypt: An Assessment." *Middle East Forum* 48:2 (1972): 19–28.

2233   "The Trouble in Arab-Soviet Relations." *Middle East Newsletter* 6:4 (July–Aug. 1972): 5–9.

October 1973 War

2234   al-Bitar, Salah al-Din. "The Implications of the October War for the Arab World." *Journal of Palestine Studies* 3:2 (1974): 34–45.

2235   Battle, L. "The Arabs: Why Now?" *New York Times Magazine* (Oct. 21, 1973): 34.

2236   Brown, David A. "Israel Airlift Flights Underscore C-5 Rapid Deployment Capability." *Aviation Week & Space Technology* (Dec. 10, 1973): 16–19.

2237 Coleman, Herbert J. "Gabriel Outmatches Soviet Styx in Mideast Engagements at Sea." *Aviation Week & Space Technology* (Dec. 10, 1973): 20.

2238 ———. "Israeli Air Force Decisive in War." *Aviation Week & Space Technology* (Dec. 3, 1973): 18–21.

2239 DeVore, Ronald M. "The Arab-Israeli Arms Race and the Superpowers." *Current History* 66 (Feb. 1974): 70–73.

2240 El-Ayouty, Yassin. "The Palestinians and the Fourth Arab-Israeli War." *Current History* 66 (Feb. 1974): 74–78.

2441 Ghareeb, Edmund. "The U.S. Arms Supply to Israel During the October War." *Journal of Palestine Studies* 3:2 (1974): 114–21.

2242 Griffith, William E. "The Fourth Middle East War, the Energy Crisis and U.S. Policy." *Orbis* 17:4 (1974): 1161–88.

2243 Leslie, S. C. "Crisis in the Middle East: The Israeli Dimension: Facing the Facts." *Round Table* 253 (Jan. 1974): 25–34.

2244 Mansfield, Peter. "Crisis in the Middle East: The Arab Dimension: Renewed Self-Confidence." *Round Table* 253 (Jan. 1974): 13–24.

2245 "The Middle East War." *Armed Forces Journal International* 111 (Jan. 1974): 33–38.

2246 Oudes, Bruce. "In the Wake of the Middle East War." *Africa Report* 19:1 (Jan.–Feb. 1974): 11–13.

2247 Reich, Bernard. "Israel Between War and Peace." *Current History* 66 (Feb. 1974): 49–52.

2248 "Resolutions Passed by the Security Council of the United Nations on the Arab-Israeli Conflict, October 22, 23, and 25, 1973." *Middle East Journal* 27 (Autumn 1973): 534.

2249 Richardson, John P. "Arab Civilians and the October War." *Journal of Palestine Studies* 3:2 (1974): 122–29.

2250 Rodwell, Robert R. "The Mideast War: A Damned Close-Run Thing." *Air Force Magazine* 57 (Feb. 1974): 36–41.

2251 Ropelewski, Robert R. "Egypt Assesses Lessons of October War." *Aviation Week & Space Technology* (Dec. 17, 1973): 14–17.

2252 Rubinstein, A. "The Israelis: No More Doves." *New York Times Magazine* (Oct. 21, 1973): 34.

2253 Sax, Cmdr. Samuel W., and Avigdor Levy. "Arab-Israeli Conflict Four: A Preliminary Assessment." *Naval War College Review* 26:4 (Jan.–Feb. 1974): 7–16.

2254 Sella, Amnon. "Soviet Training and Arab Performance." *Jerusalem Post* [Weekly Overseas Edition] (Feb. 14, 1974): 18.

2255 Shoufani, Elias. "Israeli Reactions to the War." *Journal of Palestine Studies* 3:2 (1974): 46–64.

2256 Sus, Ibrahim. "Western Europe and the October War." *Journal of Palestine Studies* 3:2 (1974): 65–83.

2257 Whetten, Lawrence, and Michael Johnson. "Military Lessons of the Yom Kippur War." *World Today* 30 (Mar. 1974): 101–9.

Strategic Considerations, Post–1973: Suez, Red Sea, Sinai

2258 Bell, J. Bowyer. "Bab el Mandeb, Strategic Troublespot." *Orbis* 16:4 (1973): 975–89.

2259 Bindra, A. P. S. *Suez Thrombosis—Causes and Prospects.* London: Vikas, 1972.

2260 Burrell, R. "Canal, Pipeline or Cape?" *New Middle East*, no. 41 (Feb. 1972): 29–32.

2261 Cottrell, A. "Implications of Reopening the Canal for the Area East and South of Suez." *New Middle East*, no. 34 (July 1971): 29–32.

2262 Gray, Colin S. "The Security of Israel." *Military Review* 53 (Oct. 1973): 22–35.

2263 Legum, Colin. "Red Sea Politics: Implications Beyond the Fringe." *New Middle East,* no. 51 (Dec. 1972): 7–8.

2264 *The Meaning of "Secure Borders."* Tel Aviv: Israelis Reply, n.d.

2265 Mortimer, Edward. "Israel: 'Danger from Within': General Peled Attacks Leadership." *Times* (London) (Dec. 19, 1973).

2266 Nutting, A. "Changing Attitudes in Britain from Suez to Today." *Middle East Forum* 45:3 (1969): 5–14.

2267 Safran, Nadav. "The War and the Future of Arab-Israeli Conflict." *Foreign Affairs* 52 (Jan. 1974): 215–36.

2268 Shoufani, E. "The Sinai Wedge." *Journal of Palestine Studies* 1:3 (1972): 85–94.

2269 Stanford, Maj. Melvin J. "Strategic Factors within the Middle East." *Military Review* 53 (Dec. 1973): 78–91.

2270 Stevens, Georgiana G. "Suez." *Atlantic Monthly* (July 1971): 16–19.

Spies

2271 Aldouby, Zwy, and Jerrold Ballinger. *The Shattered Silence: The Eli Cohen Affair.* New York: Coward, McCann & Geoghegan, 1971.

2272 Alia, J. "Israël: L'Opération des services secrets." *Le nouvel observateur* (Apr. 21, 1973): 44–47.

2273 Bar-Zohar, Michael. *Spies in the Promised Land: Iser Harel and the Israeli Secret Service.* Boston: Houghton Mifflin, 1972.

2274 Ben-Hanan, Eli. *Our Man in Damascus: The Story of Elie Cohen, Israel's Greatest Spy.* New York: Crown, 1969.

2275 Dan, Uri, and Y. Ben-Porath. *The Secret War: The Spy Game in the Mideast.* New York: Amis, 1971.

2276 Dekel, Efraim. *Shai: Exploits of Haganah Intelligence.* London: Yoseloff, 1959.

2277 Lotz, Wolfgang. *The Champagne Spy.* London: Vallentine, Mitchell, 1972.

2278 Salpeter, E. "The Kibbutz Boy Who Became a Spy." *New Leader* (Jan. 8, 1973): 4–6.

VII / THE UNITED NATIONS & PEACE EFFORTS

A / The United Nations & the Arab-Israeli Problem

2279 Bentwich, Norman. "The Middle East and the United Nations." *Middle Eastern Affairs* 2 (Nov. 1951): 351-60.

2280 Brook, David. *Preface to Peace: The United Nations and the Arab-Israel Armistice System.* Washington, D.C.: Public Affairs, 1964.

2281 Dib, G. Moussa. *The Arab Bloc in the United Nations.* Amsterdam: Djambatan, 1956.

2282 Gruen, George E. *Israel, the United States and the United Nations.* New York: American Jewish Committee and Jewish Publication Society of America, 1968.

2283 Hadawi, Sami. *Palestine before the United Nations.* Beirut: Institute for Palestine Studies, 1966.

2284 Hamzeh, Fuad S. *United Nations Conciliation for Palestine 1949-1967.* Monograph Series, no. 17. Beirut: Institute for Palestine Studies, 1968.

2285 Hebrew University of Jerusalem. *Israel and the United Nations.* New York: Manhattan, 1956.

2286 Howard, Harry N. "The Arab-Asian States in the United Nations." *Middle East Journal* 7 (Summer 1953): 279-92.

2287 ———. "The United Nations in the Middle East." *Current History* 60 (Jan. 1971): 7–12.

2288 Leonard, Larry. *The United Nations and Palestine*. International Conciliation, no. 454. New York: Carnegie, Oct. 1949.

2289 Little, Tom. "Arabs and Neutralism at the United Nations." *Arab World* 7:1 (Jan. 1961): 6–9.

2290 Mates, L. "The United Nations and the Middle East." *Review of International Affairs* (Belgrade) (July 5–20, 1967): 1–4.

2291 Mezerik, A. G., ed. *Arab-Israel Conflict and the United Nations*. New York: International Review Service, 1962.

2292 Nes, D. "Israel and the United Nations." *Middle East International* (Feb. 1973): 11–12.

2293 Rodley, N. "The United Nations and Human Rights in the Middle East." *Social Responsibility* 38:2 (1971): 217–40.

2294 Sayegh, Fayez A. "The United Nations and the Palestine Question, 1947–1964." *Islamic Review* 52:11 (Nov. 1964): 5–9.

2295 Stevens, G. "The Middle East: A View from the U.N." *Atlantic Monthly* (Sept. 1969): 4–12.

2296 Urquhart, Brian. *Hammarskjöld*. New York: Knopf, 1972.

International Military Force

2297 Bloomfield, Lincoln P., et al. *International Military Forces: The Question of Peace-keeping in an Armed and Disarming World*. Boston: Little, Brown, 1964.

2298 Bowett, D. W. *United Nations Forces*. New York: Praeger, 1965.

2299 Burns, Arthur Lee, and Nina Heathcote. *Peace-Keeping by U.N. Forces*. New York: Praeger, 1963.

2300 Harbottle, M. "Peacekeeping and Peacemaking." *Military Review* 49 (Sept. 1969): 43–59.

2301 Rikye, Maj. Gen. I. J. *Preparation and Training of United Nations Peace-Keeping Forces.* Adelphi Papers, no. 9. London: Institute for Strategic Studies, Apr. 1964.

United Nations Truce Supervision Organization (UNTSO)

2302 Burns, E. L. M. *Between Arab and Israeli.* London: Harrap, 1962.

2303 Leary, B. "An UNTSO Executive's View 1956–58." *Mid East* 8:4 (1968): 34–39.

2304 von Horn, Maj. Gen. Carl. *Soldiering for Peace.* New York: David McKay, 1967.

B / Prospects for Peace

2305 Al-Abid, Ibrahim. *Israel and Negotiations.* Palestine Essays, no. 20. Beirut: Palestine Liberation Organization Research Center, July 1970.

2306 Belyaev, I. "How the Soviet Union Visualizes a Middle East Settlement." *New Middle East,* no. 21 (June 1970): 30–33.

2307 Ben-Dak, Joseph D. "Some Directions for Research Toward Peaceful Arab-Israeli Relations: Analysis of Past Events and Gaming Simulation of the Future." *Journal of Conflict Resolution* 16:2 (June 1972): 281–95.

2308 Ben Porath, Yeshayahu. "Greater Israel or Withdrawal?" *New Middle East,* no. 51 (Dec. 1972): 12–14.

2309 Bourguiba, H. "Negotiations the Only Means for Settling Disputes." *Review of International Affairs* (Belgrade) (Jan. 5, 1969): 6–8.

2310 Caradon, Baron Hugh M. F. "A Plan for Middle East Peace." *War/Peace Report* 10 (Dec. 1970): 7–11.

2311 Church, Senator Frank. *Prospects for Peace in the Middle East: The View from Israel.* Washington, D.C.: U.S.G.P.O., 1972.

2312 Clark, C. "Middle East Conflict: The Basis for Negotiations and Some Proposals for a Settlement." *Australian Outlook* 27:1 (1973): 50–72.

2313 Cooley, John K. "'Most Prejudices Just Look Silly' When You Study Together." *Christian Science Monitor* (Mar. 29, 1973).

2314 Davis, John H. "The Arabs and Israel: Blighted Hopes, Arid Future?" *Middle East Forum* 40:5 (June 1964): 19–23.

2315 Dowty, A. "The Application of International Guarantees to the Egypt-Israel Conflict." *Journal of Conflict Resolution* 16:2 (June 1972): 253–68.

2316 Eckardt, A. Roy. "The Fantasy of Reconciliation in the Middle East." *Christian Century* (Oct. 13, 1971): 1198–1202.

2317 Ehrlich, M. "The Road to Peace in the Middle East." *Political Affairs* 48 (Aug. 1969): 42–50.

2318 Fisher, Roger D. *Dear Israelis, Dear Arabs: A Working Approach to Peace.* New York: Harper & Row, 1972.

2319 Fulbright, Senator J. W. "The Middle East: Perspectives for Peace." *Survival* 12 (Nov. 1970): 360–68.

2320 Hadawi, Sami. "Israel's Sham Peace Offers." *Middle East Forum* 40:2 (Feb.–Mar. 1964): 27–29.

2321 Hart, P. "An American Policy Toward the Middle East." *Annals of the American Academy of Political and Social Science* 390 (July 1970): 98–113.

2322 Kimche, Jon. *There Could Have Been Peace.* New York: Dial Press, 1973.

2323 Laqueur, Walter Z. "Is Peace in the Middle East Possible?" *New York Times Magazine* (Aug. 27, 1967): 38.

2324 Love, K. "The Art of the Impossible: Peace Talks in the Middle East." *Mid East* 10:5 (Oct. 1970): 12-17.

2325 Lumer, H. "The Fight for Peace in the Middle East." *Political Affairs* 52 (Mar. 1973): 5-17.

2326 Mallison, W. "The Diplomatic Methods to Achieve Minimum Order in the Middle East." *Journal of International Law & Economics* 6:1 (July 1971): 113-24.

2327 Merlin, S. *The Search for Peace in the Middle East*. Cranbury, New Jersey: Yoseloff, 1968.

2328 "The Middle East: Some Basic Issues and Alternatives." *Peace Research Society Papers* 15 (1970): 1-167.

2329 Monroe, Elizabeth. "The Arab-Israel Frontier." *International Affairs* 29 (Oct. 1953): 439-48.

2330 Oxtoby, Willard G. "The Middle East: From Polemic to Accommodation." *Christian Century* (Oct. 13, 1971): 1192-97.

2331 Peretz, Don. "The United States, the Arabs and Israel: Peace Efforts of Kennedy, Johnson, and Nixon." *Annals of the American Academy of Political and Social Science* 401 (May 1972): 116-25.

2332 Rafael, Amnon E. "A Proposal for Peace in the Middle East." *Orbis* 16:1 (1972): 119-52.

2333 Reisman, Michael. *The Art of the Possible: Diplomatic Alternatives in the Middle East*. Princeton, New Jersey: Princeton University Press, 1970.

2334 Rogers, W. "The Need for a Negotiating Process in the Middle East." *U.S. Department of State Bulletin* (Feb. 5, 1973): 129-31.

2335 Safran, Nadav. "The Alternatives in the Middle East." *Commentary* 47:5 (May 1969): 45-55.

2336 *Search for Peace in the Middle East.* Philadelphia: American Friends Service Committee, 1970.

2337 Stone, I. F. "For a New Approach to the Israeli-Arab Conflict." *New York Review of Books* (Aug. 3, 1967): 1–6.

2338 "To Make War or To Make Peace: Proceedings of the International Symposium on Inevitable War or Initiatives for Peace, Tel Aviv, March 27–30, 1969." *New Outlook* 12:5–6 (June–Aug. 1969): 1–285. [Special Issue]

2339 Tuma, Elias H. *Peacemaking and the Immoral War: Arabs and Jews in the Middle East.* New York: Harper & Row, 1972.

C / Peace Efforts

United Nations Resolution 242

2340 Dorsey, William. "Resolution 242: Focus of All Attempts to Secure a Settlement." *New Middle East,* no. 44 (May 1972): 27–29.

2341 Lapidoth, R. "UN Resolution 242." *Wiener Library Bulletin* 26:1–2 (1973): 2–9.

2342 Radovanovic, L. "Reflections on the November 22, 1967, Security Council Resolution." *Journal of Palestine Studies* 1:2 (1972): 61–69.

Jarring Mission

2343 Bar-Nir, D. "Israel Must Answer Jarring." *New Outlook* 14:6 (Aug. 1971): 20–24.

2344 Gillon, D. "The Prospects for the Jarring Talks." *World Today* 27 (Feb. 1971): 50–55.

2345 Gottlieb, Gidon. "Of Suez, Withdrawal and Jarring: The Search for a Compromise." New York University Center for International Studies Policy Papers, n.d.

2346 Kanowitz, K. "Back to Jarring." *New Outlook* 14:1 (Jan. 1971): 37–42.

2347 "Mrs. Meir's Statement on Jarring Peace Talks." *New Middle East,* no. 29 (Feb. 1971): 45–50.

2348 Murphy, Cornelius F. "The Middle East Crisis." *St. John's Law Review* 44 (Jan. 1970): 390–98.

2349 Reich, B. "The Jarring Mission and the Search for Peace in the Middle East." *Wiener Library Bulletin* 26:1–2 (1973): 13–20.

2350 "The Situation in the Middle East: Report of the Secretary-General on the Activities of the Special Representative to the Middle East." *Middle East Journal* 26 (Winter 1972): 69–77.

2351 "United States Calls for Resumption of Negotiations on Interim Middle East Settlements." *U.S. Department of State Bulletin* (Jan. 17, 1972): 72–75.

2352 U Thant. "The Story of the Jarring Mission." *New Middle East,* no. 29 (Feb. 1971): 30–35.

Rogers Plan

2353 "Assistant Secretary Sisco Interviewed on 'Meet the Press'." *U.S. Department of State Bulletin* (Aug. 3, 1970): 150–55.

2354 Belyaev, I. "Who Is Obstructing a Middle East Settlement." *International Affairs* (Moscow) (Nov. 1970): 86–90.

2355 Hanauer, E. R. "The U.S. and Peace in the Middle East: A New Approach." *Mid East* 9:4 (July–Aug. 1969): 3–10.

2356 "Israel Looks Toward Peace: A Symposium." *Midstream* 17:9 (Nov. 1971): 3–19.

2357 Nixon, President Richard M. "U.S. Foreign Policy for the 1970's: A New Strategy for Peace." *U.S. Department of State Bulletin* (Mar. 9, 1970): 274–331.

2358   Pranger, Robert J. *American Policy for Peace in the Middle East 1969–1971: Problems of Principle, Maneuver and Time.* A.E.I. Foreign Affairs Studies, no. 1. Washington, D.C.: American Enterprise Institute for Public Policy Research, 1971.

2359   Rogers, William. "A Lasting Peace in the Middle East: An American View." *U.S. Department of State Bulletin* (Jan. 5, 1970): 7–11.

2360   Rubinstein, Amnon. "A Plan for the Sinai—'Something Less than Peace in Return for Something Less than Total Withdrawal'." *New York Times Magazine* (Jan. 17, 1971): 12.

2361   ———. "Why the Israelis Are Being Difficult." *New York Times Magazine* (Apr. 18, 1971): 32.

2362   Salpeter, Eliahu. "Nearing Sadat's Deadline: Shadows in the Middle East." *New Leader* (Dec. 27, 1971): 7–9.

2363   Seymour, G. "The Middle East, September–October 1970." *Contemporary Review* 217:1259 (Dec. 1970): 303–8.

2364   "Transcript of Assistant Secretary of State Joseph Sisco's Interview on the NBC Television Programme 'Meet the Press,' July 12, 1970." *New Middle East*, no. 23 (Aug. 1970): 9–12.

2365   U.S. Congress. House of Representatives. Committee on Foreign Affairs. Subcommittee on the Near East. Hearings: *Approaches to Peace in the Middle East.* 92d Cong., 2d sess., 1972.

2366   *United States Middle East Policy: Peace or Appeasement.* Boston: American Professors for Peace in the Middle East, Jan. 1970.

2367   "U.S. Policy Defined: The Rogers' Press Conference (March 16, 1971)." *New Middle East,* no. 31 (Apr. 1971): 48–49.

Kissinger's Efforts

2368 Alpern, D. M. "Henry's Frantic Year." *Saturday Review World* (Apr. 20, 1974): 14.

2369 "Back to Shuttle Diplomacy: Israeli-Syrian Negotiations." *Time* (Mar. 4, 1974): 25–26.

2370 "Disengagement Talks Proceed as Syria Calls for Next Stage of Warfare." *Middle East Information Media Brief* (May 1–15, 1974): 1.

2371 Draper, T. "Road to Geneva: The U.N. and the Arab-Israeli Conflict." *Commentary* 57:2 (Feb. 1974): 23–39.

2372 "Edging toward Mideast Peace: New Success for Kissinger." *U.S. News & World Report* (Mar. 11, 1974): 55.

2373 Fromm, J. "Can the Superpowers Bring Peace to the Middle East?" *U.S. News & World Report* (Nov. 12, 1973): 24–25.

2374 Griffith, T. "How Deep Is the U.S. Commitment to Israel?" *Time* (Oct. 29, 1973): 52.

2375 "It's a Bird, It's a Plane, It's Super *K*." *Newsweek* (Apr. 1, 1974): 33–34.

2376 Kissinger, Henry A. "News Conference of December 6, 1973." *U.S. Department of State Bulletin* (Dec. 24, 1973): 753–63.

2377 ———. "News Conference of January 3, 1974." *U.S. Department of State Bulletin* (Jan. 28, 1974): 77–86.

2378 ———. "News Conference of January 22, 1974." *U.S. Department of State Bulletin* (Feb. 11, 1974): 137–45.

2379 "Kissinger as Crisis Manager." *Newsweek* (Nov. 5, 1973): 42.

2380 "Kissinger Tries to Grease the Wheels." *Newsweek* (Jan. 21, 1974): 37–38.

2381 "Middle East Peace Conference Opens in Geneva: Statements by Henry Kissinger." *U.S. Department of State Bulletin* (Jan. 14, 1974): 21–24.

2382 "Mideast: Both Sides Hope for a Miracle from U.S." *U.S. News & World Report* (Nov. 26, 1973): 35–36.

2383 "Return of the Magician: Syrian-Israeli Negotiations." *Time* (Mar. 11, 1974): 41–42.

2384 "Secretary Kissinger Visits Middle East and Europe." *U.S. Department of State Bulletin* (Jan. 14, 1974): 25–26.

2385 "Shuttle to Disengagement: Agreement to Disengage Israeli and Egyptian Forces along the Suez Canal." *Time* (Jan. 28, 1974): 36.

2386 Sidey, H. "International Natural Resource: Work of Henry Kissinger." *Time* (Feb. 4, 1974): 24.

2387 "Superpower Search for a Settlement: U.S.-Russia Meetings." *Time* (Oct. 29, 1973): 20–21.

2388 "U.S. Announces Egypt-Israel Agreement on Force Separation." *U.S. Department of State Bulletin* (Feb. 11, 1974): 145–46.

2389 "U.S. Warns Russia: Limits beyond which We Cannot Go." *U.S. News & World Report* (Nov. 5, 1973): 72–74.

2390 Van Voorst, B. "Travels with Henry." *Newsweek* (Feb. 4, 1974): 76–77.

2391 "Victory for Shuttle Diplomacy." *Newsweek* (Jan. 28, 1974): 30–32.

2392 "Whew! Pressures on Israel and Arabs to Begin Cease-Fire." *National Review* (Nov. 23, 1973): 1317.

VIII / THE WEST, THE SUPERPOWERS, & THE MIDDLE EAST

2393 Campbell, John C., and Helen Caruso. "The West and the Middle East." *Military Review* 52 (Oct. 1972): 75–83.

2394 ———. *The West and the Middle East.* Papers on International Affairs Series, 15:10. New York: Council on Foreign Relations, 1972.

2395 Hanania, Farid S. "Tension in the Arab Near East." *Annals of the American Academy of Political and Social Science* 288 (July 1953): 56–62.

2396 Hourani, Albert. "The Decline of the West in the Middle East, I." *International Affairs* 29 (Jan. 1953): 22–42.

2397 ———. "The Decline of the West in the Middle East, II." *International Affairs* 29 (Apr. 1953): 156–83.

2398 Issawi, Charles. "Negotiation from Strength? A Reappraisal of Western-Arab Relations." *International Affairs* 35 (Jan. 1959): 1–9.

2399 Kedourie, Elie. "Western Illusions about the Middle East." *Commentary* 25 (Jan. 1958): 16–22.

2400 Lewis, Bernard. *The Middle East and the West.* Bloomington: Indiana University Press, 1964.

2401 Longrigg, Stephen. "The Decline of the West in the Middle East." *International Affairs* 29 (July 1953): 326–29.

2402 Sachar, Howard M. *Europe Leaves the Middle East, 1935–1954*. New York: Knopf, 1972.

A / Superpowers in the Middle East

2403 Base, Tarun. *The Superpowers and the Middle East*. New York: Asia Publishing House, 1972.

2404 Brown, Neville. "After the Summit: Shifts in the Superpower Balance." *New Middle East,* no. 46 (July 1972): 14–16.

2405 Campbell, John C. *The Middle East in the Muted Cold War*. Social Science Foundation and the Department of International Relations Monograph, no. 1. Denver: University of Denver, 1965.

2406 ———. "The Soviet Union and the United States in the Middle East." *Annals of the American Academy of Political and Social Science* 401 (May 1972): 126–35.

2407 Curtis, Michael. "Soviet-American Relations and the Middle East Crisis." *Orbis* 15:1 (1971): 403–27.

2408 Dimeshkie, Nadim. "The Impact of the Cold War on the Arab World." *Middle East Forum* 39:10 (Dec. 1963): 15–20.

2409 Donovan, John, ed. *U.S. and Soviet Policy in the Middle East*. New York: Facts on File, 1972.

2410 Evron, Yair. *The Middle East: Nations, Superpowers and Wars*. New York: Praeger, 1973.

2411 Frye, Richard N., ed. *The Near East and the Great Powers*. Port Washington, New York: Kennikat, 1951.

2412 Hurewitz, J. C., ed. *Soviet-American Rivalry in the Middle East.* New York: Praeger, 1969.

2413 Ibrahim, S. "Arab Images of the United States and the Soviet Union Before and After the June War of 1967." *Journal of Conflict Resolution* 16:2 (June 1972): 227–40.

2414 Lewis, B. "The Great Powers, the Arabs and the Israelis." *Foreign Affairs* 47 (July 1969): 542–52.

2415 Merlin, Samuel, ed. *The Big Powers and the Present Crisis in the Middle East.* Rutherford, New Jersey: Fairleigh Dickinson University Press, 1968.

2416 Milenkovic, M. "The Big Powers and the Middle East." *Review of International Affairs* (Belgrade) (July 5–20, 1969): 10–13.

2417 Milstein, Jeffrey S. "American and Soviet Influence, Power Balance, and Arab-Israeli Violence." In *Peace, War, and Numbers,* edited by Bruce M. Russet. Beverly Hills, California: Sage, 1972.

2418 Nahumi, M. "The Powers in the Middle Eastern Conflict." *New Outlook* 10:6 (July–Aug. 1967): 11–19.

2419 Peabody, James B. "Escalation or Detente in the Middle East." *Military Review* 52 (Apr. 1972): 35–49.

2420 Reese, H. "The Arab-Israeli Dispute and the Major Powers." *Military Review* 46 (Apr. 1966): 53–64.

2421 Said, Edward. "U.S. Policy and the Conflict of Powers in the Middle East." *Journal of Palestine Studies* 2:3 (1973): 32–50.

2422 Sheehan, Edward R. F. "The United States, the Soviet Union and Strategic Considerations in the Middle East." *Naval War College Review* 23:10 (June 1971): 22–30.

2423 Whetten, L. "The Military Consequences of Mediterranean Superpower Parity." *New Middle East,* no. 38 (Nov. 1971): 14–25.

B / United States & the Middle East

Historical Ties

2424 DeNovo, John A. *American Interests and Policies in the Middle East, 1900–1939.* Minneapolis: University of Minnesota Press, 1963.

2425 Dodge, Bayard. "American Educational and Missionary Efforts in the Nineteenth and Early Twentieth Centuries." *Annals of the American Academy of Political and Social Science* 401 (May 1972): 15–22.

2426 Field, James A., Jr. "Trade, Skills, and Sympathy: The First Century and a Half of Commerce with the Near East." *Annals of the American Academy of Political and Social Science* 401 (May 1972): 1–14.

2427 Finnie, David H. *Pioneers East: The Early American Experience in the Middle East.* Cambridge, Massachusetts: Harvard University Press, 1967.

2428 Grabill, Joseph L. *Protestant Diplomacy and the Near East: Missionary Influence in American Policy, 1810–1927.* Minneapolis: University of Minnesota Press, 1971.

2429 Howard, Harry N. "The American Tradition and U.S. Policy in the Middle East." *Middle East Forum* 40:3 (April 1964): 17–22.

2430 Tibawi, A. L. *American Interests in Syria, 1800–1901.* New York: Oxford University Press, 1966.

2431 Wright, L. C. *United States Policy Toward Egypt, 1830–1914.* New York: Exposition, 1969.

2432 Wright, Quincy. "American Historical and Present Concerns in the Middle East." *Issues* 19:3 (1965): 44–56.

Policy in the Contemporary Middle East

2433 "ABC's of Israeli-Arab Conflict—The U.S. Role." *U.S. News & World Report* (June 19, 1967): 44–46.

2434 Campbell, John C. *The United States in World Affairs, 1947-1948*. New York: Council on Foreign Relations, 1948.

2435 Cleveland, Ray L. "The United States, Israel and the Arab States: The View from 1965." *Middle East Forum* 43:2-3 (1967): 65-76.

2436 Davids, Jules. "The United States and the Middle East: 1955-1960." *Middle Eastern Affairs* 12 (May 1961): 130-40.

2437 Fulbright, James William. "The Case for a New Internationalism." *War/Peace Report* 11 (May 1971): 3-7.

2438 Hanna, Paul L. "America in the Middle East." *Middle Eastern Affairs* 10 (May 1959): 178-90.

2439 Hart, P. "Where We Stand." *Annals of the American Academy of Political and Social Science* 401 (May 1972): 136-42.

2440 Hoskins, Halford L. "The U.S. in the Middle East: Policy in Transition." *Current History* 48 (May 1965): 257-62.

2441 Howard, Harry N. "The U.S. in the Middle East Today." *Current History* 57 (July 1969): 36-41.

2442 Hunter, Robert E. "In the Middle in the Middle East." *Foreign Policy*, no. 5 (1971-1972): 137-50.

2443 Johnson, Joseph E. "Arab vs. Israeli: Challenge for Americans." *Issues* 18:2 (1964): 1-13.

2444 Kerr, Malcolm H. "Nixon's Second Term: Policy Prospects in the Middle East." *Journal of Palestine Studies* 2:3 (1973): 14-29.

2445 Lilienthal, Alfred M. *The Other Side of the Coin: An American Perspective of the Arab-Israeli Conflict*. New York: Devin-Adair, 1965.

2446 Morgenthau, Hans J. "The U.S. and the Mideast." *New Leader* (June 19, 1967): 3-6.

2447 Nahumi, Mordechai. "The United States and the Middle East." *New Outlook* 7:2 (Feb. 1964): 25–33.

2448 Nes, D. "No New Ideas in Washington." *Middle East International* (Apr. 1973): 6–7.

2449 ———. "Our Middle East Involvement." *Middle East Forum* 45:3 (1969): 15–27.

2450 Patterson, Gardner. *Declining American Involvement in the Middle East.* New York: World, 1965.

2451 "Prime Minister Meir of Israel Visits Washington." *U.S. Department of State Bulletin* (Mar. 26, 1973): 355–57.

2452 Rostow, E. "The Middle East Crisis and Beyond." *U.S. Department of State Bulletin* (Jan. 8, 1968): 41–48.

2453 Said, A. "The United States and the Middle East and North Africa." *Naval War College Review* 22:10 (June 1970): 41–47.

2454 Sakran, F. "The United States and the Arab-Israeli Conflict." *Middle East Newsletter* 2:8 (Oct. 1968): 1–2.

2455 Sams, James F. "United States Policy and the Middle East." *Middle East Forum* 43:2–3 (1967): 45–56.

2456 Sisco, Joseph J. "The Arab-Israeli Confrontation: A Challenge to International Diplomacy." *U.S. Department of State Bulletin* (May 26, 1969): 443–46.

2457 ———. "The United States and the Arab-Israeli Dispute." *Annals of the American Academy of Political and Social Science* 384 (July 1969): 66–72.

2458 Speiser, Ephraim A. *The United States and the Near East.* Cambridge, Massachusetts: Harvard University Press, 1950.

2459 Stevens, Georgiana G., ed. *The United States and the Middle East.* Englewood Cliffs, New Jersey: Prentice-Hall, 1964.

2460   Stork, Joe. "The American New Left and Palestine." *Journal of Palestine Studies* 2:1 (1972): 64–69.

2461   U.S. Department of State. Report: *United States Foreign Policy, 1969–1970*. Washington, D.C.: U.S.G.P.O., 1971.

2462   Winocour, Jack. "The United States and the Middle East." *Middle Eastern Affairs* 5 (Aug.–Sept. 1954): 260–68.

2463   Wright, Quincy. "The Middle East Problem." *American Journal of International Law* 64 (Apr. 1970): 270–81.

2464   Yost, C. "U.S. Gives Views in U.N. General Assembly Debate on the Situation in the Middle East." *U.S. Department of State Bulletin* (Nov. 23, 1970): 656–63.

United States Interests & Policy Goals

2465   "Assistant Secretary Sisco Discusses Middle East Policy for Israeli Television." *U.S. Department of State Bulletin* (Nov. 13, 1972): 566–73.

2466   Badeau, J. "Let's Broaden Our Options." *Mid East* 10:5 (Oct. 1970): 34–37.

2467   Battle, L. "Objectives and Directions of U.S. Policy in the Near East." *U.S. Department of State Bulletin* (June 3, 1968): 710–14.

2468   Beling, Willard A., ed. *The Middle East: Quest for an American Policy*. Albany, New York: State University of New York Press, 1973.

2469   Belyaev, I. "Middle East Crisis and Washington's Manoeuvres." *International Affairs* (Moscow) (Apr. 1970): 30–35.

2470   Berger, E. "Problems of American Policy-Makers in the Middle East." *Middle East Forum* 45:1–2 (1968): 61–81.

2471   Bernstein, M., and L. Bolling. "Alternatives for the U.S. in the Middle East." *Mid East* 10:5 (Oct. 1970): 38–41.

2472 Brownell, George A. "American Aviation in the Middle East." *Middle East Journal* 1 (Oct. 1947): 401–16.

2473 Campbell, John C. "The Arab-Israeli Conflict: An American Policy." *Foreign Affairs* 49 (Oct. 1970): 51–69.

2474 ———. *Defense of the Middle East: Problems of American Policy.* 2d ed. New York: Harper, 1960.

2475 ———. "There *Is* a New Look in Washington: The Change in America's Middle East Perspective." *New Middle East,* no. 9 (June 1969): 11–14.

2476 Crabb, Cecil, Jr. *Bipartisan Foreign Policy: Myth or Reality.* Evanston, Illinois: Row, Peterson, 1957.

2477 Dmitriyev, E. "Washington's 'Quiet Diplomacy' and Middle East Realities." *International Affairs* (Moscow) (Apr. 1972): 40–45.

2478 ———, and V. Alexayev. "U.S. Policy in the Middle East." *International Affairs* (Moscow) (Nov. 1971): 39–43.

2479 Edelsberg, Herman. *Whose Fight in the Middle East? An Analysis of America's National Interest.* Washington, D.C.: B'nai B'rith International Council, 1970.

2480 Eliot, George. "Strategic Problems of the Middle East." *Middle Eastern Affairs* 4 (Oct. 1953): 313–23.

2481 Eller, E. M. "U.S. Destiny in the Middle East." *U.S. Naval Institute Proceedings* 82 (Nov. 1956): 1160–69.

2482 Gershman, C. "Rowland Evans' Complaint." *Midstream* 18:1 (Jan. 1972): 66–70.

2483 Hart, Parker T. "The Go-Between: A Role the U.S. Can No Longer Play." *New Middle East,* no. 50 (Nov. 1972): 7–10.

2484 Henderson, Loy W. "American Political and Strategic Interests in the Middle East and Southeastern Europe." *U.S. Department of State Bulletin* (Nov. 23, 1947): 996–1000.

2485 ———. "Statement Summarizing the Objectives of United States Policy in the Near and Middle East." *Middle East Journal* 1 (Jan. 1947): 85–86.

2486 Hunter, R. "American Policy in the Middle East." *Royal Central Asian Journal* 55 (Oct. 1968): 265–75.

2487 Hurewitz, J. C. "Our Mistakes in the Middle East." *Atlantic Monthly* (Dec. 1956): 46–52.

2488 Lenczowski, George, ed. *The United States Interests in the Middle East*. Washington, D.C.: American Enterprise Institute for Public Policy Research, 1968.

2489 Lesser, A., and H. Clesner. "America's Interest in the Middle East." *American Zionist* 61:9 (June 1971): 11–13.

2490 Magnus, R. "U.S. Political-Strategic Interests in the Middle East." *Military Review* 49 (Mar. 1969): 47–55.

2491 ———, ed. *Documents on the Middle East: United States Interests in the Middle East*. Washington, D.C.: American Enterprise Institute for Public Policy Research, 1969.

2492 Mark, M. "United States Foreign Policy in the Middle East." *New Outlook* 15:3 (Mar.–Apr. 1972): 48–54.

2493 Masannat, G. "Arab Neutrality and American Foreign Policy in the Middle East." *General Political Quarterly* 1:3 (1967): 19–26.

2494 Mattison, Frances C. *A Survey of American Interests in the Middle East*. Washington, D.C.: Middle East Institute, 1953.

2495 Nolte, Richard. "American Policy in the Middle East." *Journal of International Affairs* 13:2 (1959): 113–25.

2496 O'Neill, Captain Bard E. "The Middle East, 1973: Cold War Changes and American Interests." *Air University Review* 24;5 (July–Aug. 1973): 57–62.

2497 Quandt, William B. "The Middle East Conflict in U.S. Strategy, 1970–1971." *Journal of Palestine Studies* 1:1 (1971): 39–52.

2498 ———. *United States Policy in the Middle East: Constraints and Choices.* Santa Monica, California: RAND, RM–5980, 1970.

2499 Reich, B. "America in the Middle East: Changing Aspects in U.S. Policy." *New Middle East,* no. 1 (Oct. 1968): 9–13.

2500 ———. "United States Policy in the Middle East." *Current History* 60 (Jan. 1971): 1–6.

2501 Rubin, Barry. "America's Mid-East Policy: A Marxist Perspective." *Journal of Palestine Studies* 2:3 (1973): 51–67.

2502 Rustow, Dankwart A. "Defense of the Near East." *Foreign Affairs* 34 (Jan. 1956): 271–86.

2503 *The Security of the Middle East: A Problem Paper.* Washington, D.C.: Brookings Institution, 1950.

2504 Sisco, Joseph J. "U.S. Objectives in the Middle East." *U.S. Department of State Bulletin* (Aug. 10, 1970): 175–78.

2505 Thompson, Carol L. "American Policy in the Middle East." *Current History* 35 (Oct. 1958): 234–39.

2506 U.S. Congress. House of Representatives. Committee on Foreign Affairs. Subcommittee on the Near East. Hearings: *U.S. Interests in and Policy Toward the Persian Gulf.* 92d Cong., 2d sess., 1972.

2507 U.S. Congress. Senate. Committee on Armed Services. Report: *The Middle East and American Security Policy,* by Senator Henry M. Jackson. 91st Cong., 2d sess., 1970.

2508 Welles, Sumner. *We Need Not Fail.* Boston: Houghton Mifflin, 1948.

2509 Westerfield, H. Bradford. *Foreign Policy and Party Politics.* New Haven, Connecticut: Yale University Press, 1955.

2510 Wright, Edwin M. "U.S. Strategic Involvement in the Middle East." *Naval War College Review* 18:10 (June 1966): 1–11.

2511 Wright, Quincy. *A Foreign Policy for the United States.* Chicago: University of Chicago Press, 1947.

2512 Wright, Walter L., Jr. "Contradictory Foreign Policies in the Near East." *Virginia Quarterly Review* 23 (Spring 1947): 179–92.

Relations with the Arab World

2513 Abu-Jaber, F. "American-Arab Relations from the Balfour Declaration to the Creation of the State of Israel, 1917–1948." *Middle East Forum* 44:4 (1968): 5–20.

2514 Badeau, John S. *The American Approach to the Arab World.* New York: Harper & Row, 1968.

2515 ———. "U.S.A. and U.A.R.: A Crisis in Confidence." *Foreign Affairs* 43 (Jan. 1965): 281–96.

2516 Berman, S. "UAR Propaganda 'Orientation' in the U.S.A." *International Problems* 8:1–2 (June 1970): 62–74.

2517 Efimenco, N. Marbury. "American Impact upon Middle East Leadership." *Political Science Quarterly* 69 (June 1954): 202–18.

2518 Fakhry, Rashed F. "Namecalling and Beyond." *al-Kulliyah* 30 (Mar. 1955): 10–11.

2519 Gaspard, J. "The Myth of the American Myth: How the Arabs See the Americans." *New Middle East,* no. 16 (Jan. 1970): 28–32.

2520 Issawi, Charles. "United States Policy and the Arabs." *Current History* 34 (Mar. 1958): 136–40.

2521   Lichtheim, George. "The U.S. Backs the Arab Monarchs." *Commentary* 23 (June 1957): 516–22.

2522   Perlmann, M. "Bagdad-Gaza Bandung." *Middle Eastern Affairs* 6 (May 1955): 141–51.

2523   Polk, William R. *The United States and the Arab World.* Rev. ed. Cambridge, Massachusetts: Harvard University Press, 1969.

2524   Said, Edward. "The Arab Portrayed." *Arab World* 14:10–11 (Oct.–Nov. 1968): 5–7.

2525   Wright, Esmond. "Defence and the Bagdad Pact." *Political Quarterly* 28 (Apr.–June 1957): 158–67.

Eisenhower Doctrine & Lebanon, 1958

2526   Atyeo, Henry C. "The United States in the Middle East." *Current History* 32 (Mar. 1957): 106–64.

2527   Baldridge, Elward F. "Lebanon and Quemoy—The Navy's Role." *U.S. Naval Institute Proceedings* 87:2 (Feb. 1961): 94–100.

2528   Campbell, John C. "From 'Doctrine' to Policy in the Middle East." *Foreign Affairs* 35 (Apr. 1957): 441–43.

2529   Holloway, J. L., Jr.; John R. Binns; and Robert Tepper. "'The American Landing in Lebanon': 'Orders Firm but Flexible'—Comment and Discussion." *U.S. Naval Institute Proceedings* 89 (Sept. 1963): 3.

2530   Houston, J. A. "The Eisenhower Era." *Current History* 57 (July 1969): 24.

2531   Howard, Harry N. "The Regional Pacts and the Eisenhower Doctrine." *Annals of the American Academy of Political and Social Science* 401 (May 1972): 85–94.

2532   Hughes, Emmet J. *The Ordeal of Power: A Political Memoir of the Eisenhower Years.* New York: Atheneum, 1963.

2533   Humbaraci, Arslan. *Middle East Indictment: From the Truman Doctrine, the Soviet Penetration and Britain's Downfall to the Eisenhower Doctrine.* London: Robert Hall, 1958.

United States Policy toward Israel

2534   Howard, Harry N. "The United States and Israel: Conflicts of Interest and Policy." *Issues* 18:2 (1964): 13–27.

2535   Khamis, S. "The Israeli-U.S. Alliance in Action." *World Marxist Review* 11 (July 1968): 74–81.

2536   Lilienthal, Alfred. *There Goes the Middle East.* New York: Devin-Adair, 1957.

2537   ———. *What Price Israel?* Rev. ed. Chicago: Regnery, 1956.

2538   "Nixon Offers a Kosher Lunch: Jews Wooed as Election Warms Up." *Jewish Observer and Middle East Review* (Mar. 17, 1972): 8.

2539   Reich, B. "The Israel-U.S. Relationship." *Wiener Library Bulletin* 23:4 (1969): 2–12.

2540   Safran, Nadav. "The United States: How Firm an Ally in War?" *New Middle East,* no. 40 (Jan. 1972): 18–19.

2541   ———. *The United States and Israel.* Cambridge, Massachusetts: Harvard University Press, 1963.

2542   "United States Aid to Israel." *Middle East International* (Jan. 1973): 6.

2543   "The U.S. Presidential Election: An Analysis and a Choice." *Israel Horizons* 20:9 (Sept.–Oct. 1972): 3–6.

Zionism: Israel & American Jewry

2544   Arnoni, M. "Doing What Comes Unnatural." *Israel Magazine* 2:2 (1969): 57–59.

2545   Carvely, Andrew. *U.S.-U.A.R. Diplomatic Relations and Zionist Pressures.* St. Louis, Missouri: D.H.-T.E. International, 1969.

2546 Coleman, Clarence L., Jr. "U.S. Rejects the 'Jewish People' Concept." *Issues* 18:4 (1964): 2.

2547 Halperin, Samuel. *The Political World of American Zionism.* Detroit, Michigan: Wayne State University Press, 1961.

2548 Halpern, Ben. *The American Jew.* New York: Theodor Herzl Foundation, 1956.

2549 Hertzberg, A. "Israel and American Jewry." *Commentary* 44:2 (Aug. 1967): 69–73.

2550 Howard, Harry N. "The Senate Inquiry into Zionist Activities." *Arab Journal* 1:1 (1964): 30–35.

2551 ———. "The State Department and the Charge of Anti-Semitism." *Issues* 20 (1966): 1–8.

2552 Mallison, W. "Jewish Fund Bores Holes in U.S. Tax Laws." *Middle East International* (July 1971): 53–56.

2553 Rudeneh, O. "The Jewish Factor in U.S. Politics." *Journal of Palestine Studies* 1:4 (1972): 92–107.

2554 Serpell, C. "The Jewish Lobby in Washington." *Middle East International* (Apr. 1973): 6–7.

2555 Silverberg, Robert. *If I Forget Thee, O Jerusalem: American Jews and the State of Israel.* New York: Morrow, 1970.

2556 Stevens, Richard P. *American Zionism and U.S. Foreign Policy.* New York: Pageant, 1962.

2557 Taylor, A. "Israel and the Modern Jewish Identity Crisis." *Mid East* 11:3 (July 1970): 18–20.

United States Economic & Military Aid

2558 Coleman, Herbert J. "Mulley Airs U.S. Role in Saudi Jet Order." *Aviation Week & Space Technology* (May 23, 1966): 32–33.

2559 Daniel, Robert L. *American Philanthropy in the Near East.* Athens: Ohio University Press, 1970.

2560 Gardiner, Arthur Z. "Point Four and the Arab World: An American View." *Middle East Journal* 4 (July 1950): 296–306.

2561 Hakim, George. "Point Four and the Middle East: A Middle East View." *Middle East Journal* 4 (Apr. 1950): 183–95.

2562 Hoskins, Halford L. "Aid and Diplomacy in the Middle East." *Current History* 51 (July 1966): 14–19.

2563 Lindberg, John. "Technical and Economic Aid to the Middle East." *Current History* 38 (May 1960): 285–89.

2564 Meyer, A. J. "Reflections on American Economic Policy in the Middle East." *Middle Eastern Affairs* 10 (June–July 1959): 233–37.

2565 Peretz, Don. "United States Aid in the Middle East." *Current History* 33 (Aug. 1957): 95–100.

2566 "Secretary Rogers' News Conference of June 25, 1970." *U.S. Department of State Bulletin* (July 13, 1970): 25–30.

2567 U.S. Congress. Senate. Committee on Government Operations. Subcommittee on Reorganization and International Organizations. Report: *United States Foreign Aid in Ten Middle Eastern and African Countries,* submitted by Senator Ernest Gruening. 88th Cong., 1st sess., 1963.

2568 Young, Lewis. "American Blacks and the Arab-Israeli Conflict." *Journal of Palestine Studies* 2:1 (1972): 70–85.

United States Mediterranean Fleet

2569 Blair, Leon B. "Mediterranean Geopolitics." *U.S. Naval Institute Proceedings* 77 (Feb. 1951): 135–39.

2570 Field, James A., Jr. *America and the Mediterranean World.* Princeton, New Jersey: Princeton University Press, 1969.

2571 Kafman, A. "U.S. Big Stick in the Mediterranean." *International Affairs* (Moscow) (Aug. 1967): 71–75.

2572 Palmer, J. M. "NATO and the Mediterranean." *Revue militaire générale* 7 (July 1972): 52–67.

2573 Pfaff, R. "The American Military Presence in the Middle East." *Middle East Forum* 48:2 (1972): 29–42.

2574 Reitzel, William. "The American Position in the Mediterranean." *Yale Review* 35 (June 1947): 673–88.

2575 ———. *The Mediterranean: Its Role in America's Foreign Policy.* New York: Harcourt, Brace, 1948.

2576 Shub, Louis. *The United States and Israel in the Mediterranean.* Jewish Affairs Background Reports, vol. 1, no. 1. Los Angeles: Center for the Study of Contemporary Jewish Life, University of Judaism, 1970.

2577 Xydis, Stephen G. "The Genesis of the Sixth Fleet." *U.S. Naval Institute Proceedings* 84 (Aug. 1958): 40–50.

C / Soviet Union & the Middle East

Historical Ties

2578 "Early Soviet Contacts with Arab and African Countries." *Mizan* 8:2 (Mar.–Apr. 1966): 87–94.

2579 Hopwood, Derek. *The Russian Presence in Syria and Palestine, 1843–1914: Church and Politics in the Near East.* London: Oxford University Press, 1969.

2580 Joudah, A. "The Historical Origins of Russia in the Middle East." *Middle East Forum* 48:2 (1972): 7–18.

2581 Laqueur, Walter Z. *The Struggle for the Middle East: The Soviet Union in the Mediterranean, 1948–1968.* New York: Macmillan, 1969.

2582 Lenczowski, George. *Russia and the West in Iran, 1918–1948: A Study in Big-Power Rivalry.* 1949. New York: Greenwood Reprint, 1968.

2583 Psomiades, Harry J. "Soviet Russia and the Orthodox Church in the Middle East." *Middle East Journal* 11 (Autumn 1957): 371–81.

2584 Smith, Jay C. *The Russian Struggle for Power, 1914–1917: A Study of Russian Foreign Policy During the First World War.* New York: Philosophical Library, 1956.

2585 Spector, Ivar. *The Soviet Union and the Muslim World, 1917–1956.* Seattle: University of Washington Press, 1959.

2586 Stavrou, Theofanis George. "Russian Interest in the Levant 1843–1848: Porfirii Uspenskii and Establishment of the First Russian Ecclesiastical Mission in Jerusalem." *Middle East Journal* 17 (Winter–Spring 1963): 91–103.

2587 ———. *Russian Interests in Palestine, 1882–1914: A Study of Religious and Education Enterprises.* Thessalonica, Greece: Institute for Balkan Studies, 1963.

2588 Tibawi, A. L. "Russian Cultural Penetration of Syria—Palestine in the Nineteenth Century." *Royal Central Asian Journal* 53 (June 1966): 166–82; 53 (Oct. 1966): 309–23.

Relations with Contemporary Middle East

2589 Borodin, N. "The Soviet Union and the Middle East—Facts and Fictions (A Soviet View)." *New Middle East,* no. 34 (July 1971): 14–17.

2590 Campbell, J. C. "The Soviet Union and the Middle East." *Russian Review* 29 (Apr. 1970): 143–53; 29 (July 1970): 247–61.

2591 Cottrell, A. "The Soviet Union in the Middle East." *Orbis* 14:3 (1970): 588–98.

2592 De Carmoy, G. "Soviet Penetration in the Mediterranean." *Military Review* 50 (Mar. 1970): 83–90.

2593   Druks, H. "The Soviet Role in the Middle East." *Eastern Europe* 20:2 (Fall 1971): 19–27.

2594   Forsythe, David P. "The Soviets and the Arab-Israeli Conflict." *World Affairs* 134 (Fall 1971): 132–42.

2595   Golan, Galia. *The Soviet Involvement in the Middle East.* Jerusalem: Hebrew University Press, 1971.

2596   Goodman, M. "Russia and the Middle East." *Foreign Service Journal* 46:5 (Apr. 1969): 14.

2597   Hughes, E. "The Russians Drill Deep in the Middle East." *Fortune* (July 1968): 102–5.

2598   Kimche, J. "New Soviet Moves in the Middle East." *Midstream* 18:4 (Apr. 1972): 3–11.

2599   Kirk, George. "Hammer, Sickle, and Crescent." *al-Kulliyah* 29 (Nov. 1954): 2–7.

2600   Klieman, Aaron S. *Soviet Russia and the Middle East.* Baltimore: Johns Hopkins Press, 1970.

2601   Klinghoffer, A. "Pretext and Context: Evaluating the Soviet Role in the Middle East." *Mizan* 10:3 (May–June 1968): 86–93.

2602   Kulski, W. W. *The Soviet Union in World Affairs: A Documented Analysis, 1964–1972.* Syracuse, New York: Syracuse University Press, 1973.

2603   Laqueur, Walter Z. "Russia Enters the Middle East." *Foreign Affairs* 47 (Jan. 1969): 296–308.

2604   ———. *Soviet Russia and the Middle East.* New York: Praeger, 1959.

2605   Lenczowski, George. *Soviet Advances in the Middle East.* Washington, D.C.: American Enterprise Institute for Public Policy Research, 1971.

2606 Leshem, Moshe. "Soviet Propaganda to the Middle East." *Middle Eastern Affairs* 4 (Jan. 1953): 1–10.

2607 Lewis, Bernard. "Russia in the Middle East." *Survival* 12 (Oct. 1970): 332–36.

2608 M., D. L. "Middle East: Soviet Emphasis on Realism." *Mizan* 9:5 (Sept.–Oct. 1967): 215–17.

2609 Martin, H. G. "The Soviet Union and the Middle East." *Middle Eastern Affairs* 7 (Feb. 1956): 49–56.

2610 Merz, Robert. "The Reddening Middle East." *Ordnance* 57 (Jan.–Feb. 1973): 295–98.

2611 "The Middle East in the Soviet Press." *Mizan Supplement* A:2 (Mar.–Apr. 1966): 1–7.

2612 Mumford, Major Jay C. "Soviet Motivation in the Middle East." *Military Review* 52 (Sept. 1972): 40–49.

2613 Nes, David G. "The Russians in the Middle East." *Middle East International* (Mar. 1972): 12–13.

2614 ———. "The Soviets in the Middle East." *Military Review* 52 (June 1972): 80–85.

2615 Schuyler, G. "Middle East: It Is All Sinking in a Red Sea." *American Opinion* 14:7 (July–Aug. 1971): 31–36.

2616 Shwadran, Benjamin. "The Soviet Role in the Middle East Crisis." *Current History* 60 (Jan. 1971): 13–18.

2617 ———. "The Soviet Union in the Middle East." *Current History* 52 (Feb. 1967): 72–77.

2618 "Soviet Interests in the Middle East." *Mizan* 8:3 (May–June 1966): 142–44.

2619 Spector, Ivar. "Russia in the Middle East." *Current History* 32 (Feb. 1957): 83–88.

2620 Vucinich, Wayne S. "Russia and the Near and Middle East." *Current History* 28 (Feb. 1955): 80–88.

2621 Wheeler, Geoffrey E. "Russia and the Middle East." *International Affairs* 35:3 (July 1959): 295–304.

2622 ———. "Russia and the Middle East." *Political Quarterly* 28 (Apr.–June 1957): 127–36.

Soviet Interests & Policy

2623 Dallin, David. "Soviet Policy in the Middle East." *Middle Eastern Affairs* 6 (Nov. 1955): 337–44.

2624 Fisher, Harold H. "Russia's Interest in the Middle East." *Current History* 33 (Nov. 1957): 277–82.

2625 Heitmann, G. "Soviet Policy and the Middle East Crisis." *Survey* 69 (Oct. 1968): 133–44.

2626 Hirshmann, Ira A. *Red Star Over Bethlehem: Russia Drives to Capture the Middle East.* New York: Simon & Schuster, 1971.

2627 Hunter, R. E. *The Soviet Dilemma in the Middle East, Part I: Problems of Commitment.* Adelphi Papers, no. 59. London: Institute for Strategic Studies, Sept. 1969.

2628 ———. *The Soviet Dilemma in the Middle East, Part II: Oil and the Persian Gulf.* Adelphi Papers, no. 60. London: Institute for Strategic Studies, Oct. 1969.

2629 Issawi, Charles. "Through a Glass Darkly: A Recent Soviet Study on the Middle East." *Middle East Journal* 14 (Autumn 1960): 470–75.

2630 Lenczowski, G. "Soviet Policy in the Middle East." *Current History* 55 (Nov. 1968): 268–74.

2631 Millar, Thomas B. *Soviet Policies in the Indian Ocean Area.* Canberra Papers on Strategy and Defence, no. 7. Canberra: Australian National University Press, 1970.

2632 Primakov, Yevgeny. "Why the Suez Canal Must Be Reopened—A Russian View." *New Middle East,* no. 46 (July 1972): 7–8.

2633 Sick, G. "The U.S.S.R. and the Suez Canal Closure." *Mizan* 12:2 (Nov. 1970): 91–99.

2634 Smolansky, O. M. "Soviet Policy in the Arab East: 1945–1947." *Journal of International Affairs* 13:2 (1959): 126–40.

2635 "Soviet Aims and Interests in the Middle East." *Middle East International* (Apr.–May 1972): 10–12.

2636 "Soviet Policy in the Middle East." *World Today* 11 (Dec. 1955): 518–29.

2637 Thomas, John R. "The Dilemmas of Soviet Policy in the Middle East." *Parameters* [Journal of the Army War College] 1:2 (Fall 1971): 34–42.

2638 Wesson, R. "The Soviet Interest in the Middle East." *Current History* 59 (Oct. 1970): 212–19.

2639 Whetten, L. "Empire or Revolution? The Dilemma of Russian Policy." *New Middle East,* no. 8 (May 1969): 11–15.

Attitudes toward the Arab World

2640 Ballis, W. "Soviet Foreign Policy Toward Developing States: The Case of Egypt." *Studies on the Soviet Union* 7:3 (1968): 84–113.

2641 Ben-Tzur, Avraham. "Soviet-Egyptian Relations." *New Outlook* 7:4 (May 1964): 26–34.

2642 Cottrell, A. J. "Soviet-Egyptian Relations." *Military Review* 49 (Dec. 1969): 69–77.

2643 Eran, Oded, and Jerome E. Singer. "Soviet Policy Towards the Arab World, 1955–71." *Survey* 17 (Autumn 1971): 10–29.

2644　Laqueur, Walter Z. "The Moscow-Cairo Axis." *Commentary* 21 (May 1956): 409–17.

2645　———. "Russians vs. Arabs." *Commentary* 53:4 (Apr. 1972): 60–69.

2646　London, Isaac. "Evolution of the U.S.S.R.'s Policy in the Middle East, 1950–1956." *Middle Eastern Affairs* 7 (May 1956): 169–78.

2647　Petrov, R. "The Soviet Union and the Arab Countries." *International Affairs* (Moscow) (Oct. 1972): 22–29.

2648　"Soviet Interest in Syria." *Mizan* 8:1 (Jan.–Feb. 1966): 23–33.

2649　Spector, Ivar. "Soviet Foreign Policy in the Arab World." *Current History* 36 (Jan. 1959): 13–17.

2650　Wheeler, Geoffrey E. "Russia and the Arab World." *World Today* 17 (July 1961): 307–18.

Soviet Union & Israel

2651　Dagan, Avigdor. *Moscow and Jerusalem: Twenty Years of Relations Between Israel and the Soviet Union.* Introduction by Abba Eban. New York: Abelard-Schuman, 1970.

2652　Dmitriev, Y. "The Arab World and Israel's Aggression." *International Affairs* (Moscow) (Sept. 1970): 20–24.

2653　"Israel's Very Special Relationship—With Russia." *Middle East International* (Apr. 1973): 27–29.

2654　Katz, Ze'ev. "A Change in Soviet-Israel Relations." *New Outlook* 7:3 (Mar.–Apr. 1964): 6–10.

2655　Khan, Rais A. "Israel and the Soviet Union: A Review of Postwar Relations." *Orbis* 9:4 (1966): 999–1012.

2656　Shweitzer K. "Soviet Policy Towards Israel 1946–1952." *Mizan* 11:1 (Jan.–Feb. 1969): 18–30.

Soviet Jewry Question

2657 Errera, Leo Abram. *The Russian Jews: Extermination or Emancipation?* Translated from the French by Bella Lowy, with a prefatory note by Theodore Mommsen. London, 1894.

2658 Meyer, Peter, et al. *The Jews in the Soviet Satellites.* 1953. New York: Greenwood Reprint, 1971.

2659 "Russian Jews and the Canal: Part of a New Initiative?" *New Middle East,* no. 41 (Feb. 1972): 3–4.

2660 Teller, Judd L. *The Kremlin, the Jews, and the Middle East.* New York: Yoseloff, 1957.

2661 Tzion, Ben. "On the Jewish Question in the Soviet Union." *New York Times Magazine* (May 3, 1970): 24.

2662 Zander, Walter. *Soviet Jewry, Palestine and the West.* London: Gollancz, 1947.

Soviet Military Aid

2663 Joshua, Wynfred. "Arms for the Love of Allah." *U.S. Naval Institute Proceedings* 96 (Mar. 1970): 30–39.

2664 ———, and Stephen P. Gilbert. *Arms for the Third World: Soviet Military Aid Diplomacy.* Baltimore: Johns Hopkins Press, 1969.

2665 "The Middle East: Background to the Russian Intervention." *World Today* 11 (Nov. 1955): 463–77.

Economic Policy & Aid

2666 Alan, Ray. "Russia Enters the Levant." *Commentary* 22 (Dec. 1956): 512–17.

2667 Berliner, Joseph S. "Soviet Economic Policy in the Middle East." *Middle Eastern Affairs* 10 (Aug.–Sept. 1959): 286–91.

2668 Dmitriev, E. "Soviet-Arab Friendship: A New Stage." *International Affairs* (Moscow) (Aug. 1971): 66–68.

2669 Freedman, Robert O. "The Soviet Union and the Middle East: The High Cost of Influence." *Naval War College Review* 24:5 (Jan. 1972): 15–34.

2670 Gaspard, J. "The Kremlin without Abdul Nasser—A New Relationship with Egypt." *New Middle East*, no. 26 (Nov. 1970): 17–19.

2671 Goldman, Marshall I. "A Balance Sheet of Soviet Foreign Aid." *Foreign Affairs* 43 (Jan. 1965): 340–60.

2672 ———. *Soviet Foreign Aid*. New York: Praeger, 1967.

2673 Kovner, Milton. "Soviet Aid Strategy in Developing Countries." *Orbis* 8:3 (1964): 624–40.

2674 Ofer, G. "The Economic Burden of Soviet Involvement in the Middle East." *Soviet Studies* 24:3 (Jan. 1973): 329–47.

2675 Safran, Nadav. "The Soviet-Egyptian Treaty—As Seen from Washington." *New Middle East*, no. 34 (July 1971): 10–13.

2676 Smirnov, V., and I. Matyukhin. "U.S.S.R. and the Arab East: Economic Contacts." *International Affairs* (Moscow) (Sept. 1972): 83–87.

2677 "Text of the Soviet Iraqi Friendship Treaty." *New Middle East*, no. 45 (June 1972): 42.

2678 Yakovlev, D. "Soviet-Iraqi Cooperation Grows and Develops." *International Affairs* (Moscow) (July 1972): 65–67.

Soviet Mediterranean Fleet

2679 Ackley, Richard T. "The Soviet Navy's Role in Foreign Policy." *Naval War College Review* 24:9 (May 1972): 48–63.

2680 Anthem, T. "Russia in the Mediterranean." *Contemporary Review* 212:1226 (Mar. 1968): 132–37.

2681 Brown, N. "Soviet Naval Expansion: The Global Scene Assessed." *New Middle East,* no. 30 (Mar. 1971): 17–21.

2682 Cox, D. "Sea Power and Soviet Foreign Policy." *U.S. Naval Institute Proceedings* 95 (June 1969): 32–44.

2683 Douglas-Home, A. "Red Fleet Off Suez: Mediterranean Challenge." *Atlantic Community Quarterly* 7:1 (Spring 1969): 78–89.

2684 Guriel, B. "The Mediterranean in Soviet Strategic Thinking: Gateway to the Atlantic." *New Middle East,* no. 26 (Nov. 1970): 20–23.

2685 Hashavia, Arie. "The Soviet Fleet in the Mediterranean." *Military Review* 47 (Feb. 1967): 79–81.

2686 Mertens, R. "The Soviet Fleet in Arab Politics: History Reconsidered." *New Middle East,* no. 14 (Nov. 1969): 21–25.

2687 Miksche, F. "The Soviet Union as a Mediterranean Power." *Military Review* 48 (July 1968): 32–36.

2688 Murphy, Capt. F. M. "The Soviet Navy in the Mediterranean." *U.S. Naval Institute Proceedings* 93 (Mar. 1967): 38–44.

2689 Sick, G. "Russia and the West Mediterranean: Perspectives for the 1970's." *Naval War College Review* 22:10 (June 1970): 48–69.

2690 "The Soviet Naval Threat: Reality and Illusion." [Center for Defense Information] *Defense Monitor* 1:1 (May 1972): 1–8.

2691 "The Soviet Navy on NATO's Flanks." *NATO Review* 20:7–8 (July–Aug. 1972): 17–21.

2692   Whetten, Lawrence L. *The Soviet Presence in the Eastern Mediterranean.* New York: National Strategy Information Center, 1971.

2693   Zoppo, C. "Soviet Ships in the Mediterranean and the U.S.-Soviet Confrontation in the Middle East." *Orbis* 14:1 (1970): 109–28.

D / Communism in the Middle East: Arab World

2694   Bakdash, Khalid. "For the Successful Struggle for Peace, National Independence, and Democracy We Must Resolutely Turn toward the Workers and Peasants [Document]." *Middle East Journal* 7 (Spring 1953): 206–21.

2695   Ellis, Harry B. *Challenge in the Middle East: Communist Influence and American Policy.* New York: Ronald, 1960.

2696   Kodsy, Ahmad El. "Nationalism and Class Struggles in the Arab World." In *The Arab World and Israel,* edited by Kodsy and Lobel. New York: Monthly Review Press, 1970.

2697   Laqueur, Walter Z. "The Appeal of Communism in the Middle East." *Middle East Journal* 9 (Winter 1955): 17 27.

2698   ———. *Communism and Nationalism in the Middle East.* New York: Praeger, 1956.

2699   ———. "The 'National Bourgeoisie'—A Soviet Dilemma in the Middle East." *International Affairs* 35 (July 1959): 324–31.

2700   Pennar, Jaan. "The Arabs, Marxism and Moscow: A Historical Survey." *Middle East Journal* 22 (Autumn 1968): 433–47.

2701 Schopflin, George. "Russia's Expendable Arab Communists." *New Middle East,* no. 45 (June 1972): 20–21.

2702 Spector, Ivar, trans. "Program of Action of the Communist Party of Egypt [Document]." *Middle East Journal* 10 (Autumn 1956): 427–37.

E / China, Sino-Soviet Relations, & the Middle East

2703 Adie, W. A. C. "China's Middle East Strategy." *World Today* 23 (Aug. 1967): 317–26.

2704 Ben-Dak, Joseph. "China in the Arab World." *Current History* 59 (Sept. 1970): 157–62.

2705 "China, the Arab World and Africa." *Mizan* 6:5 (May 1964): 1–66. [Special issue]

2706 Cooley, J. "China and the Palestinians." *Journal of Palestine Studies* 1:2 (1972): 19–34.

2707 Farra, R. "The Chinese People's Republic and the Arab World." *Middle East Forum* 42:1 (1966): 43–50.

2708 Fowler, R. "China's Middle East Objectives." *Middle East International* (Mar. 1972): 14–15.

2709 Katz, Ze'ev. "The Sino-Soviet Conflict and the Arabs." *New Outlook* 7:4 (May 1964): 35–37.

2710 U.S. Congress. House of Representatives. Committee on Foreign Affairs. Subcommittee on the Near East. Hearings: *A Sino-Soviet Perspective in the Middle East.* 92d Cong., 2d sess., 1972.

2711 Wheeler, Geoffrey E. "Soviet and Chinese Policies in the Middle East." *World Today* 22 (Feb. 1966): 64–78.

F / Europe & the Arabs & Israel

2712 Abdul-Rahman, As'ad. *United States and West German Aid to Israel.* Facts and Figures Series, no. 6. Beirut: Palestine Liberation Organization Research Center, 1966.

2713 Aruri, Naseer H., and Natalie Hevener. "France and the Middle East, 1967-1968." *Middle East Journal* 23 (Autumn 1969): 484-502.

2714 Astakhov, S. "Bonn-Tel Aviv Axis." *International Affairs* (Moscow) (Nov. 1968): 41-45.

2715 Brown, Neville. "European Foreign Policy—Myth or Reality." *New Middle East,* no. 40 (Jan. 1972): 25-27.

2716 Day, A. "Israel's Quest for Friends on the International Left." *New Middle East,* nos. 52-53 (Jan.-Feb. 1973): 57-58.

2717 Dessouki, Ali. *Canadian Foreign Policy and the Palestine Problem.* Publication no. 1. Ottawa: Middle East Research Centre, 1969.

2718 Gendzier, Irene L. "Arabs and Israelis: French Views." *Middle East Journal* 22 (Spring 1968): 213-18.

2719 Godin, M. "What Do the French Want? A Look at De Gaulle's Mideastern Policy." *New Middle East,* no. 6 (Mar. 1969): 6-9.

2720 Hauenstein, Fritz. "West Germany and the Middle East." *Middle Eastern Affairs* 7 (Jan. 1956): 11-19.

2721 Kiesewetter, Wolfgang. "The Middle East: An Important Phase in the International Class Struggle." *German Foreign Policy* 10:3 (1971): 189-99.

2722 Laqueur, Walter Z. "Bonn, Cairo, Jerusalem: The Triple Crisis." *Commentary* 39:5 (May 1965): 29-38.

2723 Medzini, M. "Israel's Changing Image in the German Mass Media." *Wiener Library Bulletin* 26:3-4 (1972-1973): 8-13.

2724 Ramazani, Rouhollah K. *The Middle East and the European Common Market*. Charlottesville: University Press of Virginia, 1964.

2725 Rouleau, E. "French Policy in the Middle East." *World Today* 24 (May 1968): 209-18.

2726 Stevens, G. "France and the Middle East." *Atlantic Monthly* (Aug. 1970): 8.

IX / CONTINUING PROBLEMS

A / Jordan Waters Conflict

2727   Bochenski, Feliks, and William Diamond. "TVA's in the Middle East." *Middle East Journal* 4 (Jan. 1950): 52–82.

2728   Colvin, Ian. "Sharing the Waters of Jordan." *Royal Central Asian Journal* 51 (July–Oct. 1964): 245–50.

2729   Doherty, Kathryn B. *Jordan Waters Conflict.* International Conciliation, no. 553. New York: Carnegie, May 1965.

2730   Glueck, Nelson. *The River Jordan.* New York: McGraw-Hill, 1968.

2731   Hays, James B., and A. E. Barrekette. *T.V.A. on the Jordan: Proposals for Irrigation and Hydro-Electric Development in Palestine.* Washington, D.C.: Public Affairs, 1948.

2732   Hudson, James. "The Litani River of Lebanon: An Example of Middle Eastern Water Development." *Middle East Journal* 25 (Winter 1971): 1–14.

2733   Ionides, M. G. "The Disputed Waters of Jordan." *Middle East Journal* 7 (Spring 1953): 153–64.

2734   ———. "The Jordan Valley." *Royal Central Asian Journal* 38 (Oct. 1951): 217–25.

2735   Jansen, G. H. "The Problem of the Jordan Waters." *World Today* 20 (Feb. 1964): 60–68.

2736 Khouri, Fred J. "The Jordan River Controversy." *Review of Politics* 27:1 (Jan. 1965): 32–57.

2737 "Light on the Litani." *al-Kulliyah* 29 (Dec. 1954): 5–12.

2738 Meissner, Frank. "Prospectives for Artificial Rain Enhancement in the Jordan Valley Development." *Middle East Journal* 7 (Autumn 1953): 484–98.

2739 Saliba, Samir N. *The Jordan River Dispute*. The Hague: Nijhoff, 1968.

2740 Stevens, Georgiana G. *Jordan River Partition*. Hoover Institution Studies, no. 6. Stanford, California: Stanford University Press, 1965.

2741 ———. *The Jordan River Valley*. International Conciliation, no. 506. New York: Carnegie, Jan. 1956.

The Johnston Plan

2742 Abu-Jaber, F. S. "Eisenhower, Israel and the Jordan Valley Authority Scheme." *Middle East Forum* 45:2 (1969): 51–63.

2743 "Eric Johnston Reports Agreement on Sharing Jordan Waters." *U.S. Department of State Bulletin* (July 26, 1954): 132.

2744 "Eric Johnston Reports on Near East Talks." *U.S. Department of State Bulletin* (Nov. 30, 1953): 749–50.

2745 "Eric Johnston to Resume Talks on Jordan Valley Development." *U.S. Department of State Bulletin* (June 14, 1954): 913.

2746 Johnston, Eric. "Jordan Valley River Development." *U.S. Department of State Bulletin* (Dec. 28, 1953): 891–93.

2747 ———. "Mission to the Middle East." *U.S. Department of State Bulletin* (Feb. 22, 1954): 282–84.

2748 ——. "The Near East and the West." *U.S. Department of State Bulletin* (May 28, 1954): 788–91.

2749 Peretz, Don. "Development of the Jordan Valley Waters." *Middle East Journal* 9 (Autumn 1955): 397–412.

2750 Schmidt, Dana Adams. "Prospects for Solution of the Jordan River Valley Dispute." *Middle Eastern Affairs* 6 (Jan. 1955): 1–12.

Water Diversion

2751 Dees, Joseph L. "Jordan's East Ghor Canal Project." *Middle East Journal* 13 (Autumn 1959): 357–71.

2752 Gritz, S. "The Jordan Waters." *Military Review* 47 (Dec. 1967): 56–64.

2753 Gruen, George E. "Jordan's East Ghor Irrigation Project." *New Outlook* 7:5 (June 1964): 34–37.

2754 Hammad, Khairi. "The Arab Summit Conference and the Israeli Water Projects." *Egyptian Political Science Review* 35 (Feb. 1964): 3–12.

2755 Hasan, Saadat. "Israeli Diversion of the Jordan Waters: A Threat to Peace in the Middle East." *Arab Journal* 1:1 (1964): 21–29.

2756 Khouri, Fred J. "The U.S., the U.N. and the Jordan River Issue." *Middle East Forum* 40:4 (May 1964): 20–24.

2757 Khoury, Victor. "Plans to Divert the Jordan River Waters." *Middle East Forum* 40:6 (Summer 1964): 18–21.

2758 Kinen, I. L., ed. "Water—To Work or to Waste." *Near East Report* (Jan. 14, 1964): 5–7.

2759 Manners, I. "The East Ghor Irrigation Project." *Focus* 20:8 (Apr. 1970): 8–11.

2760 Mehlman, William. "Jordan's Troubled Waters." *Reporter* (Jan. 30, 1964): 29–33.

2761 Misri, B. A. "Jordan Waters." *Islamic Review* 52:10 (Oct. 1964): 9–12.

2762 Nimrod, Yoram. "Conflict over the Jordan." *New Outlook* 8:6 (Sept. 1965): 5–18.

2763 ———. "The Jordan's Angry Waters." *New Outlook* 8:5 (July–Aug. 1965): 19–33.

2764 ———. "The Unquiet Waters." *New Outlook* 8:4 (June 1965): 38–49.

2765 Peretz, Don. "River Schemes and Their Effect on Economic Development in Jordan, Syria, and Lebanon." *Middle East Journal* 18 (Summer 1964): 293–305.

2766 Rizk, Edward. *The River Jordan.* Information Paper, no. 23. New York: Arab Information Center, 1964.

2767 Shepherd, Naomi. "The Water Carrier." *New Statesman* 67 (Jan. 17, 1964): 66.

2768 Smith, C. G. "Diversion of the Jordan Waters." *World Today* 22 (Nov. 1966): 491–98.

2769 Stewart, Desmond. "The Waters of the Jordan." *Spectator* (Jan. 17, 1964): 73–75.

B / Jerusalem

2770 Blyth, Estelle. *When We Lived in Jerusalem.* London: Murray, 1927.

2771 Bovis, H. Eugene. *The Jerusalem Question, 1917–1968.* Stanford, California: Hoover Institution Press, 1971.

2772 Efrat, Elisha. *Changes in the Town Planning Concepts of Jerusalem, 1919–1969.* Jerusalem: Ministry of the Interior, 1971.

2773   Gray, John. *A History of Jerusalem*. New York: Praeger, 1969.

2774   Pfeiffer, C. F. *Jerusalem through the Ages*. Grand Rapids, Michigan: Baker, 1967.

2775   Tibawi, A. L. "The City of Jerusalem." *Islamic Quarterly* 16 (Jan.–June 1972): 3–11.

2776   Vester, Bertha Spafford. *Our Jerusalem: An American Family in the Holy City 1881–1949*. Beirut: Middle East Export, 1950.

2777   Williams, Albert N. *The Holy City: The Pageant of Jerusalem's Thirty Centuries of History*. New York: Duell, 1954.

Jerusalem Holy City

2778   Great Britain. Colonial Office. *Statement of Policy*.... Parliamentary Papers, Cmd. 3229. London: H.M.S.O., Nov. 1928. [Wailing Wall]

2779   Hollis, Christopher, and Ronald Brownrigg. *Holy Places: Jewish, Christian and Muslim Monuments in the Holy Land*. New York: Praeger, 1969.

2780   Karmi, H. "How Holy Is Palestine to the Muslims?" *Islamic Quarterly* 14 (Apr.–June 1970): 63–90.

2781   Kotker, Norman. "The Holy City." *Horizon* 7:2 (Spring 1965): 4–19.

2782   Mawlawi, R. "Israeli Aggression and Desecration of Sanctities in Palestine." *Middle East Forum* 45:3 (1969): 45–60.

2783   Tibawi, A. L. "Jerusalem: Its Place in Islam and Arab History." *Arab World* 14:10–11 (Oct.–Nov. 1968): 9–22.

2784   ———. *Jerusalem: Its Place in Islam and Arab History*. Monograph Series, no. 19. Beirut: Institute for Palestine Studies, 1969.

2785 ———. "Jerusalem through History: A City of Three Faiths." *New Middle East,* nos. 52-53 (Jan.-Feb. 1973): 9-11.

2786 Zander, Walter. *Israel and the Holy Places of Christendom.* London: Weidenfeld & Nicolson, 1971.

Jerusalem, 1948-1967

2787 Abu Shilbaya, Muhammad. "Jerusalem Before and After 1967: An Arab View." *New Middle East,* nos. 42-43 (Mar.-Apr. 1972): 45.

2788 Bishop, Eric F. F. "Jerusalem Byways of Memory: Leaders [IV]." *Muslim World* 55 (July 1965): 230-36.

2789 Dov, Joseph. *The Faithful City: The Siege of Jerusalem 1948.* New York: Simon & Schuster, 1960.

2790 Ethridge, Willie Snow. *Going to Jerusalem.* New York: Vanguard, 1950.

2791 Levin, Harry. *Jerusalem Embattled.* London: Gollancz, 1950.

2792 Perowne, Stewart. *The One Remains: A Report from Jerusalem.* London: Hodder & Stoughton, 1954.

2793 Weltsch, Robert. "What Chance for Arab-Jewish Accord?" *Commentary* 6 (July 1948): 8-17.

Jerusalem, 1967-1973

2794 Adams, M. "Jerusalem." *Arab Palestinian Resistance* 3:9 (Sept. 1971): 28-38.

2795 Al-Khatib, Rouhi. *The Judaization of Jerusalem.* Palestine Essays, no. 19. Beirut: Palestine Liberation Organization Research Center, July 1970.

2796 Berman, S. "Recrudescence of the 'bellum justum et pirum' Controversy and Israel's Reunification of Jerusalem." *International Problems* 7:1-2 (May 1969): 29-45.

2797   Darin-Drabkin, H. "Jerusalem—City of Dissension of Peace." *New Outlook* 11:1 (Jan. 1968): 7-12.

2798   de Gramont, Sanche. "Jerusalem: Experiment in Coexistence: 70,000 Arabs Added to 200,000 Jews." *New York Times Magazine* (July 30, 1967): 14-18.

2799   Feinstein, R. "The Administration of United Jerusalem." *Public Administration in Israel and Abroad* 9 (1968): 116-23.

2800   Halkin, H. "Building Jerusalem." *Commentary* 52:3 (Sept. 1971): 59-66.

2801   Hudson, M. "Jerusalem: A City Still Divided." *Mid East* 8:4 (1968): 20-25.

2802   Jerusalem. Central Bureau of Statistics. *Census of Population and Housing 1967, East Jerusalem.* 1968.

2803   "Jerusalem: A City of Peace and Conflict." *New Outlook* 14:9 (Dec. 1971): 35-44.

2804   *The Judaization of Jerusalem 1967-1972.* Monograph Series, no. 32. Beirut: Institute for Palestine Studies, 1972.

2805   Landau, Eli. *Jerusalem the Eternal: The Paratrooper's Battle for the City of David.* Tel Aviv: Maariv, 1968.

2806   McClain, J. "Jerusalem Under Occupation." *Middle East Newsletter* 3:1 (Jan.-Feb. 1969): 5-8.

2807   Macleish, K., and T. Spiegel. "Reunited Jerusalem Faces Its Problems." *National Geographic* (Dec. 1968): 835-71.

2808   Mansour, A., and E. Stock. "Arab Jerusalem and Annexation." *New Outlook* 14:1 (Jan. 1971): 22-36.

2809   Ofner, Francis. "National and Spiritual Capital: Israeli View of Jerusalem." *Christian Science Monitor* (Dec. 17, 1970): 7.

2810 Peretz, Don. "Impressions of Jerusalem." *Mid East* 8:4 (1968): 16-19.

2811 Rabinovich, Abraham. *The Battle for Jerusalem: June 5-7, 1967*. Philadelphia: Jewish Publication Society of America, 1972.

2812 "Report: Jerusalem." *Atlantic Monthly* (July 1968): 24.

2813 Schleifer, Abdullah. "The Fall of Jerusalem." *Evergreen Review* (Dec. 1967): 26.

2814 ———. *The Fall of Jerusalem*. New York: Monthly Review Press, 1972.

2815 Segal, R. *Whose Jerusalem? The Conflicts of Israel*. London: Jonathan Cape, 1973.

2816 "Spotlight on Jerusalem." *Israel Magazine* 1:2 (1968): 9-54.

2817 Stevens, Georgiana. "Israeli Bulldozers vs. Arab Identity." *Christian Science Monitor* (Dec. 7, 1971): 13.

2818 Tekoah, Ambassador Josef. *Barbed Wire Shall Not Return to Jerusalem*. New York: Israel Information Services, 1968.

2819 "United Nations: Security Council Resolution on Jerusalem." *International Legal Materials* 10:6 (1971): 1294.

2820 United Nations. "UN Resolution: Jerusalem Statement [Document]." *Middle East International* (Jan. 1972): 36.

2821 U Thant. "Report on Jerusalem." *U.N. Monthly Chronicle* 8 (Dec. 1971): 108-15.

Jerusalem Solution

2822 Bush, G. "U.S. Position on Jerusalem." *U.S. Department of State Bulletin* (Oct. 25, 1971): 469-70.

2823 Fitzgerald, Sir William. "An International Regime for Jerusalem." *Royal Central Asian Journal* 37 (July–Oct. 1950): 273–83.

2824 Jones, S. "The Status of Jerusalem: Some National and International Aspects." *Law and Contemporary Problems* 33:1 (1968): 169–82.

2825 Pfaff, Richard H. *Jerusalem: Keystone of an Arab-Israeli Settlement*. Washington, D.C.: American Enterprise Institute for Public Policy Research, 1969.

2826 Sykes, C. "Holy City." *Encounter* 30:2 (Feb. 1968): 39–43.

2827 U.S. Congress. House of Representatives. Committee on Foreign Affairs. Subcommittee on the Near East. *Jerusalem: The Future of the Holy City for Three Monotheisms*. 92d Cong., 1st sess., 1971.

2828 "United States Reaffirms Position on Jerusalem." *U.S. Department of State Bulletin* (July 28, 1969): 76–78.

2829 Wilson, Evan M. "The Internationalization of Jerusalem." *Middle East Journal* 23 (Winter 1969): 1–13.

2830 ———. *Jerusalem: Key to Peace*. Washington, D.C.: Middle East Institute, 1970.

C / Middle East Oil

Concessions & Early Efforts to 1950

2831 Cattan, Henry. *The Evolution of Oil Concessions in the Middle East and North Africa*. Dobbs Ferry, New York: Oceana, 1967.

2832 "The Great Oil Deals." *Fortune* (May 1947): 138–43.

2833 Hearn, Sir Arthur. "Oil and the Middle East." *International Affairs* 24 (Jan. 1948): 63–75.

2834 Hewins, Ralph. *Mr. Five Per Cent: The Story of Calousie Gulbenkian.* New York: Rinehart, 1958.

2835 Kliemer, Don. "Lid on Kirkuk Output Lifted." *World Oil* (June 1952): 285–86.

2836 Lees, G. M. "Oil in the Middle East." *Royal Central Asian Journal* 33 (Jan. 1946): 47–57.

2837 Lloyd, Seton. *Oil in the Middle East.* New York: Oxford University Press, 1954.

2838 Loftus, John A. "Middle East Oil: The Pattern of Control." *Middle East Journal* 2 (Jan. 1948): 17–32.

2839 Longrigg, Stephen. "The Liquid Gold of Arabia." *Royal Central Asian Journal* 36 (Jan. 1949): 20–33.

2840 ———. *Oil in the Middle East: Its Discovery and Development.* 3d. ed. London: Oxford University Press, 1968.

2841 Mikdashi, Zuhayr. *A Financial Analysis of Middle Eastern Oil Concessions, 1901–1965.* New York: Praeger, 1966.

2842 Mikesell, Raymond F., and Hollis B. Chenery. *Arabian Oil: America's Stake in the Middle East.* Chapel Hill: University of North Carolina Press, 1949.

2843 Mughraby, Muhamad A. *Permanent Sovereignty over Oil Resources: A Study of Middle East Oil Concessions and Legal Change.* Beirut: Middle East Research and Publishing Center, 1966.

2844 Philby, H. St. John. *Arabian Oil Ventures.* Washington, D.C.: Middle East Institute, 1964.

Oil Developments, 1950–1970

2845 Finnie, David H. *Desert Enterprise: The Middle East Oil Industry in Its Local Environment.* Cambridge, Massachusetts: Harvard University Press, 1958.

2846 ———. "Recruitment and Training of Labor: The Middle East Oil Industry." *Middle East Journal* 12 (Spring 1958): 127–43.

2847 Frank, Helmut J. *Crude Oil Prices in the Middle East: A Study in Oligopolistic Price Behavior.* New York: Praeger, 1965.

2848 Frankel, Paul. *Oil: The Facts of Life.* London: Weidenfeld & Nicolson, 1964.

2849 Hamilton, Charles W. *Americans and Oil in the Middle East.* Houston, Texas: Gulf, 1963.

2850 Hartshorn, J. E. *Oil Companies and Governments: An Account of the International Oil Industry in Its Political Environment.* London: Faber, 1967.

2851 Hirst, David. *Oil and Public Opinion in the Middle East.* New York: Praeger, 1966.

2852 Issawi, Charles, and Mohammed Yeganeh. *The Economics of Middle Eastern Oil.* New York: Praeger, 1963.

2853 Lebkicher, Roy. *Aramco and World Oil.* New York: Moore, 1952.

2854 Lenczowski, George. *Oil and State in the Middle East.* Ithaca, New York: Cornell University Press, 1960.

2855 Longrigg, Stephen H. "The Economics and Politics of Oil in the Middle East." *Journal of International Affairs* 19:1 (1965): 111–22.

2856 ———. "Middle-Eastern Oil: Blessing or Curse?" *Royal Central Asian Journal* 42 (Apr. 1955): 150–64.

2857 Lubell, Harold. *Middle East Oil Crises and Western Europe's Energy Supplies.* Baltimore: Johns Hopkins Press, 1963.

2858 Lutfi, Ashraf. *Arab Oil: A Plan for the Future.* Beirut: Middle East Research and Publishing Center, 1960.

2859   M., D. L. "Soviet Interest in Middle East Oil." *Mizan* 10:3 (May–June 1968): 79–85.

2860   Mann, Clarence. *Abu Dhabi: Birth of an Oil Sheikdom*. Beirut: Khayats, 1964.

2861   Marlowe, John. "Oil as Hostage." *Encounter* 30:2 (Feb. 1968): 33–34.

2862   Melamid, Alexander. "The Oil Fields of the Sinai Peninsula." *Middle Eastern Affairs* 10 (May 1959): 191–95.

2863   "Oil Production in the Middle East, 1967–1971." *Middle East Economic Digest* (Jan. 14, 1972): 32.

2864   Rachkov, V. "The Middle East Crisis and U.S. Oil Monopolies." *International Affairs* (Moscow) (Apr. 1969): 31–35.

2865   Roberts, Dick. *Mideast Oil & U.S. Imperialism*. New York: Pathfinder Press, 1971.

2866   Sayegh, Kamal S. *Oil and Arab Regional Development*. New York: Praeger, 1968.

2867   Shwadran, Benjamin. *The Middle East, Oil, and the Great Powers*. New York: Praeger, 1955.

2868   ———. "Middle East Oil 1961." *Middle Eastern Affairs* 13 (Oct. 1962): 226–35.

2869   Snodgrass, C. Stribling, and Arthur Kuhl. "U.S. Petroleum's Response to the Iranian Shutdown." *Middle East Journal* 5 (Autumn 1951): 501–4.

2870   U.S. Department of the Interior. Office of Oil and Gas. *The Middle East Petroleum Emergency of 1967*. 2 vols. Washington, D.C.: U.S.G.P.O., 1969.

2871   Yaari, S. "The Markets for Middle East Oil." *Middle Eastern Affairs* 7 (June–July 1956): 213–21.

2872 Yeganeh, Mohammed. "Investment in the Petroleum Industry of the Middle East [Economic Review]." *Middle East Journal* 6 (Spring 1952): 241–46.

Organization of Petroleum Exporting Countries (OPEC)

2873 Adelman, M. "Is the Oil Shortage Real? Oil Companies as OPEC Tax-Collectors." *Foreign Policy*, no. 9 (1973): 69–107.

2874 Drayton, Geoffrey. "The Travails of OPEC." *World Today* 19 (Nov. 1963): 485–91.

2875 Itayim, Fuad."The Organization of Petroleum Exporting Countries." *Middle East Forum* 38:9 (Dec. 1962): 13–19.

2876 "OPEC Members' Production (in thousands of tons) for 1970 and 1971." *Middle East Economic Digest* (Jan. 14, 1972): 33.

2877 Stevens, Harley C. "Some Reflections on the First Arab Petroleum Congress." *Middle East Journal* 13 (Summer 1959): 273–82.

Oil in the 1970s

2878 Adelman, M. "Is the Oil Shortage Real?" *Middle East Information Series* 23 (May 1973): 26–35.

2879 Akins, James E. "The Oil Crisis: This Time the Wolf Is Here." *Foreign Affairs* 51 (Apr. 1973): 462–90.

2880 ———. "A State Department View." *Middle East Information Series* 23 (May 1973): 61–64.

2881 Baldwin, Hanson W. "The Stakes Are Oil." *Army* 21:8 (Aug. 1971): 10–15.

2882 Barger, Thomas C. "Middle Eastern Oil since the Second World War." *Annals of the American Academy of Political and Social Science* 401 (May 1972): 31–44.

2883   Berry, Maj. John A. "The Growing Importance of Oil." *Military Review* 52 (Oct. 1972): 2–16.

2884   Fellowes, Peregrine. "Time of Troubles for the Oil Industry." *New Middle East*, no. 47 (Aug. 1972): 29–31.

2885   Issawi, Charles. *Oil, the Middle East and the World.* New York: Library Press, 1972.

2886   Kimche, Jon. "Oil and Arab Nationalism." *Journal of the Middle East Society* 1 (Spring 1947): 72–79.

2887   Laqueur, W., and E. Luttwak. "Oil." *Commentary* 56:4 (Oct. 1973): 37–43.

2888   Medzini, M. "Japan, Israel and the Arab States." *Middle East Information Series* 22 (Feb. 1973): 27–29.

2889   Medzini, R. "Japan's Vital Stake in Middle Eastern Stability." *New Middle East*, nos. 42–43 (Mar.–Apr. 1972): 51–54.

2890   Mosley, Leonard. *Power Play: Oil in the Middle East.* New York: Random House, 1973.

2891   Odell, Peter R. *Oil and World Power: A Geographical Interpretation.* Baltimore: Penguin, 1970.

2892   Owen, L. "The Year 2001: When the Oil Boom Runs Dry." *New Middle East*, no. 46 (July 1972): 25–27.

2893   Pensin, D. "Oil and Independence." *International Affairs* (Moscow) (Nov. 1972): 34–40.

2894   Remba, O., and A. Sinai. "The Energy Problem and the Middle East: An Introduction." *Middle East Information Series* 23 (May 1973): 2–7.

2895   Schurr, Sam H., and Paul T. Homan. *Middle Eastern Oil and the Western World.* New York: American Elsevier, 1971.

2896 Shwadran, Benjamin. "Middle East Oil." *Current History* 66 (Feb. 1974): 79-82.

2897 Stocking, George W. *Middle East Oil: A Study in Political and Economic Controversy.* Nashville, Tennessee: Vanderbilt University Press, 1970.

2898 Thomas, T. "World Energy Resources: Survey and Review." *Geographical Review* 63:2 (Apr. 1973): 246-59.

2899 Wilson, C. "A Plan for Energy Independence." *Foreign Affairs* 51 (July 1973): 657-75.

Oil as a Political Weapon

2900 Best, G. "Middle East Oil and the U.S. Energy Crisis: Prospects for New Ventures in a Changed Market." *Law and Policy in International Business* 1 (1973): 215-73.

2901 Cass, W. "Middle East Oil: The Subsurface Weapon." *U.S. Naval Institute Proceedings* 99 (Jan. 1973): 18-25.

2902 Frankel, E., et al. "The 'Energy Crisis' and U.S.-Middle East Policy." *Middle East Information Series* 23 (May 1973): 8-16.

2903 Hirst, David. "Faisal, Jihad for Jerusalem." *Manchester Guardian Weekly* (Nov. 24, 1973): 1.

2904 Kostanick, Huey Louis. "Oil in World Politics." *Current History* 33 (Nov. 1957): 263-71.

2905 Lichtblau, J. "The Politics of Petroleum." *Reporter* (July 13, 1967): 26-28.

2906 Mitchell, D. "Oil: The Shifting Balance of Power." *Middle East International* (Apr. 1973): 8-10.

2907 Nes, D. "The U.S. Energy Crisis and the Middle East." *Military Review* 53 (Mar. 1973): 3-7.

2908 Shwadran, Benjamin. "Oil in the Middle East Crisis." *Middle Eastern Affairs* 8 (Apr. 1957): 126-34.

2909 Silbey, F. "Will Arab Oil Change the U.S.-Middle East Stance?" *Middle East Information Series* 23 (May 1973): 40-52.

2910 Stone, I. F. "What Price Arab Oil?" *Nation* (Oct. 4, 1947): 358-60.

2911 Tariki, A. "Oil in the Service of the Arab Cause." *Middle East Forum* 42:1 (1966): 23-35.

Soviet Interests in Middle East Oil

2912 Becker, Abraham S. *Oil and the Persian Gulf in Soviet Policy in the 1970's*. Santa Monica, California: RAND, P-4743, Dec. 1971.

2913 Berry, John A. "Oil and Soviet Policy in the Middle East." *Middle East Journal* 26 (Spring 1972): 149-60.

2914 DeNezza, Eugene J. "The Soviet Need for Middle East Oil." *Air University Review* 22:4 (May-June 1971): 52-57.

2915 Ebel, Robert E. *Communist Trade in Oil and Gas: An Evaluation of the Future Export Capacity of the Soviet Bloc*. New York: Praeger, 1970.

2916 Goldman, M. "The Soviet Role in Oil, Economics and the Middle East." *Middle East Information Series* 23 (May 1973): 87-96.

2917 Hassmann, Heinrich. *Oil in the Soviet Union*. Translated by Alfred M. Leeston. Princeton, New Jersey: Princeton University Press, 1953.

2918 Knowles, R. S. "A New Soviet Thrust." *Mid East* 9:6 (Dec. 1969): 5-9.

2919 Landia, L. "Soviet Interest in Middle East Oil." *New Middle East,* no. 3 (Dec. 1968): 16-21.

2920 Mazour, Anatole G. "Russia, the Middle East, and Oil." *World Affairs Interpreter* 22 (Winter 1952): 415-23.

2921 Rachkov, B. "The Russian Stake in the Middle East: A Noted Soviet Oil Expert Answers the Recent Western Criticisms of the Kremlin's Policy." *New Middle East*, no. 8 (May 1969): 36–37.

D / Conflict Continued, 1967–1973

2922 Arnoni, M. "The Near East and World Strategy." *New Outlook* 14:8 (Oct.–Nov. 1971): 20–24.

2923 Aron, Raymond. *De Gaulle, Israel and the Jews*. Translated by John Sturrock. New York: Praeger, 1969.

2924 Aronsfeld, C. "The Historical Boundaries of Palestine." *Contemporary Review* 213:1235 (Dec. 1968): 289–97.

2925 Avineri, S. "The New Status Quo." *Commentary* 45:3 (Mar. 1968): 49–54.

2926 Basiouni, M. Cherif, and Eugene M. Fisher. "The Arab-Israeli Conflict—Real and Apparent Issues: An Insight into Its Future from the Lessons of the Past." *St. John's Law Review* 44 (Jan. 1970): 399–465.

2927 Beaufre, A. "Réflexions sur la crise du Moyen-Orient." *Stratégie* (Oct.–Dec. 1970): 49–66.

2928 Beit-Hallahmi, B. "Some Psychosocial and Cultural Factors in the Arab-Israel Conflict: A Review of the Literature." *Journal of Conflict Resolution* 16:2 (June 1972): 269–80.

2929 Berger, Elmer. "The Crisis in the Middle East in Depth and Perspective." *Arab World* 15:9 (1969): 11–17.

2930 Cleveland, R. "Some 'Middle East Experts': More Dangerous Than Non-Professionals." *Arab World* 14:12 (Dec. 1968): 10–14.

2931 Dobbing, Herbert. *Cause for Concern: A Quaker's View of the Palestine Problem*. Monograph Series, no. 24. Beirut: Institute for Palestine Studies, 1970.

2932 Elkordy, Abdul-Hafez M. *Crisis of Diplomacy: The Three Wars . . . and After. . . .* San Antonio, Texas: Naylor, 1971.

2933 Elon, Amos. "The Israel-Arab Deadlock." *New York Review of Books* (Aug. 1, 1968): 14–20.

2934 Galtung, Johan. "Conflict Theory and the Palestine Problem." *Journal of Palestine Studies* 2:1 (1972): 34–63.

2935 ———. "Middle East and the Theory of Conflict." *Journal of Peace Research* 8:3–4 (1971): 173–206.

2936 Geyer, Georgie A. "Love and Hate in the Middle East." *Progressive* 36 (Apr. 1972): 27–30.

2937 Gleditsch, Nils P. "Interaction Patterns in the Middle East." *Cooperation and Conflict* 6:1 (1971): 15–30.

2938 Goldberg, A., and C. Yost. "The Middle East: Two Views." *Vista* 6:5 (May–June 1971): 33–37.

2939 Grant, Z. B. "Arab-Israeli Impasse." *New Republic* (Jan. 3, 1970): 15–17.

2940 Huntley, C. O. "Arab versus Jew: The Evolution of Two National Strategies." *Naval War College Review* 22:3 (Nov. 1969): 69–91.

2941 Kent, G. "Foreign Policy Analysis: The Middle East." *International Problems* 9:3–4 (Nov. 1970): 40–56.

2942 Kerr, Malcolm H. *The Middle East Conflict*. Headline Series, no. 191. New York: Foreign Policy Association, Oct. 1968.

2943 Khadduri, Majid, ed. *The Arab-Israeli Impasse: Expressions of Moderate Viewpoints on the Arab-Israeli Conflict by Well Known Western Writers*. Washington, D.C.: Luce, 1969.

2944 ———, ed. *Major Middle Eastern Problems in International Law.* Washington, D.C.: American Enterprise Institute for Public Policy Research, 1972.

2945 Kimche, Jon. "Where Do We Go Now? Agenda for 1972." *New Middle East,* no. 38 (Nov. 1971): 3–6.

2946 Koch, Howard, Jr. *Six Hundred Days: A Reappraisal of the Arab-Israeli Confrontation since June 1967.* Permanent Observer of the League of Arab States to the United Nations. New York, Mar. 1969.

2947 Kodsy, Ahmad El, and Eli Lobel. *The Arab World and Israel.* New York: Monthly Review Press, 1970.

2948 Laqueur, Walter Z. "The Middle East Is Potentially More Dangerous than Vietnam." *New York Times Magazine* May 5, 1968): 35.

2949 Lewis, Bernard. "Conflict in the Middle East." *Survival* 13 (June 1971): 192–98.

2950 Mason, Herbert. "Reflections on the Middle East Crisis." *Muslim World* 60 (Jan. 1970): 1–5.

2951 ———, ed. *Reflections on the Middle East Crisis.* The Hague: Mouton, 1970.

2952 Nutting, Anthony. "The Tragedy of Palestine from the Balfour Declaration to Today." *Arab World* 14:1–2 (Jan.–Feb. 1968): 3–6.

2953 Peres, Y. "The New Left and Israel." *New Outlook* 13:2 (Feb. 1970): 18–27.

2954 Reinhardt, G. Frederick. "The Middle East of the 1970's." *Air University Review* 21:4 (May–June 1970): 41–50.

2955 Rostow, E. "The Middle Eastern Crisis in the Perspective of World Politics." *International Affairs* 47 (Apr. 1971): 275–88.

2956 Toynbee, Arnold, and Louis Eaks. "Arnold Toynbee on the Arab-Israeli Conflict." *Journal of Palestine Studies* 2:3 (1973): 3-13.

2957 "The Unending Middle East Crisis." *Reporter* (June 29, 1967): 12-22.

2958 U.S. Congress. House of Representatives. Committee on Foreign Affairs. Subcommittee on the Near East. Hearings: *The Near East Conflict*. 91st Cong., 2d sess., 1970.

2959 Vatikiotis, P. J. *Conflict in the Middle East*. Chicago: Aldine-Atherton, 1971.

2960 Yost, C. "Israel and the Arabs: The Myths that Block Peace." *Atlantic Monthly* (Jan. 1969): 80-85.

Israeli Positions & Views

2961 Al-Roy, G. C. "Israeli Anxiety and War in the Middle East." *International Review of History and Political Science* 5:4 (Nov. 1968): 1-8.

2962 Avnery, Uri. "Unofficial and Unrepresentative, But...." *New Middle East*, no. 12 (Sept. 1969): 23-28.

2963 Ben Porath, Yeshayahu. "Greater Israel or Withdrawal?" *New Middle East*, no. 51 (Dec. 1972): 12-14.

2964 Bentwich, Norman. *Israel: Two Fateful Years, 1967-1969*. New York: Drake, 1972.

2965 "Can Arab and Jew Live Together in Palestine?" *Middle East International* (May 1971): 23-25.

2966 Carmel, H. "Who's who in the Israeli Protest Movement." *New Outlook* 17:4 (May 1974): 33-37.

2967 "Dayan's New Initiative." *New Middle East*, no. 37 (Oct. 1971): 32-34.

2968 Gellenor, J. "The Middle East: The Israeli Case." *Commentator* 14:3 (Mar. 1970): 9-12.

2969 Goldman, N. "The Future of Israel." *Foreign Affairs* 48 (Apr. 1970): 443–59.

2970 Harkabi, Y. "We Must Learn to Understand the Substance of the Arab Case." *New Middle East,* no. 2 (Nov. 1968): 26–30.

2971 Heradstveit, Daniel. "Israeli Elite Perceptions of the Arab-Israeli Conflict." *Journal of Palestine Studies* 2:3 (1973): 68–93.

2972 "How Young Israeli-Arabs See Their Future." *Atlas* 20:4 (Apr. 1971): 26–27.

2973 Kutler, Y. "Moshe Dayan: The Peace Map Needn't Be the Same as the Cease-Fire Lines. . . ." *Atlas* 18:12 (Dec. 1969): 48–50.

2974 Landau, J. "Israel's War of Words." *Jewish Observer and Middle East Review* (Feb. 7, 1969): 18–19.

2975 Leslie, S. C. "The Rift in Israel, I." *International Affairs* 45 (July 1969): 436–51.

2976 ———. "The Rift in Israel, II." *International Affairs* 45 (Oct. 1969): 617–30.

2977 Lipski, Sam. "Survival in the Seventies [Interview of Itzhak Rabin by Sam Lipski on Israel's Future]." *Jewish Observer and Middle East Review* (Jan. 16, 1970): 14–17.

2978 Meir, Golda. "Israel in Search of Lasting Peace." *Foreign Affairs* 51 (Apr. 1973): 447–61.

2979 ———. "The Right of Peoples to Live in Freedom." *Jewish Observer and Middle East Review* (July 4, 1971): 12–17.

2980 Ofner, Francis. "Young Arabs and Jews Extend Their Hands." *Christian Science Monitor* (Mar. 30, 1973): 9.

2981 Rayner, J. "The State of Israel: A Progressive Jewish View." *Anglo-Jewish Association Quarterly* 15:4 (Apr. 1971): 8–19.

2982 Schnall, David J. "Notes on the Political Thought of Dr. Moshe Sneh." *Middle East Journal* 27 (Summer 1973): 342–52.

2983 Shamir, Moshe. *My Life with Ishmael*. London: Vallentine, Mitchell, 1970.

Arab Positions & Views

2984 Abu-Lughod, I. "The Arab-Israeli Confrontation: Some Comments on the Future." *Arab Journal* 5:1–2 (1968): 12–23.

2985 ———. "The Quest for an Arab Future." *Arab Journal* 4:2–4 (1967): 22–29.

2986 Daher, Adel. *Current Trends in Arab Intellectual Thought*. Santa Monica, California: RAND, RM–5979, Dec. 1969.

2987 El Messiri, A. "Israel: Base of Western Imperialism." *Arab Journal* 5:3 (1968): 61–71.

2988 Fisher, Eugene M., and M. Cherif Bassiouni. *Storm over the Arab World*. Chicago: Follett, 1973.

2989 Gareeb, Edmund. "Mohammed Hassanein Heykal Discusses War and Peace in the Middle East." *Journal of Palestine Studies* 1:1 (1971): 3–20.

2990 Hadawi, Sami. *Palestine in Focus*. Palestine Essays, no. 7. Beirut: Palestine Liberation Organization Research Center, Aug. 1969.

2991 Halliday, Fred. "Egypt Moves West." *Ramparts* (Aug. 1971): 41–44.

2992 Harkabi, Yehoshafat. *Arab Attitudes toward Israel*. New York: Hart, 1972.

2993 Heradstveit, Daniel. "Arab Demands and Desires in the Conflict with the State of Israel." *Cooperation and Conflict* 6:2 (1971): 115–35.

2994 Hottinger, Arnold. "The Depth of Arab Radicalism." *Foreign Affairs* 51 (Apr. 1973): 491–504.

2995 Kerr, Malcolm H. *Regional Arab Politics and the Conflict with Israel*. Santa Monica, California: RAND, RM-5966, 1969.

2996 Losman, D. L. "The Arab Boycott of Israel." *International Journal of Middle East Studies* 3 (Apr. 1972): 99-122.

2997 Nutting, Anthony. "Israel through Middle Eastern Eyes: A Western Beachhead." *Arab World* 13:3 (Mar. 1967): 6.

2998 Pogson, W. "The Middle East: The Arab Case." *Commentator* 14:3 (Mar. 1970): 7-9.

2999 Rejwan, N. "Arab Intellectuals and Israel." *New Outlook* 14:6 (Aug. 1971): 25-31.

3000 Scheer, R. "The Nasser Thesis: Oil and the Arabs." *Ramparts* (Jan. 1968): 37-42.

3001 *Seminar of Arab Jurists on Palestine* (Algiers, 22-27 July 1967). Translated from the French by Edward Rizk. Monograph Series, no. 18. Beirut: Institute for Palestine Studies, 1968.

3002 Sharabi, H. "Modernity and the Arab World." *Middle East Forum* 44:3 (1968): 21-25.

3003 Trabulsi, F. "The Palestine Problem: Zionism and Imperialism in the Middle East." *New Left Review* 47 (Sept.-Oct. 1969): 53-90.

INDEX

The transliteration of proper names from Arabic and Hebrew into the Roman alphabet frequently results in a number of variant spellings. When authoritative sources such as Webster's *Biographical Dictionary* or the *Writer's Directory* provide accepted English spellings for a name, that version is used in the index for the variant spellings of the same name found in the text. If the variation in spelling is too extreme, the names are listed as separate entries.

In the entries below, the authors' names should read as follows: Abdel-Malek (1973); Bassiouni, M. Cherif (2926); Bethmann, Erich W. (18); Dmitriyev, E. (2668); Eisenstadt, S. N. (868); Granott, A. (1483); Hirschmann, Ira A. (2626); Leslie, S. Clement (905); Mogannam, E. Theodore (523); Nasser, G. A. (1672); Rachkov, B. (2864); Radovanovic, L. (649); Rosensaft, Menachem, Z. (1900); Sachar, Howard Morely (857); Schechtman, Joseph B. (1625); Seton-Williams, M. V. (1427).

Abbady, I. A., 139
Abbass, Abdul Majid, 1499
Abcarius, M. F., 1579
Abdel-Malek, Anouar, 480, 1973
Abdul-Rahman, As'ad, 2712
Abdullah, King (of Jordan), 219
Al-Abid, Ibrahim, 14, 1133, 2305
Abidi, Aqil Hyder Hasan, 500
Abi Mershed, Walid, 1811
Abouchdid, Eugenie Elie, 538
Abuetan, Barid, 1805
Abu-Ghazaleh, Adnan M., 1481
Abu-Lughod, Ibrahim, 317, 1095, 1132, 1885, 2017, 2984, 2985
Abu-Jaber, F. S., 1453, 1724, 2009, 2513, 2742
Abu Jaber, Kamel S., 501, 539

Abu Shilbaya, Muhammad, 2787
Acheson, Dean G., 1634
Ackley, Richard T., 2679
Adams, C. C., 385
Adams, Michael, 1789, 2794
Adams, Sherman, 1846
Adamson, David, 575
Adelman, M., 2878
Adie, W. A. C., 2703
Agwani, M. S., 572
Ahmed, Jamal Mohammad, 1320
Akins, James E., 2879, 2880
Akzin, Benjamin, 761
al- (names beginning with. *See* under second segment of name)
Alami, Musa, 1013
Alan, Ray, 2666

Alder, Bill, 734
Alder, C., 864
Aldington, Richard, 1382
Aldouby, Zwy, 2271
Aldrich, Winthrop W., 1853
Alexander, Lyle T., 328
Alexander, Yonah, 53, 1904
Alexayev, V., 2478
Alia, J., 2272
Allon, Yigal, 1119, 1725
Alpern, D. M., 2368
Alport, E. A., 865
Alter, R., 1264
Altoma, Salih J., 1096
American University, Foreign Area Studies Division, 369, 540, 577, 596
Amiran, D. H. K., 762
Ammar, Hamed, 370
Anabtawi, S. N., 1110, 1886
Andrews, Fannie F., 1454
Anglo-American Committee of Inquiry, 1580
Ansari, Zafar Ishaq, 1304
Anthem, T., 2680
Anthony, John D., 15, 16
Antic, P., 2063
Antonius, George, 1314
Antonovsky, Aaron, 763
Antoun, R., 346
Appel, Benjamin, 735
Arafat, Y., 2088
Arendt, Hannah, 1573
Arfa, Hassan, 578
Arian, Alan, 736, 763, 892, 893
Armstrong, Hamilton Fish, 1920
Armstrong, Harold Courtenay, 541
Arnold, G. L., 1620
Arnoni, M. S., 318, 972, 2544, 2922
Aron, Raymond, 2923
Aronsfeld, C., 2924
Arsenian, Seth, 1651
Aruri, Naseer H., 502, 2018, 2713
Asfour, John, 1482
Ash, J., 847
Ashhab, N., 2089
Ashkar, Riad, 2176
Astakhov, S., 949, 1070, 2010, 2714
Aston, Maj. Gen. Sir George, 1416
Atallah, R., 1939
Atiyah, E., 617
Atiyah, Edward, 1635
Atyeo, Henry C., 406, 1854, 2526
Avineri, Shlomo, 989, 990, 2925
Aviram, A., 1186, 1187
Avnery, Uri, 1265, 2189, 2962
Avram, Benno, 1740

El-Ayouty, Yassin, 483, 2240
Ayres, Henry F., 419
Ayrout, Father Henry Habib, 371
Azar, Edward E., 1790
Azcarate, Pablo de, 1628

Babcock, F. Lawrence, 1546
Badeau, John S., 336, 407, 1305, 1887, 2466, 2514, 2515
Badi, Joseph, 737, 894
Baer, Gabriel, 297, 372, 450
Bailey, G., 1071
Bakdash, Khalid, 2694
Baker, Henry E., 895
Balabkins, Nicholas, 937
Baldridge, Elward F., 2527
Baldwin, Hanson W., 1855, 2881
Balfour, Arthur J., 1225
Ballinger, Jerrold, 2271
Ballis, W., 2640
Baly, Dennis, 689, 1306
Banai, Margalit, 778
Barakat, Halim, 1072, 1073, 2075
Baratz, Joseph, 503
al-Barawy, Rashed, 405
Barbour, Nevill N. 451, 1315, 1500, 1581, 1629, 1717
Barclay, Brig. Cyril N., 1940
Bar-David, Molly Lyons, 233
Bardin, Shlomo, 1266
Barer, S., 1941
Barger, Thomas C., 2882
B'ari, S., 1138
Barjot, P., 1824
Barker, A. J., 1791
Barkes, G., 1878
Barman, T., 1687
Barnes, Wyatt E., 1726
Bar-Nir, D., 2343
Bar-On, Mordechai, 1942
Barrekette, A. E., 2731
Bartholomew, John, 130
Bartsch, William H., 17
Baruth, K. H., 1464
Bar-Yaacov, N., 1652
Bar-Zohar, Michael, 234, 1888, 2273
Base, Tarun, 2403
Bashan, Raphael, 1943
Bassiouni, M. Cherif, 2926, 2988
Baster, Albert S. James, 326, 504, 1024, 1045
Batal, James, 408, 1253
Battle, L., 2235, 2467
Bauer, Yehuda, 1515, 1516, 1557, 1558

Bawly, Dan, 1960
Baxter, R. R., 1741
Al-Bazzaz, A. R., 1303
Beaton, Leonard, 2011, 2212
Beatty, Ilene, 1428
Beaufre, Gen. Andre, 1825, 1944, 2213, 2927
Bechtold, Peter K., 635
Becker, Abraham S., 1139, 2912
Beecher, William, 505
Be'eri, Eliezer, 287, 348
Begin, Menachem, 1559, 1560
El-Behairy, M., 1742
Behrman, Lucy, 792
Bein, Alex, 235
Beit-Hallahmi, B., 2928
Beling, Willard A., 1321, 2468
Bell, Gertrude M. L., 542, 1344
Bell, J. Bowyer, 950, 1678, 1879, 2019, 2214, 2258
Beller, J., 866
Belyaev, I., 2306, 2354
Belyayev, I., 1889
Ben-Dak, Joseph D., 2307, 2704
Ben-Gurion, David, 236, 667, 668, 1198, 1211, 1267
Ben-Hanan, Eli, 2274
Ben-Horin, Meir, 237
Benor, J. L., 793
Ben Porath, Yeshayahu, 2275, 2308, 2963
Ben-Porath, Yoram, 794
Bentov, M., 1097
Bentwich, Norman, 238, 669, 690, 938, 1120, 1316, 1417, 1455, 1456, 2279, 2964
Bentwick, Joseph S., 764
Ben-Tzur, Avraham, 2641
Ben-Zur, A., 349
Berding, Andrew H., 1773
Berger, Earl, 652
Berger, Elmer, 1242–46, 1254, 1255, 1612, 2470, 2929
Berger, L., 877
Berger, Monroe, 298, 373, 420, 452
Bergmann, A., 1046
Berkman, Ted, 1945
Berliner, Joseph S., 2667
Berman, M., 795
Berman, S., 2516, 2796
Bermant, Chaim, 671
Bernadotte, Counte Folke, 1679, 1680
Bernard, Edward Fergusson, 1826
Bernstein, Marver H., 718, 2471
Berque, Jacques, 374
Berry, Maj. John A., 2883, 2913
Bess, Demaree, 1827

Best, G., 2900
Besterman, Theodore, 1
Bethmann, Erich W., 18, 1322
Bevis, Richard, 1340
Bevis, Vivian, 1074
Bharier, Julian, 17
Bilby, Kenneth W., 672
Binder, Leonard, 288, 562, 636
Bindra, A. P. S., 2259
Binns, John R., 2529
Birdwood, Lord (Christopher Bromhead), 220
Birnbaum, Ervin, 896
Bishop, Eric F. F., 2788
al-Bitar, Salah al-Din, 2234
Blair, Leon B., 2569
Blanc, Haim, 691, 796
Blanchard, Allan E., 1946
Blechman, Barry M., 928, 929
Bloomfield, L. M., 1928, 2297
Blumber, H., 1268
Blunt, Wilfrid S., 387
Blyth, Estelle, 2770
Boardman, Francis, 23
Bober, Arie, 1247
Bochenski, Feliks, 66, 2727
Bodenheimer, Henriette Hanna, 239
Bodman, Herbert L., Jr., 567
Boehm, Adolf, 1489
Bolling, L., 2471
Bolshakov, V., 1269, 1270
Bonne, Alfred, 299, 327, 711
Borochow, Baer, 1501
Borodin, Nikolai, 2020, 2589
Boskovic, M., 2090
Bourguiba, H., 2309
Boustany, Wedi Fr., 1429
Boutros-Ghali, B. Y., 618
Bovis, H. Eugene, 2771
Bowett, D. W., 2298
Bowle, John, 1472
Bowman-Manifold, Michael G. E., 1345
Boyd, James, 1921
Braham, Randolph L., 765
Bransten, Thomas R., 240
Brecher, M., 724, 973
Brenner, Y., 1561
Brill, J., 289
Brilliant, Moshe, 930
Bromberger, M., 1828
Bromberger, S., 1828
Brook, David, 2280
Broomfield, William S., 2012
Brown, David A., 2236
Brown, Neville, 1974, 2064–66, 2118, 2404, 2681, 2715
Brownell, George A., 2472

INDEX / 259

Brownrigg, Ronald, 2779
Bruegel, J., 437
Bruhns, Fred C., 1025
Bruno, Michael, 848, 878
Buber, Martin, 1212, 1248, 1249, 1630, 1633
Buchan, Alastair, 1689, 1947
Buehrig, Edward H., 1056
Buffum, W., 2076
Bullard, Sir Reader, 1690, 1691
Burdett, Winston, 319
Burgoyne, Elizabeth, 1346
Burns, Arthur Lee, 2299
Burns, E. L. M., 1922, 2302
Burrell, R., 2260
Burrowes, R., 1890
Burrows, Millar, 1537
Busch, Briton Cooper, 68, 1347, 1692
Bush, G., 2822
Bustani, Emile, 1856
Buzzard, A., 1709
Byford-Jones, W., 692, 1829
Byrnes, James F., 1538

Cadett, Thomas, 1604
Cagle, Malcolm W., 1929
Caiden, Gerald E., 719
Calvocoressi, Peter, 1804, 1857
Campbell, D., 506
Campbell, John C., 2393, 2394, 2405, 2406, 2434, 2473-75, 2528, 2590
Canaan, Muhammad Tawfiq, 1517
Capil, M., 350
Caradon, Baron Hugh M. F., 2310
Carmel, H., 2966
Carmi, S., 1230
Carmichael, Joel, 263, 300
Carr, J., 2177
Carr, Winifred, 507
Carrol, R., 2178
Carson, William Morris, 453
Carthew, Anthony, 1975, 1976
Carvely, Andrew, 1977, 2545
Cass, W., 2901
Castro y Rossi, Adolfo de, 1199
Cattan, Henry, 991, 992, 993, 1047, 2831
Cavanaugh, Sandy, 1830
Cecil, Charles O., 605
Chaliand, Gerard, 2021
Chapra, M., 2147
Charteris, M. M. C., 1595
Chase, Francis, 1582
Chejne, Anwar G., 637
Chenery, Hollis B., 2842
Cherson, Randolph, 1775

Chesnoff, Richard, 1891
Childers, Erskine B., 301, 1014, 1026, 1792, 1812, 1858
Chouraqui, Andre N., 1200
Chowdhuri, R. N., 1418
Christman, Henry M., 113, 114
Churba, J., 438
Church, Senator Frank, 2311
Churchill, Charles W., 302
Churchill, R. S., 1948
Churchill, W. S., 1948
Clark, C., 2312
Clark, D. M. J., 1831
Clark, Senator Joseph S., 1905
Clawson, Marion, 328
Cleland, Wendell, 454, 619
Clesner, H., 2489
Cleveland, Ray L., 1978, 2435, 2930
Coate, Winifred, 1027
Cobban, Alfred, 1637
Cohen, Abner, 797
Cohen, Aharon, 320, 1250
Cohen, E., 766, 867
Cohen, G., 767
Cohen, Geula, 922, 1562
Cohen, H., 579, 1201
Cohen, Israel, 1191, 1213, 1231
Cohen, Iva, 54
Cohen, Michael, 1431, 1490, 1518, 1519, 1923
Cohn, David, 1638
Coleman, Clarence L., Jr., 2546
Coleman, Herbert J., 2237, 2238
Colombe, Marcel, 409
Colombos, C. John, 1930
Colvin, Ian, 2728
Colvin, Robert D., 2201
Comay, M., 951
Comstock, Alzada, 1776
Cooke, Hedley V., 725
Cooley, John K., 611, 1098, 1140, 2022, 2313, 2706
Coon, Carleton S., 303
Cooper, B., 1256
Copeland, Miles, 410
Copeland, Paul W., 508
Corditz, D., 1979
Cottrell, Alvin J., 69, 2119, 2261, 2591, 2642
Council on Foreign Relations, 105
Courtney, Lord, 1348
Cox, D., 2682
Cox, Frederick J., 2202
Crabb, Cecil, Jr., 2476
Cragg, Kenneth, 279
Creamer, Daniel, 1590
Crecelius, Daniel, 455

Cremeans, Charles D., 439
Cressey, George, 304
Crossman, Richard H. S., 1596, 1597
Crown, Alan D., 834
Crum, Bartley C., 1621
Cumberbatch, A. N., 388
Cumming, H. H., 1419
Cunningham, Sir Alan, 1598
Curtis, Michael, 2407
Cust, Archer, 1502
Cygielman, Victor, 1183
Czudnowski, Moshe M., 897

Dadiani, L., 739
Dagan, Avigdor, 2651
Daher, Adel, 2986
Dajani, Burhan, 1613
Dallin, David, 2623
El Daly, S., 456
Dan, Uri, 2275
Daniel, Robert L., 2559
Dann, Uriel, 509, 580
Darin-Drabkin H., 712, 835, 2797
Darwish, I., 1924
Davids, Jules, 2436
Davidson, Brian, 879
Davis, Helen, 115
Davis, John H., 1075, 1121, 2314
Davis, Moshe, 673
Davis, U., 1251
Dawn, C. Ernest, 1296, 1297, 1307, 1383, 1907
Day, Alan, 939, 2716
Dayan, David, 1949
Dayan, Moshe, 1141, 1806, 1813, 1880, 2148
Dayan, Yael, 241, 1950
Dearden, Ann, 510
Decalo, S., 952
De Carmoy, G., 2592
Decraene, P., 953
Dees, Joseph L., 2751
Defrates, J., 1057
De Gaury, Gerald, 597, 674
de Gramont, Sanche, 2798
Deighton, H. S., 1599
Dekel, Efraim, 2276
Dekmejian, Hrair R., 375
DeNezza, Eugene J., 2914
DeNovo, John A., 2424
Denoyan, Gilbert, 2044
Dershowitz, A., 1142
Deshen, Shlomo A., 849
Dessouki, Ali, 2004, 2717
Deutscher, I., 2005

Devlin, K., 898
DeVore, Ronald M., 2120, 2239
Diab, Zuhair, 116
Diamond, William, 2727
Dib, George Moussa, 1143, 2281
Dimeshkie, Nadim, 2408
Dinstein, Yoram, 2023
Dinur, Ben-Zion, 978
Diqs, Isaak, 351
Dmitriev, Y., 2652
Dmitriyev, E., 2477, 2478, 2668
Dobbing, Herbert, 2931
Dobb, C. H., 321
Dobb, Peter C., 482, 1076, 1077
Dodge, Bayard, 2425
Doerr, Arthur H., 880
Doherty, Kathryn B., 2729
Donovan, John, 2409
Donovan, R. J., 1951
Dorsey, William H., Jr., 2045, 2340
Dotan, Uri, 24
Doty, L. L., 1881
Douglas-Home, A., 2683
Douglas-Home, C., 2121
Dov, Joseph, 2789
Dowty, A., 2315
Draper, Theodore, 940, 941, 2371
Dror, Yehezkel, 761
Druks, H., 2593
Dubnov, Semen Markovich, 1197
Duchene, François, 2122

Eaks, Louis, 2956
Eaton, Joseph W., 768
Eayrs, James, 1793
Eban, Abba (Audrey S.), 653, 726, 727, 769, 942, 1202, 1662, 1814
Ebel, Robert E., 2915
Ebon, Martin, 1653
Eckardt, A. Roy, 2316
Edelman, Maurice, 242
Edelsberg, Herman, 2479
Eden, Sir Anthony, 1832, 1833
Edgerton, Glen E., 1859
Edlund, Milton C., 330
Edmonds, C. J., 581
Efimenco, N. Marbury, 2517
Efrat, Elisha, 2772
Ehrlich, M., 2317
Eisenberg, J., 1257
Eisenhower, Dwight D., 1847
Eisenstadt, S. N., 702, 770, 868
el- (names beginning with. See under second segment of name)
Elath, Eliahu, 771, 1931

Elazar, D., 1144
Eliot, George, 2480
Elkashef, Ahmed R., 1883
Elkordy, Abdul-Hafez M., 2932
Eller, E. M., 2481
Elliot, Ward, 458
Ellis, Harry B., 728, 2695
Elon, Amos, 772, 1145, 1952, 2933
Elston, D. R., 675
Emanuel, Muriel, 55
Entelis, J., 335, 2077
Epstein, Leon D., 1834
Eran, Oded, 2223, 2643
al-Eran, Tahany, 44
Ereli, Eliezer, 1815
Errera, Leo Abram, 2657
Ethridge, Willie Snow, 2790
Ettinghausen, Richard, 25
Evans, A., 2091, 2092
Evans, Laurence, 1401
Evenari, Michael, 740
Evron, Yair, 1932, 2123, 2124, 2410
Eyal, E., 798
Eytan, Walter, 729

Faherty, Robert, 1058
Fakhry, Rashed F., 2518
Falk, R. D., 931
Fall, Bernard B., 1816
Falls, Cyril, 1350, 1727
Fancher, Michael, 1059
Farah, Caesar E., 1323
Farbenstein, Leonard, 2012
Farhi, D., 1173
Faris, N. A., 1324
Farjo, Ya'akov, 899
Farnie, D. A., 1743
Farouki, H., 1099
Farra, R., 2707
Farrell, James Thomas, 703
Fatemi, Nasrollah S. 1325
Al-Fattal, R. K., 2042
Faulkner, Brian, 390
Fay, Sidney, 1639
Fein, Leonard J., 900
Feiner, Leon, 1762
Feinstein, R., 2799
Feis, Herbert, 676, 1861
Feiwel, T. R., 1520
Fellowes, Peregrine, 2884
Fernea, Elizabeth Warnock, 484, 582
Fernea, Robert A., 583
Field, James A., Jr., 2426, 2570
Field, M., 543
Fielding, George, 1583

Finbert, Elian-J., 741
Fine, Helen, 773
Finer, Herman, 1326, 1794
Finger, Nachum, 881
Fink, Reuben, 1539
Finkelstein, Louis, 1203
Finnie, David H., 2427, 2845, 2846
Fisher, Eugene M., 2988
Fisher, Harold H., 2624
Fisher, Roger D., 2318
Fisher, Sidney Nettleton, 267, 352, 353
Fisher, W. B., 131
Fishman, Aryei, 699
Fitzgerald, Sir William, 2823
Fitzsimmons, Matthew A., 1457
Flapan, Simha, 460, 923, 1188
Fletcher, M. E., 1744
Fletcher-Cooke, J., 742
Florsheim, Joel, 693
Foda, Ezzeldin, 1147, 2110
Forsythe, David P., 1060, 1631, 2594
Fowler, R., 2708
Fox, S., 1214
Franjieh, S., 2093
Frank, Gerold, 1563, 1564
Frank, Helmut J., 2847
Frank, L. A., 2203
Frank, M. Z., 694, 695, 869, 955
Frankel, E., 2902
Frankel, Paul, 2848
Frankenstein, Carl, 704
Frankl, Ludwig August, 1204
Freedman, Robert O., 2669
Freeman, R., 485
Fried, Jerome J., 330
Friedman, George, 979
Friedman, Isaiah, 1205, 1361
Friedrich, Carl J., 1540
Friendly, A., Sr., 2024
Frischwasser Ra'anan, H. F., 1458
Froelich, J. C., 956
Fromm, J., 2373
Frye, Richard N., 2411
Fulbright, Senator James William, 2319, 2437
Furlonge, Geoffrey, 512, 1100

Gabbay, Rony E., 1028
Gabelic, A., 2224
Gabrieli, Francesco, 280
Gagnon, M. H., 1925
Galatoli, Anthony M., 391
Gallagher, Charles F., 612, 613
Gallman, Waldemar, 584
Galtung, Johan, 2934, 2935

Garber-Talmon, Yonina, 836
Garcia-Granados, Jorge, 1654
Gardiner, Arthur Z., 2560
Gardner, Brian, 1349
Garrett, W. B., 1848
Gaspard, J., 598, 2046, 2519
Gazit, S., 1148
Geddes, C. L., 4, 5
Gellenor, J., 2968
Gendzier, Irene L., 2025, 2078, 2718
Gerling, Shalom, 1565
Gershman, C., 2482
Gervasi, Frank, 1566, 1892
Geva, Ahron, 901
Geyer, Georgie A., 2936
Ghareeb, Edmund, 2241, 2989
El-Ghonemy, Mohammad Riad, 329
Gibb, H. A. R., 281, 1503
Gidney, James B., 1402
Gillon, D., 2344
Gilmour, I., 1078
Gleditsch, Nils P., 2937
Glick, Edward B., 1640
Glubb, Lt. Gen. Sir John Bagot, 354, 513, 514, 932, 1718, 1807, 1835, 1893
Gluek, Nelson, 2730
Godin, M., 2719
Goitein, S. D., 322, 799, 1206
Golan, Galia, 2595
Goldberg, A., 2938
Goldberg, Harvey E., 850, 851, 852
Goldman, Marshall I., 2671, 2672, 2916
Goldman, N., 2969
Goldmann, Nahum, 243, 980, 1271
Golomb, Eliyahu, 1341
Goodman, M., 2596
Gordon, Cyrus H., 1817
Gordon, Helen C., 544
Gorkin, Michael, 837
Gottlieb, Gidon, 2345
Grabill, Joseph L., 2428
Graham, R., 2114
Granovsky (Granott), Abraham, 713, 1483, 1601
Granqvist, Hilma, 306, 1484
Grant, Z. B., 2047, 2939
Grassmuck, George, 47, 563
Graves, Philip P., 221, 1432
Graves, Robert, 1384
Graves, R. M., 1433
Gray, Colin S., 2262
Gray, John, 2773
Gray, Richard A., 6
Great Britain
    Admiralty, Naval Intelligence Division, 323
    Colonial Office, 1362, 1363, 1411–

Great Britain *(Continued)*
    13, 1459, 1460, 1473–76, 1504–6, 1521–25, 1535, 2778
    Foreign Office, 106
Green, S. J., 995
Greener, Leslie, 1763
Greenspan, Morris, 1149
Grieb, Conrad K., 1368
Griffith, T., 2374
Griffith, William E., 2242
Grimwood-Jones, D., 27
Gritz, S., 2752
Gross, Feliks, 1224
Gruber, Ruth, 677, 1605
Gruen, George E., 2282, 2753
Gruenbaum, Ludwig, 1606
Gubser, Peter, 564
Guenther, H. P., 565
Gulick, John, 566
Guriel, B., 2684

Haberman, Stanley John, 585
Hadawi, Sami, 800, 996, 1029, 1079, 1083, 1403, 1434, 1435, 1615, 2283, 2320, 2990
Haddad, George M., 290, 291, 355
Haddad, W., 2068
Haim, Sylvia G., 1298, 1308, 1317, 1327
Hakim, George, 1084, 2561
Halbrook, Stephen, 1215
Halderman, John W., 1933
Halevi, Nadav, 882
Halkin, H., 902, 1272, 2800
Hallberg, Charles, 1745
Halliday, Fred, 2991
Halpern, Ben, 1192, 1233, 2548
Halpern, Manfred, 268, 461
Hamilton, Charles W., 2849
Hamlett, Bruce D., 1693
Hammad, Khairi, 2754
Hammad, M. B., 1150
Hamzeh, Fuad S., 1681, 1682, 2284
Hanania, Farid S., 2395
Hanauer, E. R., 2355
Hanna, Elias W., 2110
Hanna, Paul L., 1461, 1602, 1778, 2438
Harari, Yechiel, 801
Harbottle, M., 2300
Harbutt, C., 1953
Hare, Raymond A., 1622
Harkabi, Yehoshafat, 654, 655, 1954, 2026, 2048, 2049, 2215, 2216, 2970, 2992
Harlech, L., 1862
Harman, Zena, 853
Harrigan, Anthony, 1719

Harris, Christina Phelps, 422
Harris, Frank, 1894
Harris, George L., 376, 515
Harris, Mervyn, 1273
Harrison, Joseph G., 337
Harrison, P. W., 1414
Hart, Parker T., 2321, 2439, 2483
Hartshorn, J. E., 2850
Hasan, Saadat, 2040, 2755
Hashavia, Arie, 2685
Hassmann, Heinrich, 2917
Hattis, Susan Lee, 1111, 1112
Hauenstein, Fritz, 2720
Haupert, J. S., 1685
Hauslich, A., 870
Hays, James B., 2731
Hearn, Sir Arthur, 2833
Heathcote, Nina, 2299
Hebrew University of Jerusalem, 2285
Heikal, Mohamed H., 411
Heiman, Leo, 1884, 1955, 2125
Heitmann, G., 2625
Heller, Joseph, 1193
Henderson, Loy W., 2484, 2485
Henkin, Louis, 981
Henricus [pseud.], 1616
Henriques, Robert, 1818
Heradstveit, Daniel, 2094, 2971, 2993
Herman, Simon N., 943
Herrmann, Klaus J., 1369
Hertzberg, Arthur, 1113, 1194, 2549
Heruthi, E., 1174
Herzl, Theodor, 1216
Herzog, C., 1956
Hess, Clyde G., Jr., 567
Hessler, William H., 1863
Heth, Meir, 883
Hewins, Ralph, 1683, 2834
Heymont, Irving, 2149-52, 2191
Higgins, R., 1908
Hilmy, H., 1122
Himadeh, Sa'id, 1485
Hinden, Rita, 1507
Hindle, P., 1934
Hinteroff, E., 1864
Hirschmann, Ira A., 1607, 2626
Hirst, D., 2050, 2851, 2903
Hirszowicz, Lukasz, 1547
Hishmeh, G., 2126
Hitti, Philip K., 282, 545
Hochman, L., 2106
Hodes, Aubrey, 1114, 2217
Hodson, H. V., 1694
Hofman, John E., 802
Holborn, L., 1102
Hollis, Christopher, 2779
Holloway, J. L., Jr., 2529

Holt, Peter, 377
Homan, Paul T., 2895
Hopkins, Harry, 486
Hopkins, Lister G., 1436
Hopwood, Derek, 27, 2579
Horowitz, David, 678, 1507
Horrocks, Gen. Brian, 1779
Hoskins, Halford L., 338, 1728, 1780, 1865, 2440, 2562
Hottinger, Arnold, 2115, 2994
Hourani, Albert H., 283, 307, 546, 1781, 2396, 2397
Hourani, Cecil A., 621, 1048, 1981
Hourani, George, 998
Houston, J. A., 2530
Howard, Harry N., 28, 29, 70-72, 487, 656, 1030, 1061, 1062, 1404-7, 1866, 2013, 2069, 2286, 2287, 2429, 2441, 2531, 2534, 2550, 2551
Howard, M., 1895
Howard, Norman F., 516, 1370, 2070
Howarth, David, 599
Hudson, James, 2732
Hudson, Michael C., 568, 2028, 2051, 2079, 2801
Hughes, Emmet J., 2532, 2597
Humbaraci, Arslan, 2533
Hunter, Robert E., 1895, 2442, 2486, 2627, 2628
Huntley, C. O., 2940
Hurewitz, J. C., 73, 118, 292, 339, 356, 657, 1584, 2127, 2128, 2412, 2487
Husayn, M. T., 1324
al-Husri, Sati, 1390
Hussein, Aziza, 462
Hussein, King (of Jordan), 222, 223, 517
Husseini, Mohammed Y. al, 1486
Hutchison, Cmdr. E. H., 1808
Hutton, J., 1878
Hyamson, Albert, 1462

Ibish, Yusuf, 119
Ibrahim, S., 2413
Ingrams, D., 1371, 1395
International Bank for Reconstruction and Development, 518
Institute for Mediterranean Affairs, 1031
Ionides, Michael G., 641, 2733, 2734
Ireland, Philip, 586
Ismael, Tareq Y., 440, 441, 2029
Israel
    Army, General Headquarters, Historical Branch, 1819
    Central Bureau of Statistics, 1152
    Ministry of Defense, 1155-57

Israel *(Continued)*
  Ministry for Foreign Affairs, 803, 958, 1153, 1154, 1957, 1982, 2030
Issawi, Charles, 392, 463, 464, 642, 658, 1867, 2398, 2520, 2629, 2852, 2885
Ivanov, Yuri, 1217
Iwan, James L., 465
Izzeddin, Nejla, 284

Jabara, Abdeen, 1328, 2014
Jabbarah, 'Abidin, 1686
Jabber, Fuad, 1143, 2031, 2218, 2219
Jabbour, George, 854
Jabotinsky, Vladimir, 1585. *See also* Zhabotinskii, Vladimir Evgan'evich
Jackh, Ernest, 659
Jackson, Robert, 2169
Jacob, Abel, 959
Jacoby, F. J., 139
Jalis, A., 1983
Janowsky, Oscar I., 714
Jansen, G. H., 1234, 2735
Jansen, Michael E., 1541, 1542
Jargy, S., 2052
Jeffries, Joseph M. N., 1372, 1526
Jerusalem, Central Bureau of Statistics, 2802
Jewish Agency for Palestine, 1508
Jiryis, Sabri, 805–8
Joesten, Joachim, 1765
Johns, R., 1695
Johnson, John J., 293, 1085
Johnson, Joseph E., 1124, 2443
Johnson, Lyndon Baines, 1896
Johnson, Michael, 2257
Johnson, Paul, 1836
Johnston, Eric, 2746–48
Johnston, Scott D., 903
Johnston, Sir Charles H., 520
Jones, David L., 933
Jones, S., 2824
Joseph, Bernard, 1463
Joshua, Wynfred, 2663, 2664
Joudah, A., 2580
Judd, Denis, 1373
Jutkowski, A., 57

Kabeel, Soraya M., 48
Kac, Arthur W., 679
Kafman, A., 2571
Kagan, Col. Benjamin, 1729
Kahn, A. E., 1548
El-Kammash, Magdi, 457

Kanovsky, Eliyahu, 643, 838, 872, 1984, 1985
Kanowitz, K., 2346
Kaplan, Mordecai Menahem, 1274
Kardouche, George K., 466
Karmi, H., 2780
Karmon, Yehuda, 132
Karpat, Kemal H., 269
Kashin, Y., 960
Katsh, Abraham I., 745
Katz, Samuel, 1438
Katz, Ze'ev, 2654, 2709
Kazin, A., 1986
Kaznelson, Siegmund, 1632
Kedourie, Elie, 587, 1357, 1439, 1477, 2399
Keesing's Research Report, 1959
Keith-Roach, Edward, 1442
Kemp, Geoffrey, 2129, 2130, 2131, 2132
Kendall, Henry, 1464
Kennedy, James R., Jr., 8
Kenny, L. M., 660, 1329, 1987
Kent, G., 2941
Kerr, Malcolm H., 340, 357, 423, 442, 443, 467, 547, 644, 2444, 2942, 2995
Khadduri, Majid, 224, 294, 341, 588, 623, 645, 2943, 2944
Khalidi, Ahmed, 2176
Khalidi, E., 809
Khalidi, U., 1032
El-Khalidi, W., 1015, 1016
Khalidi, Walid, 119, 1440
Khalil, Muhammad, 624
Khan, Raisa, 2655
Khan, Rasheeduddin, 1299, 1421
Kharmis, S., 2535
Al-Khatib, Rouhi, 2795
Khouri, Fred J., 270, 548, 934, 2736, 2756
Khoury, Victor, 2757
Kiesewetter, Wolfgang, 2721
Kimche, David, 1491, 1656, 1657, 1663, 1960
Kimche, Jon, 1103, 1318, 1374, 1491, 1655–57, 1663, 1710, 2322, 2598, 2886, 2945
Kinen, I. L., 2758
King, Gillian, 1720
Kingsbury, Robert C., 133
Kinross, Lord, 1746
Kirk, George E., 271, 1049, 1586, 2599
Kirshner, S., 2133
Kisch, Frederick H., 1509
Kissinger, Henry A., 2376–78
Kitchen, Helen A., 393
Klausner, Samuel Z., 706

Klayman, Maxwell I., 839
Klein, Edward, 1891
Klieman, Aaron S., 1358, 1415, 2600
Kliemer, Don, 2835
Klinghoffer, A., 2601
Knatchbull-Hugessen, Hughe (Brabourne), 1549
Knight, M. M., 1838
Knightly, Philip, 1385
Knisbacher, M., 855
Knohl, Dov, 1664
Knowles, R. S., 2918
Koburger, Charles W., Jr., 1782
Koch, Howard, Jr., 1961, 2946
Kochan, R., 961
Kodsy, Ahmad El, 2696, 2947
Koestler, Arthur, 1441
Kolesnichenko, T., 1889
Korczyn, A., 2220
Korn, R., 982
Kostanick, Huey Louis, 2904
Kosut, Hal, 1911
Kotch, W. J., 1962
Kotker, Norman, 2781
Koury, Enver M., 295
Kovner, Milton, 2673
Kraft, E., 1912
Kraines, Oscar, 904
Krammer, A., 1642
Kreinin, Mordechai E., 962
Kuhl, Arthur, 2869
Kujoth, Jean Spealman, 91
Kulski, W. W., 2602
Kuroda, A., 1104
Kuroda, Yasumasa, 1104, 2095
Kurzman, Dan, 1658
Kushner, Gilbert, 856
Kushnir, S., 1492
Kutler, Y., 2973
Kutten, A., 58

L., T. R., 1783
Lacoutre, Jean, 424
Lacoutre, Simone, 424
Lall, Arthur, 1897
Lamar, Lt. Col. Kirby, 2108
Landau, Eli, 2805
Landau, Jacob M., 59, 394, 810, 897, 2974
Landia, L., 2919
Landis, Lincoln, 2015
Landsberg, Hans H., 328
Landshut, Siegfried, 983
Lane, Edward W., 378
Lanteri, R., 2205

Lapidoth, R., 2341
Laptev, V., 1275
Laqueur, Walter Z., 120, 661, 1195, 1235, 1276, 1277, 1898, 2006, 2225, 2323, 2581, 2603, 2604, 2644, 2645, 2697–99, 2722, 2887, 2948
Larkin, Margaret, 1665
Laufer, L., 963–65
Lau-Lavie, Naphtali, 244
Lauterpacht, E., 1868, 1926
Lawrence, T. E., 1386
Lazar, David, 1587
Leary, B., 2303
Leavitt, William, 2170
Lebkicher, Roy, 2853
Lebow, R., 1375
Lees, G. M., 2836
Le Gassick, T., 1988
Legault, Albert, 30
Legum, Colin, 2263
Lehm, W., 2096
Lehrman, Hal, 74, 680, 811, 1730, 1731
Leiden, Carl, 31, 425
Lenczowski, George, 75, 272, 358, 426, 606, 1330, 2226, 2488, 2582, 2605, 2630, 2854
Lengyel, Emil, 1465
Leonard, Larry, 2288
Leopold, Louis E., Jr., 1732
Lesch, Ann Mosely, 1001
Leshem, Moshe, 2606
Leslie, S. Clement, 905, 2243, 2975, 2976
Lesser, A., 2489
Leulliette, Pierre, 1839
Levenberg, Aliza, 1913, 1990
Levin, Harry, 1666, 2791
Levin, Nora, 1574
Levitch, Joel, 1643
Levi-Valensi, A., 984
Levy, Avigdor, 24, 2253
Lewis, Bernard, 285, 1869, 1991, 2400, 2414, 2607, 2949
Lewis, F., 743
Lewis, William H., 607, 614
Lewisohn, Ludwig, 1493
Lias, Godfrey, 1733
Lichstenstadter, Ilse, 468
Lichtblau, J., 2905
Lichtheim, George, 1840, 2521
Liddell Hart, Basil H., 1387, 1696, 1963
Likhovski, E., 906
Lilienthal, Alfred M., 2445, 2536, 2537
Lindberg, John, 2563
Lipski, Sam, 2977

Lissak, M., 907
Littell, Robert, 1891
Little, Shelby, 2053
Little, T. R., 625
Little, Tom, 379, 1766, 1767, 2054, 2289
Litvinoff, Barnet, 121, 245, 246, 1218
Lkinov-Malul, Ruth, 882
Lloyd, George Ambrose L., 395
Lloyd, Seton, 589, 2837
Lobel, Eli, 1278, 2947
Lockwood, L., 2181
Loder, J. de V., 1408
Loftus, John A., 2838
London, Isaac, 2646
London Institute of World Affairs, 141
Longgood, William F., 1784
Longrigg, Stephen H., 134, 549, 590, 2401, 2839, 2840, 2855, 2856
Lorch, Netanel, 1659, 1667
Losman, D. L., 2996
Lotz, Wolfgang, 2277
Lourie, Arthur, 1236
Love, Kenneth, 1795, 2324
Lowdermilk, Walter C., 1588
Lowenstein, R., 2153
Loya, A., 427
Lubell, Harold, 2857
Luchsinger, F., 2227
Lufti, Ashraf, 2858
Luke, Harry C., 1442
Lumer, Herman, 1279, 1280, 1644, 2325
Lurie, Jesse, 1567
Lutfiyya, Abdullah M., 302
Luttwak, Edward, 296, 2194, 2195

M., D. L., 2608
MacCallum, Elizabeth P., 551
McClain, J., 2806
McClanahan, Grant Y., 76
McClellan, Grant S., 1623
McDermott, Anthony, 2228, 2229
McDonald, James G., 681
MacDonald, Robert W., 626
McGill, Ralph, 682
McGuire, Carl, 1860
MacInnes, Archdeacon A.C., 1017
MacIntyre, Donald, 1550
McKay, Vernon, 627
MacLean, Donald, 1697
Macmillan, Harold, 1841
McMunn, Sir G., 1350
McSherry, James E., 1849

Magnes, Judah Leon, 1630, 1633, 1645
Magnus, R., 2490, 2491
Main, Ernest, 1527
Majaj, A., 1032
Makdisi, Samir A., 552
Malawer, Stuart S., 2071
Malik, Charles, 308
El Mallakh, Ragaei, 1860
Mallison, W. T., Jr., 1160, 1219, 1258, 1377, 2032, 2326, 2552
Malone, Joseph J., 1870
Mandel, Neville, 1342, 1343
Mann, Clarence, 2860
Mann, Peggy, 247
Manners, I., 2759
Mansfield, Peter, 273, 380, 488-90, 1698, 2244
Mansoor, Menahem, 122
Mansour, A., 1125, 1126, 2808
Mansur, George, 1528
Manuel, Frank E., 1396, 1543
Ma'oz, Moshe, 550
al-Marayati, Abid A., 576
Marden, Luis, 522
Mark, M., 2492
Marks, A., 774
Marks, J. H., 662
Marlowe, John, 396, 397, 628, 1319, 1466, 1529, 1747, 2861
Marr, P., 591
Marriot, J. A. R., 1699
Marshall, S. L. A., 1820, 1964, 2154
Marshall, Thomas, 2171
Martin, H. G., 2609
Marx, E., 812
Masannat, G., 2493
Mason, C., 1536
Mason, Herbert, 2950, 2951
Mates, L., 2007, 2290
Matovu, Benyamin, 873
Matthews, Charles, D., 1443
Mattison, Francis C., 2494
Maugham, Robin C. R., 1589
Mawlawi, F., 935
Mawlawi, R., 2782
Mayfield, James B., 428
Mayhew, C., 813, 1603
Mazour, Anatole G., 2920
Medding, Peter Y., 908
Medlicott, William Norton, 1700
Medvedko, L., 1281
Medzini, M., 1992, 2723, 2888
Medzini, R., 2889
Mehdi, M., 1161
Mehlman, William, 2760

Meinardus, Otto F. A., 469
Meinertzhagen, Richard, 1467
Meir, Golda, 248, 2978, 2979
Meissner, Frank, 2738
Mejcher, Helmut, 1409
Melamid, Alexander, 2862
Menuhin, Moshe, 1282
Meo, Leila M. T., 569
Merlin, Samuel, 2327, 2415
Mertens, R., 2686
Mertz, Robert Anton, 2055
Merz, Robert, 2610
Messerschmidt, E. A., 1033
El Messiri, A., 2987
Meyer, A. J., 331, 2564
Meyer, Peter, 2658
Mezerette, Jean, 2206
Mezerik, A. G., 1034, 1748, 2291
Michener, J., 1105
Mikdashi, Zuhayr, 2841
Mikes, George, 683
Mikesell, Raymond F., 2842
Miksche, F., 2687
Milenkovic, M., 2416
Millar, Thomas B., 2631
Miller, Martin J., 2172, 2182, 2183
Millis, Walter, 1624
Milner, Alfred M., 398
Milstein, Jeffrey, S., 2136, 2417
Misri, B. A., 2761
Mitchell, D., 2906
Mogannam, Matiel E. Theodore, 523, 1530
Mohy Ed-Din, K., 470
Mok, M., 2196
Mones, Hussein, 1850
Monroe, Elizabeth, 1701, 1702, 1899, 2329
Moore, Austin L., 412
Moorehead, Alan, 1551
Morgenthau, Hans J., 2446
Morris, James, 524
Morrison, S. A., 1309
Mortimer, Edward, 2265
Moskin, J., 744
Mosley, Leonard, 1531, 2890
Mousa, Suleiman, 1388
Mroue, Karim, 2033
Mruhe, Kerim, 2034
Muenzner, G., 1494
Muftic, M., 2081
Mughraby, Muhamad A., 2843
Muhsam, H. V., 814
Mumford, Maj. Jay C., 2612
Murphy, Capt. F. M., 2688
Murphy, Charles J. V., 1851

Musaelyan, G., 739
Muzzio, D., 1890

Naamani, Israel T., 745
Nachmias, David, 909
Naguib, Mohammed, 413
Nahumi, Mordechai, 966, 1162, 2418, 2447
Nakhleh, Emile A., 2097
Nardi, Noach, 1495
Nasmyth, Jenny, 884
Nasser, Gamal Abdel, 414, 415, 416, 444, 1672, 1768, 1871
Nathan, Robert R., 1590
Naufal, Sayyid, 342
Nawfal, S., 1238
Neame, Alan, 471
Nes, David G., 1914, 2292, 2448, 2449, 2613, 2614, 2907
Nevakivi, Jukka, 1359, 1360
Nevo, Y., 1018
Newcombe, Hanna, 2137
Newman, A., 744
Newton, Frances, 1444
Nihart, Brooke, 2184
Nimrod, Yoram, 2220, 2762-64
Nissenson, Hugh, 840
Nixon, President Richard M., 2357
Noble, Iris, 249
Nolte, Richard H., 77, 1331, 1872, 2495
Noth, Martin, 684
Nuseibeh, A., 1175
Nuseibeh, Hazem Saki, 1332
Nutting, Anthony, 225, 1711, 1796, 1842, 2266, 2952, 2997

O'Ballance, Edgar, 1660, 1821, 1965, 2098, 2109, 2138, 2197, 2207
Obieta, J. A., 1749
O'Brien, Patrick, 472
Oded, Yitzhak, 815, 816
Odell, Peter R., 2891
Ofer, Gur, 885, 2674
Ofner, Francis, 2809, 2980
O'Neill, Capt. Bard E., 2496
Oppenheimer, A'haron, 775
Oren, N., 975
Oren, Stephen, 910, 1176
Orni, Ephraim, 135
Ottensooser, Robert D., 715
Oudes, Bruce, 2246
Owen, Henry, 2185
Owen, L., 2892
Oxtoby, Willard G., 2330

Pack, Howard, 886
Pa'il, Meir, 2139
Palmer, J. M., 2572
Palmer, Monte, 647
Parker, J. S. F., 648
Parkes, James William, 1446–48, 1575
Parkinson, Sir Cosmo, 1712
Partridge, Burgo, 1568
Parzen, H., 1019
Patai, Josef, 250
Patai, Raphael, 251, 309, 310, 359, 525 946, 1207, 1220, 1592
Patterson, Gardiner, 2450
Patterson, J. H., 1351
Paul, J., 335
Pavel, E., 841
Peabody, Lt. Col. James B., 1333, 2419
Peake, Frederick G., 526
Pearlman, Lt. Col., Moshe, 252, 2155
Peck, M., 381
Pennar, Jaan, 2700
Pensin, D., 2893
Pepper, Curtis G., 527, 1967
Peres, Shimon, 2156
Peres, Yochanan, 817, 2953
Peretz, Don, 275, 360, 429, 663, 720, 818, 911, 1000, 1035, 1036, 1051, 1107, 1115, 1163, 1164, 2056, 2331, 2565, 2749, 2765
Peretz, Martin, 985
Peritz, R., 967
Perlmann, M., 361, 445, 1397, 1618, 1797, 1873, 2522
Perlmutter, Amos, 721, 912, 913, 1063, 1995
Perowne, Stewart, 2792
Perrett, Michael, 629, 630
Petrov, R., 2647
Petuchowski, Jakob J., 1283
Pfaff, Richard H., 1334, 2573, 2825
Pfeiffer, C. F., 2774
Philby, H. St. John, 600, 2844
Phillips, Paul G., 528
Pickering, Peter E., 60
Pinner, Walter, 1037
Plischke, Elmer, 9
Pogson, W., 2998
Poliakov, Leon, 1576
Polk, William R., 311, 362, 1468, 2523
Pollak, Adolf, 1489
Porath, Reuben, 2157
Porath, Yehoshua, 1426, 1619
Portal, R., 2158
Porter, Paul A., 1935
Prahye, B., 1284

Pranger, Robert J., 2358
Preston, Lee E., 332
Primakov, Yevgeny, 1889, 2632
Prittie, Terence, 253, 746
Prjla, A., 529, 2072
Pryce-Jones, David, 2099
Psomiades, Harry J., 2583
Pudney, John, 1750
Pundik, H., 819

Al-Qawuqji, Fauzi, 1669, 1670
Quandt, William B., 1001, 2036, 2497, 2498
Qubain, Fahim I., 573
Quester, George H., 2221
Quraishi, Zaheer, M., 399

Rabbath, Edmond, 343
Rabi, Z., 776
Rabin, Albert I., 61
Rabinovich, Abraham, 2811
Rabinovich, Itamar, 553
Rabinowicz, Oscar K., 1285
Rabinowitz, Ezekiel, 1259
Rachkov, B., 2864, 2921
Rackman, Emanuel, 722
Radmilovic, T., 631
Radovanovic, L., 649, 1116, 2342
Rafael, Amnon E., 2332
Raleigh, J. S., 632, 1735
Ramazani, Rouhollah K., 2724
Raphaeli, N., 874, 1165, 1166, 1189
Rashed, Mohammad, 1117
Rayner, J., 2981
Razzuq, As'ad, 1286, 2110
Read, James M., 1091
Reddaway, J., 1127
Reese, H., 2140, 2159, 2420
Reich, Bernard, 62, 2160, 2247, 2349, 2499, 2500, 2539
Reichmann, Eva G., 1577
Reinhardt, G. Frederick, 2954
Reischauer, Robert D., 315
Reisman, Michael 2333
Reitzel, William, 2574, 2575
Rejwan, Nissim, 473, 474, 1002, 1167, 1996, 2999
Remba, Oded, 887, 2894
Reyner, Anthony S., 1936
Richardson, Channing B., 1020
Richardson, John P., 1052, 2249
Richmond, J., 1185
Riciotti, Giuseppe, 685
Rifaat, Mohammed, 400

INDEX / 269

Rikye, Maj. Gen. I. J., 2301
Rivlin, Lt. Col. Gershon, 1736
Rizk, Edward, 2766
Robbins, P. K., 475
Roberts, Dick, 2865
Roberts, Samuel J., 976
Robertson, Terrence, 1785
Robinson, Jacob, 1128, 1647
Rodinson, Maxime, 747, 925, 926
Rodley, N., 2293
Rodwell, Robert R., 2250
Rogers, William, 2334, 2359
Rohf, S., 1422
Ro'i, Yaacov, 1226
Rolbant, Samuel, 2161
Roolvink, R., 137
Roosevelt, Kermit, 276, 401, 1648, 1673, 1674
Roots, John McCook, 1168
Ropelewski, Robert R., 2186, 2251
Rose, Norman Anthony, 1510, 1511, 1532
Rosen, Harry M., 820
Rosenberg, Leonard G., 716
Rosenblatt, Bernard A., 730
Rosenfeld, H., 1230
Rosenne, Shabtai, 686
Rosensaft, Menachem Z., 254, 1900
Rosenthal, E. I. J., 363
Roshwald, Mordecai, 777
Rostow, E., 2452
Roucek, J., 1260
Roughton, Richard A., 2008
Rouleau, Eric, 344, 492, 530, 977, 2101, 2198, 2725
Rovere, Richard H., 1997
Rowland, Howard, 927
Al-Roy, G. C., 2961
Royal Institute of International Affairs, 108, 144, 402, 1469
Rubin, Barry, 2501
Rubinstein, Alvin Z., 446, 493
Rubinstein, Amnon, 748, 2252, 2360, 2361
Rubner, Alex, 717
Rudeneh, O., 2553
Ruppin, Arthur, 1239
Russcol, Herbert, 778
Rustow, Dankwart A., 277, 2502

Saab, Gabriel S., 476
Saab, H., 633
El Sabban, Gamil, 1761
Sachar, Howard Morely, 857, 2402
Sacher, Harry, 687, 1227

Sadat, Anwar, 417, 494
Safran, Nadav, 430, 749, 914, 1737, 1901, 2267, 2335, 2540, 2541, 2675
Sager, S., 915
Said, A., 2453
Said, Edward, 2421, 2524
Sakran, Frank C., 1593, 2454
Salans, C., 1937
Salem, Elie, 365, 1310
Sales, M. E., 321
Saliba, Samir N., 2739
Salibi, Kamal S., 563, 570
Salpeter, E., 2278
Samaan, Sadek H., 477
Samo, Elias, 1902
Samra, M., 1311
Sams, James F., 2455
Samuel, Edwin, 256, 723, 731
Samuel, Horace, 1479
Samuel, Viscount Herbert, 1480
Sanger, Richard H., 531
Sanjian, Avedis K., 554
Saundby, Robert, 1703
Sax, Cmdr. Samuel W., 2253
Sayegh, Fayez A., 650, 1038, 1092, 1240, 1241, 1288, 1335, 2294
Sayegh, Kamal S., 2866
Sayegh, Yusif A., 571
al-Sayyid, Afaf Lutfi, 386
Schechtman, Joseph B., 257, 258, 707, 1022, 1289, 1552, 1625
Scheer, R., 3000
Schiff, Z., 1915
Schleifer, Abdullah, 2057, 2058, 2813, 2814
Schlesinger, B., 842
Schmidt, Dana Adams, 592, 2750
Schmidt, H. D., 1512
Schnall, David J., 2982
Scholz, P., 447
Schonfield, Hugh J., 1751, 1752
Schopflin, George, 2701
Schramm, Wilbur, 1843
Schultz, Lillie, 1661
Schurr, Sam H., 2895
Schuyler, G., 2615
Schwarz, C., 821
Schwarz, Walter, 822, 823
Schweid, E., 750
Schweitzer, K., 2656
Schofield, John, 751
Scott, Alan, 1336
Seale, Patrick, 555, 651
Searight, Sarah, 1704
Segal, R., 2815
Segre, D., 969

Segre, V. D., 779
Seligman, Lester G., 916
Selim, George Dimitri, 51
Sella, Amnon, 2254
Selzer, Michael, 780, 1208, 1221, 1290
Semaan, K., 227
El Serafy, Salah, 459
Serpell, C., 2554
Seton-Williams, M. V., 1427, 1721
Seymour, G., 2363
Sha'ath, Nabil, 1118
Shachar, A., 762
Shafei, H., 2208
Shamir, Moshe, 2983
Shapira, Avraham, 1998
Shapiro, J., 1291
Shapiro, Yonathan, 1261
Sharabi, Hisham B., 278, 312, 366, 431, 1003, 1916, 2037, 2059, 2060, 2073, 3002
Sharif, Amer A., 634
Sharon, Nahun, 888
Shatil, J., 843
Sheean, Vincent, 601
Sheehan, Edward R. F., 609, 2074, 2209, 2422
Shepherd, Naomi, 1169, 2767
Shepilov, D. T., 1798
Sherman, A., 1170
Shibl, Yusuf, 889, 1769
Shidlowsky, Benjamin, 824
Shihor, Schmuel, 259
Shimoni, Yaacov, 732
Shlomo, Hilali, 1039, 1129
Shoemaker, R., 1968
Shokeid, Moshe, 858
Shorrock, W., 1423
Shotwell, J. T., 1398
Shouby, E., 313
Shoufani, Elias, 2255, 2268
Shub, Louis, 2576
Shumsky, Abraham, 859
Shuval, Judith T., 860
Shwadran, Benjamin, 532, 936, 1040, 1179, 1786, 2616, 2617, 2867, 2868, 2896, 2908
Sick, G., 2633, 2689
Sicron, Moshe, 708
Sidebotham, Herbert, 1470
Sidey, H., 2386
Siegfried, Andre, 1787
Sights, Col. Albert P., Jr., 574
Silbey, F., 2909
Silverberg, Robert, 2555
Silverburg, S., 2112

Simon, E., 917
Simon, R., 781
Simonhoff, Harry, 1713
Simpson, Colin, 1385
Simpson, Dwight J., 79, 752–55, 1999
Simson, H. J., 1533
Sinai, Anne, 1594, 2894
Sinai, I. Robert, 1594
Singer, Jeanne G., 37
Singer, Jerome E., 2223, 2643
Sirhan, Bassem, 2038
Sisco, Joseph J., 2456, 2457, 2504
Slater, Leonard, 1738
Slocum, Robert B., 218
Slonim, R., 1080
Slonim, S., 2141
Smilansky, Moshe, 1630
Smirnov, V., 2676
Smith, C. G., 2768
Smith, Harvey H., 756
Smith, Hedrick, 495, 2222
Smith, Jay C., 2584
Smolansky, B., 2232
Smolansky, Oles M., 2231, 2232, 2634
Snodgrass, C. Stribling, 2869
Snow, Peter, 228
Sokolow, Nahum, 1209
Sousa, N., 1714
Soustelle, Jacques, 1844
Sowden, L., 918
Spain, James W., 1739
Sparrow, Gerald, 533
Spears, Sir E. L., 1705
Spector, Ivar, 2585, 2619, 2649, 2702
Speiser, Ephraim A., 314, 2458
Spender, Stephen, 696
Spiegel, Erika, 782
Spiro, Melford E., 844, 845
Srivastava, R. K., 970
St. Aubin, W. de, 1021
St. John, Robert, 226, 255, 365
Stanford, Maj. Melvin J., 2269
Stanford Research Institute, 610
Stanley, John, 2187
Stark, Freya, 1553
Stavrou, Theofanis George, 2586, 2587
Stein, G., 1399
Stein, Gabriel, 1108
Stein, Leonard Jacques, 1378, 1514
Stephens, Robert, 229
Stern, Boris, 846
Stern, G., 1399
Stern, Sol, 1262
Stetler, Russell, 1004
Stevens, Georgiana G., 448, 496, 497,

INDEX / 271

Stevens, Georgiana G. *(Continued)*
 1041, 2084, 2270, 2295, 2459, 2726,
 2740, 2741, 2817
Stevens, R., 1006, 1608
Stevens, Richard P., 1228, 2556
Stevenson, William, 1969, 2173
Stewart, Desmond, 1771, 2769
Stewart, James, 1845
Stock, Ernest, 825, 919, 1822, 2808
Stockholm International Peace
 Research Institute (SIPRI), 145, 2142
Stocking, George W., 2897
Stockman, I., 1042
Stoessinger, J. G., 1007
Stone, I. F., 664, 2337, 2910
Stork, Joe, 2460
Storrs, Sir Ronald, 1352
Streithorst, Tom, 534
Suimoni, Jacob, 826
Suleiman, M., 324, 1799, 2085
Sullivan, A., 1229
Sullivan, M. B., 1875
Sulzberger, Cyrus L., 1554
Sus, Ibrahim, 2256
Sutcliffe, Claud R., 1053
Swados, H., 1081
Swaminathan, V. S., 1555
Swartz, M., 1210
Sweet, Louise E., 38
Sweet, Miriam, L., 1904
Sykes, Christopher, 1379, 1715, 2826
Syrkin, Marie, 260, 1023, 1609
Szereszewski, Robert, 890

Tahitnen, Dale R., 2143
Talmon, Jacob, 2001
Tamarin, Georges R., 757
Tannous, Afif I., 367
Tannous, E., 2041
Tariki, A., 2911
Taslitt, Israel I., 261
Taylor, Alan R., 325, 1196, 1222, 1292,
 1626, 1627, 2557
Tedeschi, G., 920
Tekoah, Amb. Josef, 2818
Teller, Judd L., 697, 783, 1675, 2660
Temperly, H. W., 1400
Terry, Janice, 1328
Tessier, Arlette, 1190
Tetlie, Richard N., 325
Teveth, Shabtai, 262, 1180, 1970
Thayer, Philip W., 1876
Thicknesse, S. G., 1008, 1054
Thoman, Roy E., 593

Thomas, Hugh, 1800
Thomas, John, R., 2637
Thomas, Lowell, 1389
Thomas, T., 2898
Thompson, Carol L., 2505
Thompson, Jack H., 315
Thomsen, Peter, 39
Thorbecke, Ellen, 1610
Tibawi, A. L., 556, 1130, 1300, 1312,
 1353, 1365, 1391, 1392, 1487, 1716,
 2430, 2588, 2775, 2783-85
Toledano, S., 827
Tolkowsky, Samuel, 1449
Toma, E., 2162
Torrey, Gordon H., 432, 557, 558
Toynbee, Arnold, 1722, 2956
Trabulsi, F., 3003
Trevelyan, Humphrey, 345
Trevor, Daphne, 1649
Truman, Harry, 1650
Tsur, Jacob, 1809
Tuma, Elias H., 828, 2339
Turki, Fawaz, 1043
Tutsch, Hans E., 1337
Tweedy, Owen, 1009
Twitchett, K. J., 1424
Twitchill, Karl Saben, 602
Tzion, Ben, 2661

Ulitzur, Abraham, 1450
United Kingdom. *See* Great Britain
United Nations, 10, 95, 125, 146, 147,
 333, 1064-68, 1082, 1093, 1094,
 1917, 1918, 2820
United States Government
 House, Committee on Foreign
  Affairs, 1069, 2003, 2365, 2506,
  2710, 2827, 2958
 Senate, Committee on Armed
  Services, 2507
 Senate, Committee on Foreign
  Relations, 126
 Senate, Committee on
  Government Operations, 2567
 Department of State, 11-13, 109-
  11, 1044, 1788, 1801-3, 2461
 Department of the Army, 40, 41
 Department of the Interior, Office
  of Oil and Gas, 2870
 Library of Congress, 42
University of London, 52
University of the State of New York, 43
Upthegrove, Campbell L., 1471
Uri, Pierre, 947

Urquhart, Brian, 2296
U Thant, 2352, 2821
Uthmani, S., 1293

Van Cleef, Eugene, 758
Van Dusen, Michael H., 559
Van Voorst, B., 2390
Vatad, Muhammad, 829
Vatikiotis, P. J., 382, 418, 433, 434, 498, 499, 535, 2959
Verete, M., 1380
Vernant, Jacques, 1010
Vester, Bertha S., 2776
Vinogradov, A., 594
Vital, D., 1223
Vlavianos, Basil J., 1224
Vlock, Laurel, 1643
Vogel, Rolf, 948
Von Grunebaum, Gustave E., 286, 1338
von Horn, Maj. Gen. Carl, 2304
Vucinich, Wayne S., 2620

W., D., 1131
Waines, David, 1451
Wakebridge, Charles, 2199
Wakin, Edward, 478
Walker, D., 1339
Wallace-Clarke, G., 1569
Walters, D., 1078
Ward, Richard J., 1115
Warriner, Doreen, 334, 479
Waterfield, Gordon, 383
Waters, M. P., 1668
Watt, D. C., 1755
Wavell, Sir Archibald P., 1354, 1355
Weigert, Gideon, 733, 830, 831
Weinberg, A., 862
Weinberger, Siegbert J., 1810
Weingarten, Murray, 701
Weingrod, Alex, 709, 784, 785
Weinryb, Bernard D., 698, 786, 832, 1488
Weinstock, Nathan, 1496
Weintraub, Dov, 863
Weiss, Samuel, 230
Weizmann, Chaim, 264, 1578
Weizmann, Vera, 265
Weller, Jac, 2102, 2164–68, 2188
Welles, Sumner, 2508
Wellington, S., 971
Weltsch, Robert, 2793
Wenner, Lettie M., 595
Wenner, Manfred, W., 64
Werfel, Franz V., 1356

Wesson, R., 2638
Westerfield, H. Bradford, 2509
Wetmore, Warren C., 2174, 2175, 2210
Wheeler, Geoffrey E., 2621, 2622, 2650, 2711
Whetten, Lawrence L., 2144, 2145, 2200, 2257, 2423, 2639, 2692
Wigoder, G., 710
Wilber, D., 435
Wilhelm, Kurt, 1497
Wilkenfeld, Harold C., 891
Williams, Albert N., 2777
Williams, Ann, 1706
Williams, Keith, 368
Williams, L. F., 688
Willner, Dorothy, 759
Wilmington, Martin W., 1707, 1708
Wilson, Arnold, 1756
Wilson, C., 2899
Wilson, Evan M., 1115, 1545, 2829, 2830
Wilson, George C., 1109
Wilson, John A., 403
Wilson, Major R. D., 1570
Winder, R. Bayly, 603
Winocour, Jack, 2462
Wint, Guy, 1804
Wissa-Wassef, C., 449
Witkamp, F. T., 1011
Wolf, John B., 1012, 2087, 2103, 2116
Wolins, Bernard D., 786
Woolbert, Robert Gale, 1534
World Zionist Organization
  Information Department, 1294
  Research Section, 65
Wren, C., 2061
Wright, Edwin M., 2510
Wright, Esmond, 536, 2525
Wright, L. C., 2431
Wright, Quincy, 1393, 1425, 2432, 2463, 2511
Wright, Walter L., Jr., 2512
Wynn, C. Wilton, 436, 1313

Xydis, Stephen G., 2577

Yaari, D., 1938
Yaari, Ehud, 2062, 2104
Yaari, S., 2871
Yahalom, Dan, 2117
Yakovlev, D., 2678
Yale, William, 1410
Yalin-Mor, N., 1571
Yamak, Labib Zuwiyya, 560

Yaukey, David, 316
Yeganeh, Mohammed, 2872
Yin'am, S., 665
Yisraeli, D., 1556
Yodfat, A., 2039, 2211
Yost, Charles W., 1919, 2464, 2938, 2960
Young, Lewis, 2568
Young, O., 1903
Young, Peter, 537, 1971

Zahlan, Antoine, 788, 988, 2146
Zaid, K., 833
Zander, Walter, 2662, 2786
Zarhi, S., 1055
Zarour, Mariam, 1182
Zartman, I., 335

Zayid, Mahmoud Y., 404
Zebel, Sydney H., 1381
Zeine, Zeine N., 1302, 1394
Zenner, Walter P., 875, 876
Zhabotinskii, Vladimir Evgan'evich, 1572. *See also* Jabotinsky, Vladimir
Ziadeh, Nicola A., 80, 81, 561
Zidon, Asher, 921
Ziff, William Bernard, 1452
Ziman, Joshua, 1498
Zimmerman, J., 1676
Zinger, Z., 789
Zmora, Ohad, 760
Zohar, Danah, 790
Zoppo, C., 2693
Zucker, Norman L., 791
Zurayk, Constantine N., 1677
Zvyagin, Y., 666

The Arab-Israeli Conflict was compiled by Ronald M. DeVore.
Copy editing was done by Barbara Phillips,
who also designed the text.
Proofreading was performed by John R. "Jack" Raup.
Cover art by Raymond Glass.
The text was composed in 10-point Century Schoolbook
and uses Century display and heads;
composition by Chapman's Phototypesetting,
Fullerton, California.
The body is printed in black ink on a 55-pound EB Book Natural;
it is Smyth sewn with headbands over Kivar 6 Cambric which
has been applied to standard boards and plain white endsheets.
Printing and binding by Edwards Brothers, Inc.,
Ann Arbor, Michigan

Ref
Z
3479
R4
D48

JUN 6 1978